1.

GROUP PROCESS, GROUP DECISION, GROUP ACTION

MAPPING SOCIAL PSYCHOLOGY

Series Editor: Tony Manstead

Current titles:

Icek Ajzen: Attitudes, Personality and Behavior
Robert S. Baron, Norbert L. Kerr and Norman Miller: Group Process, Group Decision, Group Action
Steve Duck: Relating to Others
J. Richard Eiser: Social Judgment
Russell G. Geen: Human Aggression
Howard Giles and Nikolas Coupland: Language: Contexts and Consequences
John Turner: Social Influence
Leslie A. Zebrowitz: Social Perception

Forthcoming titles include:

Marilyn B. Brewer and Norman Miller: Intergroup Relations
Richard Petty and John Cacioppo: Attitude Change
Dean G. Pruitt and Peter J. Carnevale: Bargaining and Third Party Intervention
Wolfgang Stroebe and Margaret Stroebe: Social Psychology and Health

GROUP PROCESS, GROUP DECISION, GROUP ACTION

Robert S. Baron
Norbert L. Kerr
Norman Miller

OPEN UNIVERSITY PRESS
BUCKINGHAM

Open University Press
Celtic Court
22 Ballmoor
Buckingham
MK18 1XW

and
1900 Frost Road, Suite 101
Bristol, PA 19007, USA

First Published 1992

A catalogue record of this book is available from
the British Library

ISBN 0-335-09862-2 (pbk)
ISBN 0-335-09863-0

Printed and bound in Great Britain

Dedicated to our families

CONTENTS

FOREWORD

There has long been a need for a carefully tailored series of reasonably short and inexpensive books on major topics in social psychology, written primarily for students by authors who enjoy a reputation for the excellence of their research and their ability to communicate clearly and comprehensibly their knowledge of, and enthusiasm for, the discipline. My hope is that the *Mapping Social Psychology* series will meet that need.

The rationale for this series is twofold. First, conventional textbooks are too low-level and uninformative for use with senior undergraduates or graduate students. Books in this series address this problem partly by dealing with topics at book length, rather than chapter length, and partly by the excellence of the scholarship and clarity of the writing. Each volume is written by an acknowledged authority on the topic in question, and offers the reader a concise and up-to-date overview of the principal concepts, theories, methods and findings relating to that topic. Although the intention has been to produce books that will be used by senior level undergraduates and graduate students, the fact that the books are written in a straightforward style should make them accessible to students with relatively little previous experience of social psychology. At the same time, the books are sufficiently informative to earn the respect of researchers and instructors.

A second problem with traditional textbooks is that they are too dependent on research conducted in or examples drawn from North American society. This fosters the mistaken impression that social psychology is a uniquely North American discipline and can also be baffling for readers unfamiliar with North American culture.

To combat this problem, authors of books in this series have been encouraged to adopt a broader perspective, giving examples or citing research from outside North America wherever this helps to make a point. Our aim has been to produce books for a world market, introducing readers to an international discipline.

In this volume, Robert Baron, Norbert Kerr and Norman Miller provide a thorough introduction to the social psychology of group processes. The study of group processes is one of the cornerstones of social psychology; indeed, some of the earliest experimental studies in social psychology (those by Triplett and by Ringelmann) were investigations of the influence of groups on individual task performance. It is, nevertheless, fair to say that over the years the social psychology of groups has undergone quite dramatic shifts in popularity as a research topic. In the 1940s, 1950s and the first half of the 1960s, the study of social groups was one of the key research topics in social psychology. However, with the 'cognitive revolution' in psychology that took place in the 1960s, and which affected social psychology as much as other sub-disciplines, mainstream research became highly individualistic. Because cognitive processes were assumed to take place within individuals, rather than between them, theorists and researchers who were interested in understanding such processes were for the most part unconcerned with the workings of social groups. The decline in interest in groups was such that one leading groups researcher, Ivan Steiner, was prompted to write a paper under the title 'Whatever happened to the group in social psychology?' More recently there has been a slow, but steady revival of interest among social psychologists in the study of group processes, such that it now once again occupies a somewhat more central position within the sub-discipline.

Baron, Kerr and Miller have written a book that successfully blends the older and newer research traditions in this field. They have organized the material historically, beginning with those topics (such as social facilitation) that attracted the attention of social psychologists relatively early and ending with topics (such as stress and social support) that have only comparatively recently come to be studied by social psychologists. The book can be seen as falling into three sections. After an introductory chapter, Chapters, 2, 3 and 4 are all concerned in one way or another with the impact of groups on the task performance of individuals, examining such issues as whether the presence of an audience has a beneficial or detrimental effect on task performance, whether groups are more productive than individuals, and whether groups inevitably reduce the motivation – and therefore the performance – of their individual members. Chapters 5, 6 and 7 are concerned chiefly with social influence processes in groups; here the focus is on whether group members conform to the perceived expectations of others, how individual group members move from initial disagreement to a group decision, and how conflicts between personal gain and collective benefit are resolved. Finally, Chapters 8, 9 and 10 are concerned with more obviously 'applied' topics that are related rather directly to social problems and issues, namely aggression and conflict between social groups, the way that people can provide social support for individuals who are under stress and the psychological consequences of living in densely populated environments. Each of the authors is a leading exponent of research on social groups, and the three of them have neatly dovetailed their wisdom and experience to produce a volume that is highly readable, very interesting and right up to date. It will serve as an excellent introduction to this area, but it is also sufficiently thought-provoking to be a stimulating read for those who regard themselves as well versed in research on social groups.

Tony Manstead
Series Editor

PREFACE

Groups are a key element in human experience. Whether the group is a family, a street gang, a work group, an ethnic minority or a network of friends, group membership and influence represents one of the most powerful forces shaping our feelings, judgments and behaviors. While group processes can lead to destructive and aggressive outbursts, so too are they the source of some of our most noble actions such as love, achievement, nurturance, loyalty and sacrifice. Despite the ubiquity and importance of groups for human existence, scholarly research on group topics is a relatively recent phenomenon. While some of the earliest research on groups focused on how groups affected task performance (Triplett 1898; Ringlemann 1913) for the most part, systematic research on other topics did not become widespread until the 1940s and 1950s. Therefore, it is not surprising that group research is still very much an emerging field. As such, it provides the excitement that derives from new theory and fresh empirical phenomenon as well as the challenge (and frustration) that stems from the fact that there still is a good deal of ambiguity and uncertainty regarding many fundamental aspects of group process.

This book is designed for advanced undergraduate students in courses such as group dynamics and social psychology. In this volume we attempt to share with the reader both the excitement and the challenge of conducting research on group phenomenon. Where possible we attempt to provide historical context for the research (what inspired it, what obstacles were overcome, what controversies stimulated continued research), as well as the applied significance of what these laboratory findings mean in terms of our everyday life. Our primary objective, however, is to familiarize the reader with the theoretical perspectives and data that provide researchers with a means of interpreting group phenomenon. We place special emphasis on several aspects of group experience that we feel are of particular significance. These include processes of social influence (Chapter 5); group productivity (Chapters 2, 3 and 4); group decision-making (Chapters 5 and 6); and intergroup conflict and prejudice (Chapter 8).

The book is organized historically with early chapters presenting those research areas that first captured the attention of researchers and later chapters (crowding, social dilemmas, social support, group aggression and intergroup conflict) depicting areas that became active far more recently. Chapter 1 introduces a number of basic concepts (e.g. group structure, norms, definitional issues) fundamental to understanding group research. Chapters 2, 3 and 4 then address one of the earliest and most basic issues of group research; how groups effect the task performance of individuals. Chapter 2 focuses primarily on non-interacting groups (i.e. where one simply works in the presence of others without any need for coordination), while Chapter 3 focuses on groups that work together for some common goal and Chapter 4 discusses how group situations can suppress productivity by lowering motivation. This last topic covers some of the most recent research on group productivity. Chapters 5 and 6 cover areas of social influence and group decision-making, traditionally topics of central importance in group research and social psychology in general. The remaining Chapters (7–10) examine a number of distinctly applied topics that have captured the interest of group researchers in recent years. It is our hope that this organizational structure will aid the reader in appreciating the complexities, challenges and insights that have characterized group research since its inception.

ACKNOWLEDGEMENTS

We would like to acknowledge the invaluable assistance of the secretarial personnel who contributed to this project; specifically Beverly Hamann, Joyce Paul and Mary Vreeland. In addition, we would like to thank our students, who over the years have helped us to maintain our enthusiasm for group research. Finally, we would like to thank our colleagues David Messick and Wolfgang Stroebe for their thoughtful comments on an earlier draft, and Tony Manstead for his confidence and patience throughout the project.

1 / INTRODUCTION

Groups play a crucial role in human affairs. They dramatically shape our perceptions and attitudes, provide support in times of distress, and affect our performance and decision-making. Group processes can produce everything from destructive mob behavior to selfless loyalty. In this introductory chapter we will consider how social scientists define the term 'group'. Then we will discuss several important group characteristics that provide us with a means of both understanding and describing different forms of group experience.

The defining of a group

A mob of football (soccer) fans in Spain runs amok just prior to the World Cup; seventeen die. Soldiers in Beirut are coached to spread out when moving along a roadway; shelling begins and they group together, huddling against each other for comfort. A campus political group meets to discuss their next group action; as the discussion progresses, the group comes to embrace a more radical position than they did previously and eventually they agree to committing an act of terrorism.

These instances all illustrate principles of group dynamics. Yet the groups in question vary widely in their characteristics. These differences illustrate the difficulty of deriving a single definition of 'group' that is entirely satisfactory. Not surprisingly, a good number of definitions have been proposed. Some stress that groups must have some permanence, structure and psychological meaning for members, thereby creating a feeling of belonging. In contrast, other writers are far more flexible in their definition, arguing only that some form of communication or mutual social influence need occur if a collection of individuals are to be viewed as a group. As an example, Forsyth (1983) defines a group as 'two or more individuals who influence each other through social interaction' (p. 81).

Numerous other definitions of 'group' exist, but it seems clear that over the years, researchers have tended to feel more comfortable with the more flexible conceptualizations such as the one offered by Forsyth (1983). Thus, much of group research has focused on temporary groups which have no clear structure or lasting relationship to each other, but whose members are bound only by some brief period of mutual influence or subtle communication. The research we discuss in later chapters on mob action, bystander helping, audience impact and crowding illustrate such work.

Explaining human reliance on groups

Theorists have offered a number of reasons why groups play such a major role in human affairs. One straightforward view – *the social learning perspective* – is that since most of us are raised in a family setting, we learn to depend on others for aid, information, love, friendship and entertainment. *Social comparison theory* suggests a less obvious view. According to this theory (Festinger 1954) we feel very strong pressure to have accurate views, both about our environment and our abilities. One way to verify our views is to compare our opinions and ability-related performances to those of others. In other words, if physical reality is ambiguous we create a social reality. Therefore, according to a social comparison perspective, at least one reason we group together is to gain comparative information in an attempt to protect ourselves from inappropriate decisions and judgments.

One theoretical perspective, *exchange theory* provides a somewhat different social psychological view of group formation. It argues that groups which provide the greatest 'gains' will be most desired by members. According to this theory, group membership involves exchanging both rewards and costs with other group members. Rewards are positive elements gained through social exchange. They can be material goods or psychological goods, such as love or approval. A key feature of group interaction is that we can only obtain many of these psychological rewards by affiliating with others. For example, being accepted by high status individuals represents a very powerful, rewarding consequence of group interaction, as does having our important values and beliefs confirmed. Indeed, often social stimulation itself becomes an important resource that one can exchange (Hey, let's party tonight!). According to exchange theory, group membership also has costs. Costs can be such things as resources that we give to the group, time and effort spent on group activities, opportunities lost by belonging to the group and emotional costs associated with group activity.

This emphasis on rewards and costs allows one to think about the 'profit' one achieves through group membership (where profit = reward – costs). Because exchange theory considers psychological sources of reward as well as material rewards as a source of profit, we can view such diverse groups as friendships, and family groups and romantic couples as exchange relationships. The notion that even loved ones exchange resources amongst themselves has been most useful to family therapists and marriage counselors seeking to improve the quality of such relationships.

According to a well known exchange theory developed by Harold Kelley and John Thibaut we can explain such things as our satisfaction with a group and our dependency on it by considering this notion of profit. If our profit is greater than the profit we think is fair or normal for such a relationship we will be satisfied. Thibaut and Kelley (1959) refer to this standard of fairness as the Comparison Level (CL). According to Thibaut and Kelley, our dependency on a relationship is primarily a function of what our other options are, i.e. the 'profit' we can anticipate in our 'next best deal'. They refer to this value as comparison level for alternatives (or CLalt). As an example, we might be quite dissatisfied in a particular relationship (this implies our profit is well below our CL), but if our other options are far worse, we will be unhappily quite dependent on the relationship (our present profit is well above our CLalt).

Thus, according to Thibaut and Kelley, the further your present profit exceeds your next best option (CLalt), the greater your dependency on the group. Thibaut and Kelley's analysis explains a great many seemingly puzzling situations such as individuals who remain in unfulfilling marriages or jobs. Although the satisfaction of such individuals is low, they must perceive their other options to be even worse.

Another interesting feature of this theory is that one's satisfaction with a social relationship will depend heavily on what we use as our standard of 'fairness' (i.e. our CL). To take a recent example, the communist regime in East Germany fell, in large, part due to strong feelings of economic deprivation on the part of the East German people. Interestingly, according to most economic indicators, East Germany had a higher standard of living than Italy, England or the remaining Warsaw Pact nations. This did little to assuage feelings of dissatisfaction, however. The key issue was that West Germany was apparently the most psychologically relevant comparison group for East German citizens and by this comparison their own economic situation appeared bleak. [Note that key changes occurred in this situation only after escape and/ or migration to West Germany became possible thereby providing an extremely attractive CLalt to remaining in East Germany.]

Another theoretical view explaining the social tendency of human beings derives from theories of *sociobiology* (e.g. Bowlby 1958). These theories, which draw heavily on the work of Charles Darwin, basically argue that, on balance, grouping together has survival value for humans as well as many other species. Thus, when humans group together they are better able to protect themselves from predators and enemies, and are also able to cooperate for the purposes of farming, child rearing, hunting, and caring for the sick and injured. There are various ways in which genetic components might actually influence this tendency to congregate. One mechanism, for example, might be that more intelligent organisms are more likely to recognize the survival benefits of affiliation. If so, genetic influences on intelligence could explain why 'survival of the fittest' results in the pervasive human tendency to affiliate. Another possible example would be that humans have a genetic predisposition to bond (i.e. to respond positively to contact and nurturance). In either case, the material and psychological rewards that we gain through group membership are seen as a strong contributor to the pervasive presence of group arrangements. From our discussion so far, it should be obvious that people find groups essential for a number of different reasons. As a result, groups are likely to vary on a number of key dimensions. In the next section we will consider some of these dimensions.

Group characteristics

Group size

Group size is an obvious enough group dimension, but, it has a number of important ramifications. Larger groups are more likely to include individuals with a wide range of skills. Therefore, specialization of labor is more likely to occur. Larger groups also allow us to feel more anonymous. As a result, we may exhibit less social responsibility in larger groups, which in turn will often lead to less task involvement and lower morale on the part of many group members as group size increases.

In addition, size has a strong impact on group communication. One particularly well documented effect of increasing group size is that in larger groups a smaller percentage of individuals contribute to group discussion. This is apparently due both to the members' heightened fear of participation, and to the simple fact that there is less chance or time for individuals to express themselves in large gatherings.

Group structure

A second and most crucial dimension of groups is structure. Group structure is most likely to be well developed in permanent groups such as families, work groups, clubs, etc., where there will generally be status differences among members, well established norms of conduct and thought, leaders, followers, and various cliques and subgroups. These factors comprise some of the basic elements of group structure. That is, structure refers to the way groups are organized and how various positions in the group are related. Most writers describe group structure as being comprised of several key elements.

Roles

In almost all long-term groups, members will occupy different *social roles*. These are the expected behaviors associated with a given position within a group. Social roles may be formal or informal. Thus, a street gang might have formal officers (e.g. club president, war counselor), as well as a variety of informal roles (clown, tough guy, etc.). Often these informal roles evolve because of psychological needs within the group. Thus, the clown role noted above will often serve to relieve group tension and to provide subtly veiled social criticism and commentary through satire that otherwise might be too controversial to air.

The fact that individuals often fill multiple roles can lead to *role conflict* in which the demands of one role are incompatible with the demands of another. Such conflicts have been the source of history's more dramatic episodes. The wild west tale regarding how Sheriff Pat Garrett shot down his friend, the famous outlaw, Billy the Kid (William Bonney) exemplifies this process. This tale illustrates that roles can powerfully influence our actions, often leading us to act contrary to our private feelings or vested interest. Milgram's famous obedience studies (Milgram 1974) provide an example. In these experiments, paid adult subjects learned that, as part of a study on punishment and learning, they as 'teachers' would be asked to shock a learner (actually a confederate) every time he committed a memory error. The experimental setting was extremely realistic complete with a buzzing, blinking shock machine.

The entire point of this study was to determine when the 'teacher' would refuse to comply with the requirements of his role as obedient research participant. Almost all 'teachers' began to express reluctance and show signs of stress as the intensity of the shock they administered increased and the 'learner' cried out in pain. If they refused to administer shock, however, the experimenter urged them on by saying such things as 'please continue'; 'you must go on'. Only if the 'teacher' persisted in his reluctance despite the experimenters urgings and demands was he excused from the study. In this study, it is clear that the great majority of participants were quite disturbed and concerned about the shock they thought they were administering. Some broke out into nervous laughter, others bit their lips or dug fingernails into their palms, etc. However, this generally did not disrupt their role compliance, despite the fact that the learner appeared to be in pain. Over 60 per cent of subjects administered the maximum shock voltage (450 V) to the learner. Indeed, even when the teacher was required to hold the victim's hand to the shock plate by force, the figure only dropped to 30 per cent. Milgram's results have now been replicated in several different countries (Milgram 1974) and point out how very reluctant we are to confront authority when we are placed in a subordinate role. For those of us concerned about our susceptibility to authoritarian political regimes or about how we would react when role requirements demand immoral action from us, these data are most provocative and disturbing. It would be nice to think that we personally would act honorably under such role pressure, but the data imply that a good number of us could be pressured into committing a variety of costly, harmful or even immoral actions if role pressure is severe enough.

Status

Different social roles are usually associated with different degrees of *status*. In addition, however, status can be based on other individual characteristics as well, such as physical attractiveness, intelligence, sense of humor and skill. Status is generally a function of the degree to which an individual's contribution is crucial to the success (and prestige) of the group and how much power (control over group outcomes) that individual has. Thus, in many groups (particularly subhuman ones), status is determined by which individual is physically most dominant. Although status and power ordinarily go hand in hand, they need not. The British monarchy, for example, has exceptional status but relatively little power.

Our status can also be based on the extent to which we embody some idealized or admired characteristic. Status of this last type is often not based on our achievements or contributions. Thus, in high school social groups, physically attractive individuals tend to have unusually high status. Similarly, in most cultures racial identity is unfortunately an important determinant of status, often completely overshadowing an individual's achievements, efforts and contributions.

Status differences have a number of important effects on group process. High status individuals are likely to be valued by the group and treated more tolerantly. As a result, they will often be less affected by group norms and peer pressure than lower status members, in part because they are less likely to expect punishment for their actions. In a study by Harvey and Consalvi (1960), groups of young male offenders, all from the same clique in a youth home, were shown a stimulus (a line) and asked to estimate its length. All three friends thought they were seeing the same stimulus, but in fact, in each group one young man ('the deviate') saw a stimulus line that differed from that seen by the others. Harvey and Consalvi then assessed the extent to which this young man's estimate was affected by hearing the very different estimates made by his mates. In line with our discussion, the group opinion (the group norm) had substantially less impact on those deviates who were highest in status (clique leaders), corroborating our assertion that high status will often reduce the power of peer influences.

The opposite side of this coin is that those high in status generally have a disproportionately strong impact on group decisions and judgments whereas those low in status tend to be ignored, even when they offer intelligent and creative advice. In a classic group study, Torrance (1954b) examined the decisions made by aircraft bomber crews. Across a variety of problems, the crew was far more influenced by the opinions and answers offered by the pilot than they were by the opinions and answers offered by the tailgunner (a lowly enlisted man) This held true even in cases where the tailgunner's opinions were correct ones. These results illustrate the powerful effects status can have on group functioning.

Subgroups
The structure of many groups is dramatically affected by the existence of *cliques and subgroups*. Such subgroups can be based on such things as similarity of age, place of residence, social role or vested interest. For example, the youth gang referred to before had several subgroups. One subgrouping had to do with age. Those over the age of 18 formed the gang elite. Another subgroup had to do with neighborhood. Those from the poorest neighborhood saw themselves as 'tougher' and more daring than those from the slightly less deprived neighborhood, who in turn thought of themselves as more sophisticated and attractive to women. Subgroups can, of course, produce conflict on occasion. Older gang members were more interested in partying in bars where they could encounter more women and generally more excitement. The younger gang members, however, were too young to drink legally in bars, so they pressured the group to hold parties in motels and homes so that they could be included in the festivities. The group's general reluctance to spend group funds in this way was a source of friction between the older and younger subgroups.

Cohesion
An additional group characteristic that contributes to group structure is *group cohesion*, i.e. the overall strength of positive relationships within the group. Groups can be cohesive for a variety of reasons. Indeed, cohesion has been defined as the sum of all pressures acting to keep individuals in a group (Back 1951).

Cohesion may be high simply because group members like each other. Alternatively, group membership may be the best or only means of achieving some crucial goal. Finally, belonging to the group may provide individuals with status, a key sense of identity or some other equally important reinforcement.

Back (1951), for example, created cohesion in three ways. In one group people were told that they were likely to be emotionally compatible (our tests indicate you will like these people). Another group was told they all had high ability on the key task in the study. A third group were told that if their group succeeded they would win a valued prize. Despite the differences between these various sources of cohesion, they all produced increased conformity to group norms (but see McKelvey and Kerr 1988). Whether due to friendship, status or being a means to an end, high cohesion is a key group characteristic.

Cohesion can have a number of very powerful effects on group functioning, not the least of which is that it contributes to the loyalty, commitment and sacrifice exhibited by its members. These elements of loyalty and sacrifice were graphically illustrated in a dramatic incident from the history of the Symbionese Liberation Army (SLA). The SLA was a group of about ten men and women dedicated to the unusual goal of provoking a socialist/communist revolution in the United States. In February of 1974 they kidnapped Patricia Hearst, the daughter of socialite William Randolph Hearst, from her college apartment in Berkeley, California. Several months after Ms Hearst's kidnapping, the main SLA group was surrounded in a house in Los Angeles by hundreds of heavily armed police officers equipped with riot gear, helicopters, etc. The group had a clearly stated doctrine (or norm) to fight to the death.

Although dramatically outnumbered, not one of the SLA defenders agreed to surrender even after the house was aflame and the police again offered to hold their fire. Instead, the SLA continued the spectacular fire fight which was televised on local stations and which ended in their deaths. Indeed, when the remaining members of the SLA, learned of their SLA comrades' predicament, their first reaction was to reach the surrounded house in order to join their obviously doomed comrades (Hearst 1982). Although the SLA may have been unrealistic in its group goals, it is clear it was a most cohesive group.

Figure 1.1   Some possible communications networks

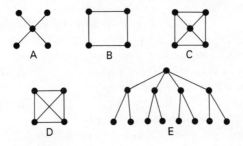

Note: People = •; Networks A, C, and E are centralized; Network D is fully decentralized.

Communication networks

A final element that defines group structure is the type of communication patterns that characterizes the group. In most small groups, there are few restrictions on who communicates with whom. However, in larger groups and organizations, unrestricted communication becomes unwieldy and inefficient, if not impossible. Consequently, *communication networks* become established. In his classic work on communication networks, Leavitt (1951) points out that a variety of communication networks are possible. Some communication networks are depicted in Figure 1.1. Notice that in Figure 1.1A all messages are routed through a centralized individual and, indeed, other individuals can only speak with the person in this central location. In Figure 1.1B, each individual can only communicate to the two individuals adjacent to them in the network. Figure 1.1C provides somewhat of a combination of Figure 1.1A and Figure 1.1B. Finally, in Figure 1.1E the lower an individual's status, the less communication options he or she has. This situation is a common one since it insulates the leaders from undue demands on their time. A good deal of experimentation indicates that in more centralized communication nets (for example, Figure 1.1A, C and E), individuals who happen to end up in the central position are most often named as leaders. Not surprisingly, those who are not in centralized positions and who, therefore, are restricted in their communication options are less satisfied with their group experience (Leavitt 1951).

These various aspects of group structure tend to serve key functions for the group. Roles encourage specialization of labor by providing a clear delineation of who should do what within the group and even specify how particular group assignments should be executed or accomplished. This reduces confusion and controversy, and facilitates the group's ability to respond to crises decisively. Status differences establish lines of authority and control, and also provide the means of rewarding and encouraging behavior that benefits the group. Subgroups often provide a power base for individuals who share a common attitude, orientation or vested interest, thereby increasing the probability that even minority positions get considered by the group. As we note above, cohesion is essential for group loyalty and inducing individual sacrifice for group benefits. Indeed, at the most basic level, groups without some source of cohesion will disband. Finally, communication networks reinforce and reflect the status and role characteristics of the group, often serve to protect group leaders from being overloaded with requests and information, and allow for rapid and efficient transmission of news, goals, information and commands throughout the group.

Group norms

In addition to group structure, a major feature of group experience is the nature of its norms, i.e. those behaviors, attitudes, and perceptions that are approved of by the group and expected (and, in fact, often demanded) of its members. Such norms will generally have powerful effects on the thoughts and actions of group members. As we will see when we discuss the conformity literature in Chapter 5, the nature of group norms has been shown in laboratory research to affect a wide range of judgments. These include artistic judgments, and visual and auditory perception. For example, in one classic study, Sherif (1936) led individuals to a totally dark room and turned on a tiny bulb. This procedure creates the illusion that the stationary light is actually moving. (Note: To maximize the illusion the room must be pitch dark and subjects should be unfamiliar with the room's size.) Sherif exposed people to a number of trials, each time asking subjects to indicate when the light began to move, when it stopped and how far it moved. Individuals were strongly influenced by the opinions of those around them. Indeed, Sherif was able to dramatically increase or decrease individuals' estimates of movement if he paid confederates to offer particularly large or small estimates. What was most impressive was that once people changed their estimates in response to group influence, they maintained similar estimates on subsequent judgments, even when they no longer were accompanied by group members. From this it would seem that people had truly changed their private perceptions about the amount of light movement they were seeing and were not simply going along with the group in order to avoid conflict.

As this implies, norms can have impressive effects. The Symbionese Liberation Army had a number of norms that exerted great influence on members. Indeed, the members' acceptance of them was so deep that they often adhered to them unthinkingly. In several cases this put the group at great risk. For example, they shared a strong normative belief that as a group, they were admired and supported by the 'common people'. Acting on this belief, members were often quite open regarding their Symbionese Liberation Army affiliation. Donal Defreeze, the group leader, went as far as canvassing the nearby neighborhood for recruits and supporters, even checking with people living in the Symbionese Liberation Army's own apartment building. ('Hello. I'm with the Symbionese Liberation Army. You know, the wanted fugitives who kidnapped Patty Hearst. We're conducting a recruitment drive. Interested?') These actions are noteworthy not only because they obviously put the group at risk, but because they were so at variance with the group's paranoid, but understandable concern about security in most other matters. Clearly, the group's belief in their popular support was a very deeply felt conviction.

Norms evolve in groups for a number of reasons.

1 Often norms are crucial for the group's survival or success. Thus, norms favoring bravery, sacrifice and loyalty (i.e. never informing) have obvious utility for groups involved in conflict and armed struggle, such as the Symbionese Liberation Army.
2 In addition, norms provide codes of behavior that render social life more predictable and efficient. Imagine the chaos that would result if people ignored the codified norms governing driving.
3 Finally, norms serve to reduce uncertainty and confusion when the environment seems unpredictable, unusual or threatening. In times of stress we seem to be particularly upset by uncertainty. A group consensus or the opinion of a group leader regarding such things as 'what's going on' and the 'best way to cope' seem to be particularly comforting and persuasive.

Leadership

The style in which the group leader manages the group's affairs represents yet another important group characteristic. Most theoretical treatments distinguish between task orientated leaders and people orientated leaders. The former are primarily concerned with group performance and maintaining the group's competitive position. The latter are more concerned with group members' feelings, needs and problems. Not surprisingly, person orientated leadership generally produces better morale than a task orientation (Shaw 1981). However, which produces superior performance? Several writers suggest that despite its poor effect on morale, a strong task orientation is useful in times of stress, time pressure or lack of structure (Fiedler 1967). Here a powerful, autocratic voice can impose order, set priorities and make rapid decisions. One sees this often enough in sports. In the closing minutes of a tight athletic contest, a successful coach cannot worry unduly about the egos of his players or take time to consider all opinions. Rather confidence and decisiveness are necessary. Several studies support the view that in times of stress, task orientated leadership is used more frequently (Fodor 1978) than people orientated leadership and is more productive (Rosenbaum and Rosenbaum 1971). A rigid autocratic leadership style is not always wise, however.

A survey by Suedfeld and Rank (1976) which examined the writings of revolutionary leaders indicated that some of history's most successful leaders varied their leadership style to fit the situation. Most revolutionary leaders used a rigid autocratic approach in the crisis period of the revolution. Those leaders however, who left office because of political or military defeat or disgrace (e.g. Trotsky, Che Guevara) were far more likely to continue this rigid approach following the revolution than those who remained in power until voluntary retirement or death (Mao Tse-Tung, George Washington, Oliver Cromwell). The latter, in contrast, were more likely to become far more flexible and less doctrinaire once the crisis period had passed. In short, a leadership style that suits one situation may be poorly adapted for another.

Stage

A final group characteristic we will consider is the *stage* of the group. A number of writers argue that groups can go through a variety of changes over time. Tuckman and Jensen (1977), for example, argue that in the earliest stages of group development, group members are most concerned about being accepted, and learning more about the group and its situation. This stage of group interaction (called *forming* by Tuckman and Jensen) is marked by polite and inhibited behavior and information seeking.

As the group matures and individual members come to feel more secure, there is a period of conflict (*storming*) where members confront their various differences. If the group survives this 'storming' stage, it will reach a stage (*norming*) in which it develops some consensus regarding roles, status and procedures. As a result of compromising during this stage, hostility and conflict will be lower and group cohesion should increase. Following this 'norming' stage, the group can begin to address more effectively its various group goals. During this period (*the performing stage*), there will be generally less conflict and emotion associated with the internal working of the group than in the prior stage. Finally, the group will reach a stage of disbanding (termed *adjournment* by Tuckman and Jensen) where group activities drop, group goals are reached or given up and the group experiences the emotions associated with separation.

As sensible as these group stages seem, their importance is often neglected. If you have ever left a 'dead' party early, only to find out the next morning that it later turned into a wild romp, you can appreciate this fact. The first hour of a big social occasion is generally in the earliest stages of group development where social interaction is constrained. As the 'ice breaks' and individuals get to know each other, they feel freer to engage in the kind of uninhibited behavior normatively appropriate at celebrations. Not all groups necessarily go through all of the stages outlined by Tuckman and Jensen (1977). Using our party example, many of social gatherings obviously avoid the conflict (or storming) stage, but after reviewing a great many studies on group process, Tuckman (1965) concluded that the stages he outlined often represent an accurate portrayal of developmental stages within groups.

Summary

Groups have a dramatic impact on human attitudes, decisions and actions. Group researchers tend to embrace a flexible working definition of 'group', often including temporary, unstructured groups in their investigations. There are a number of theoretical explanations for the pervasive influence of groups in human affairs. These include social comparison theory, exchange theory and sociobiological theories. Groups can be distinguished on the basis of several group characteristics, such as size, prevalent norms, structure and stage of development. Group structure, in turn, is based on several components, including the nature of roles and status within the group, the number and types of subgroups that exist, the degree of group cohesion and the communication network that characterizes the group. Our discussion of these various group features touched upon a number of interesting psychological phenomena, including obedience (Milgram 1974), status biases (Torrance 1954b) and the continuation of unsatisfactory relationships (Thibaut and Kelley 1959).

Suggestions for further reading

Festinger, L. (1954). A theory of social comparison processes. *Human Relations*, 7, 117–40.
Milgram, S. (1974). *Obedience to Authority*. New York: Harper & Row.
Torrance, E. P. (1954). The behavior of small groups under the stress of conditions of survival. *American Sociological Review*, 19, 751–5.
Tuckman, B. W. and Jensen, M. A. C. (1977). Stages of small group development revisited. *Group and Organizational Studies*, 2, 419–27.

2 / SOCIAL FACILITATION

In 1969, Zajonc *et al.* (1969) performed what to most people would appear to be a bizarre experiment. They found that cockroaches ran faster down a runway to escape a light source if the runway was lined with an 'audience' of onlooking fellow cockroaches (each one actually contained in its own plexiglass cubicle). This research team was re-examining one of the oldest questions in modern experimental social psychology: how the simple presence of others affects individual performance. As we will see, this study contributed to an important theory about this issue.

Norman Triplett, an American psychologist, became interested in the impact of the simple presence of fellow performers after noting that bicycle racers always turned in superior times if they had a live competitor. Triplett (1898) soon found similar results when he asked children to reel in line as quickly as possible on a fishing reel. As in cycling, *social* conditions were found to *facilitate* task performance.

This result attracted attention in part because Triplett's groups represented very elemental social units, having no history, norms or structure, and in which social interaction and cooperation seemed minimal. As such, this research focused attention on one of social psychologist's most elemental questions, namely how the mere presence of other people affects our behavior. A second reason early results were intriguing is that the earliest reports indicated that social facilitation effects occurred in a wide range of species. For example, researchers found that when conspecifics (or 'species mates') were present, dogs ran faster, chicks ate more grain, fruit flies preened their bodies more often and ants moved more sand while nest building (Zajonc 1965). In one provocative study, Larsson (1956) even found that sexual behavior among mating rats occurred more often if the couples were in the presence of other sexually active rat pairs.

In humans, social facilitation has been found on many tasks including things as diverse as jogging, word associations and computer use (cf. Bond and Titus 1983; Geen 1989; Robinson-Staveley and Cooper 1990). The early parallels between the human and non-human data suggested that social facilitation might be a basic and widespread social phenomenon. As a result, the research results drew a good deal of attention. It soon became apparent, however, that the presence of others did not invariably lead to facilitated performance. In human subjects, for example, Allport (1924) found that social facilitation occurred on certain tasks such as simple multiplication problems, but on others (such as writing refutations of Greek epigrams) working in the presence of co-actors impaired performance.

Results such as these produced a good deal of confusion. Why should social facilitation occur on some tasks and not others? These issues were so perplexing that research on social facilitation all but ceased by the 1940s. In 1965, however, things changed radically. What caused this turn round was a provocative theory of social facilitation offered by Robert Zajonc (pronounced like science with a Z).

Drive theory and social facilitation/impairment

Zajonc (1965) argued that social facilitation and social impairment both occur because we are excited and aroused by the mere physical presence of species mates. According to Zajonc, when we are around others, be they co-actors, audiences or just bystanders, we are more alert, physically excited and motivated. As a result, we try harder at the tasks we attempt. Psychologists generally refer to such feelings as a heightened state of drive. States such as hunger, fear and frustration are typical examples of drive states, but what may remain unclear to you is how this theory accounts for the fact that social conditions facilitate some tasks and impair others. If people are trying harder, why do they perform worse on some tasks?

To explain this puzzle, Zajonc referred to a well established set of findings (e.g. Spence 1956) which indicate that increasing drive increases the speed, strength and probability of an organism's dominant response. A dominant response refers to the action that an animal is most likely to emit in a given situation. This dominant tendency may be due to training, habit, personal preference or innate factors. This fact is directly relevant to social facilitation because on well learned, easy or instinctual tasks, the correct response tends to be dominant. Therefore, on easy tasks, correct responses should be facilitated or enhanced by high drive. In contrast, on counter-instinctual or difficult (i.e. poorly learned) tasks (e.g. writing one's name upside-down and backwards), the correct response would not be dominant. In such cases, increasing drive should impair performance by enhancing the tendency to perform the dominant (and incorrect) response (e.g. writing normally). In short, according to Zajonc, whether or not social facilitation or social impairment occurs is primarily a function of the type of task.

Direct tests of Zajonc's arousal/drive view were quite encouraging. In this research, investigators carefully manipulated task features so that dominant responses were either correct or incorrect. This work generally found, as predicted, that social facilitation occurred when dominant responses were correct and social impairment occurred when dominant responses were incorrect. For example, in Zajonc et al.'s (1969) cockroach study, the dominant response among such insects is to run from a sudden light source. Zajonc et al. arranged things so that, in one condition, the roaches could escape the aversive light by 'doing what comes naturally'; i.e. running down a straight runway as quickly as possible. Here, an audience of onlooking cockroaches facilitated this dominant response. In a second condition, however, roaches could only escape by making a sharp right-hand turn midway down the runway. This response required the insects to inhibit their dominant response (running fast) since they had to slow down for the turn. In this case, the audience impaired correct performance. Why? Because the audience strengthened the dominant and incorrect response of escaping at high speed.

This study and numerous other studies soon made it apparent that Zajonc was fundamentally correct in arguing that task characteristics play a crucial role in whether social facilitation or social impairment occurs. Consider some of the social facilitation studies done in sports settings.

Studies have shown social facilitation affects weightlifting (Meuman 1904) jogging (e.g. Strube *et al.* 1981); pool shooting (Michaels *et al.* 1982) and treadmill walking (Kohlfeld and Weitzel 1969). However, nothing is uncomplicated in social facilitation research. Paulus and Corneilius (1974) found that gymnastic performance of trained gymnasts was impaired by spectators while novices were unaffected. Similarly, Forgas *et al.* (1980) found that spectators were more likely to impair performance among experienced squash players than among novices while Sokill and Mynatt (1984), report that in sold out basketball arenas, free throw shooting becomes *less* accurate among collegiate players. In explaining these data, writers argue that even for accomplished intercollegiate athletes, high scoring gymnastic maneuvers and accurate basketball shooting are not 'dominant' responses, but instead require careful concentration on a number of subtle details. This view then would predict that social facilitation will most reliably occur on tasks that are relatively simple, primarily involving response speed and strength, in which the dominant response is completely mastered (e.g. sprinting, arm wrestling). Other sports, requiring precise form and accuracy (e.g. tennis, squash, figure skating) might not necessarily benefit according to such a view. This analysis assumes that some aspect of the task determines whether or not social facilitation will occur.

This assumption is shared by most researchers in this area. Here the agreement ends, however, for there is still a very active debate regarding why social facilitation occurs. Since Zajonc's 1965 theoretical statement, several different types of theoretical notions have been suggested as explanations for social facilitation. Some examples are presented below.

Zajonc's mere presence hypothesis

Zajonc's (1965, 1980) argument that the mere presence of species mates elevates drive/arousal remains one of the more provocative social facilitation theories. Zajonc feels that species mates have this effect because they are generally important and unpredictable stimuli that elevate uncertainty. This uncertainty can concern any number of issues. Will these people ridicule me, ignore me, evaluate me negatively, etc.? According to Zajonc, this increase in uncertainty will generally elevate arousal even in settings where others do not represent any obvious threat to subjects. They need not be competitors or evaluators, for example, to elevate arousal. This mere presence notion has some alarming implications. In a world where crowding and overpopulation are continuing problems (see Chapter 10), the idea that arousal increases just because other people are present suggests that crowding should be a serious source of physical stress. Not surprisingly, a number of studies have addressed this 'mere presence' issue.

For example, Schmitt et al. (1986) asked subjects to type their names on a computer in two ways; normally and then backwards, interspersing numbers among the letters (ostensibly in order to provide an identification code for the computer). This key activity occurred before the actual study began in order to minimize concerns over evaluation. Some subjects performed this action in the presence of a person who was blindfolded and fitted with earphones. This person was supposedly preparing for an upcoming study in perception. In this condition, normal typing ('the dominant response') was enhanced while difficult typing was impaired compared to subjects who typed alone. Several other studies have also found that working in the presence of either an inattentive audience or a blindfolded 'audience' has produced social facilitation effects (Haas and Roberts 1975; Rajecki et al. 1977; Robinson-Staveley and Cooper 1990). Since these studies rule out the possibility of competition and evaluation from others, they are usually interpreted as evidence favoring the mere presence hypothesis.

Although these studies may indicate that mere presence can affect responding in some settings, other studies suggest that the issue is a complex one. As we will see in Chapter 9, in stressful settings the presence of others usually produces arousal reduction rather than an increase in arousal. Thus, mere presence cannot be viewed as always increasing arousal. Moreover, several studies indicate that, on certain tasks, performance is only facilitated by the presence of an audience if it is evaluating or closely attending to the performer (e.g. Cottrell et al. 1968; Worringham and Messick 1983). Clearly, mere presence does not always trigger social facilitation/impairment. Guerin (1983) offers one explanation for why this might be so. He argues that uncertainty and arousal may not be strong in certain social situations. He feels that when we are performing with (or in front of) others, uncertainty should be strongest when we cannot monitor these persons. The reason for this, according to Guerin (1983), is that we cannot reassure ourselves that others in the setting are acting in a predictable and non-threatening manner. Guerin (Guerin and Innes 1982; Guerin 1983) has presented some evidence favoring this *social monitoring* view, but the data are, so far, a bit too inconsistent and sparse to permit strong conclusions (cf. Bond and Titus 1983).

This is an area that requires continued research since it seems clear that we do not yet fully understand when the mere presence of others will affect individual task performance. One very recent study by Cacioppo *et al.* (1990) suggests that Zajonc's notions regarding mere presence may require some revision. In this study researchers found little evidence of increased physiological arousal when people thought they were being periodically observed as they waited for a study to begin (i.e. in a non-evaluative setting). However, mere presence did have another type of effect. Those individuals who were observed showed stronger momentary changes in skin conductance when mild tones were played suggesting that they were more alert and sensitive to changes in their environment. Certainly, such results contribute to those data indicating that subtle forms of social presence have interesting (although complex) effects on behavior, perception and problem solving.

Cottrell's learned drive view

One alternative to Zajonc's mere presence/uncertainty view is Cottrell's learned drive position. Cottrell (1972) suggests that species mates elevate drive/arousal because, through learning, we have come to associate species mates with a variety of rewards (e.g. sexual satisfaction) and punishments (e.g. competing for food). As a result of this conditioning, we will often experience anticipatory excitement from the mere sight of such individuals, provided that the situational cues remind us of these past associations. An example of this process would be getting nervous seeing someone at a business meeting with whom you've had severe disagreements in past meetings. Cottrell would argue that the sight of this person at a party (a different setting) might produce little agitation, but seeing the same old enemy in a setting resembling your usual battleground would produce substantial arousal.

Cottrell's position is interesting in that it can explain both animal and human social facilitation. The theory also holds that in humans, social facilitation should primarily occur when the situation is competitive or evaluative since these settings should have the strongest past associations with rewards and punishments from others. Anyone who has experienced nervousness on stage or before an athletic contest will appreciate this view. This commonsensical notion has a good deal of support. In one of Cottrell's own studies (Cottrell *et al.* 1968), social facilitation effects did not occur if the audience was blindfolded (these blindfolded subjects were supposedly preparing for another study). In addition, a number of studies have found that competition from coworkers and attention from audiences heighten social facilitation (cf. Geen and Gange 1977). For example, both Strube *et al.* (1981), and Worringham and Messick (1983) found that the presence of spectators at a jogging track only increased jogging speed if onlookers attended to the runner's performance.

Despite these data, there is still a good deal of controversy regarding the role of evaluation and competition. Bond and Titus (1983), in an extensive meta-analytical review, found little statistical evidence that varying the degree of evaluation altered social facilitation phenomena when one 'averaged' over studies. Whether this result is due to averaging across different types of manipulations or problems in the experimental procedures in certain studies is hard to say. However, most social facilitation researchers feel that, at the very least, evaluation and competition contribute to social facilitation effects (Baron 1986; Harkins and Szymanski 1987a,b; Myers 1987; Geen 1989). A key link in this argument is that in several studies social facilitation effects are strongest in people who test high in trait anxiety (e.g. Geen 1980b, 1985) or who are particularly concerned about achievement and competition (Gastorf *et al.* 1980). However, enough nagging questions remain to encourage continued research.

Distraction/conflict theory

According to this theoretical perspective social facilitation occurs because audiences, co-actors and even bystanders often lead performers into 'attentional temptation' in which they are placed in conflict regarding whether to attend to their species mates or to their ongoing task. In such cases, the performer wishes to pay attention to more than he or she can manage, and the resulting conflict leads to drive/arousal and stress, which in turn produces the social facilitation/social impairment effects described earlier. Imagine a case where you are frantically trying to meet some typing deadline for a course, when at the same time the phone rings, the coffee begins to boil over in its pot and your puppy begins to chew on a book you borrowed from your professor. This dilemma should give you a feeling for the stress that attentional conflict involves. According to the authors of this theory (e.g. Baron *et al.* 1978; Sanders *et al.* 1978) others can be distracting for a variety of reasons. In task settings, however, a key reason will often be the desire to compare our performance to others or to check the audience's reaction to our performance.

In lower organisms, attention to others may be caused by a concern over attack, competition for scarce resources, sexual attraction or simply herding instincts. This distraction will often lead to attentional conflict in animals. Since conflict is a well established source of drive, this theoretical view can account nicely for the facilitation of dominant responding in both animals and humans that so strongly characterizes the social facilitation literature. Distraction/conflict theory is provocative, however, in that it suggests that distraction during a simple task will actually improve performance if it triggers attentional conflict. There are a number of findings which support this view (see Baron 1986 and Sanders, 1981 for reviews). For example, as early as 1933, Pessin reported that distracting subjects with lights and buzzers improved their performance on a well-learned memory task. Very similar performance increases occurred if subjects were simply observed by the experimenter. In short, an audience had precisely the same effect as a mechanical distraction. Years later Sanders and Baron (1975) added to these results, by finding that distracting subjects produced precisely the facilitation/impairment effects usually produced by the presence of others.

In one study, Moore *et al.* (1988) found that an audience and a visual distraction produced extremely similar patterns of heart rate and skin conductance during a reaction time task. In short, here again the data suggest that audiences are distracting, but distraction/conflict theory goes beyond the assertion that others are distracting. It argues that *conflict* is the crucial cause of social facilitation. This is not an easy hypothesis to test directly, but there is one relevant study. Groff *et al.* (1983) reasoned that one way to prevent attentional conflict from occurring in an audience experiment is to give subjects the task of *attending to the audience*.

In this way, the usual 'conflict' between attending to either the task or the audience is eliminated. Therefore, in a low conflict condition, subjects were told to record periodically whether a face on a TV screen was reacting positively or negatively. In this condition, this TV image was a live camera transmission of a confederate sitting several feet away from the TV screen, presumably evaluating the subject. This fact was obvious to the subject. Therefore, if subjects watched the TV screen (their primary task) they were monitoring the audience as well. In a high conflict condition the facial image on the television screen was not the face of the evaluating confederate, but instead a recorded video. As a result, in this high conflict condition, if subjects wished to examine the confederates (seated several feet from the television), they had to glance away from their primary task. In a third condition, subjects performed the rating task with no evaluator present. In all conditions, subjects were asked to squeeze a plastic bottle whenever they made a rating (see Figure 2.1). As predicted, Groff *et al.* only found evidence of social facilitation on this squeeze response in the high conflict condition. In short, the presence of an evaluating audience only had an impact on responding if attentional conflict was likely.

This study strongly suggests that attentional conflict contributes directly to social facilitation phenomenon. If so, this may explain some of the puzzling inconsistencies in the social facilitation literature. Sometimes the mere presence of others produces social facilitation, but sometimes it does not. Sometimes blindfolded audiences lead to social facilitation, but not always. In many studies, evaluation, competition or direct attention from the audience seem crucial to produce social facilitation, but others report that evaluation manipulations have little effect on social facilitation phenomena.

It seems possible that at least some of these contradictions may be due to distraction differences. Seeing others in blindfolds is curious, unusual and thought provoking, and could well distract subjects from their task in many situations. However, in some settings the cover story explaining why blindfolds are needed may be so persuasive and skillfully administered that curiosity (and consequent distraction) is minimized. Similarly, in some settings the mere presence of bystanders may provoke distraction (the bystanders could be physically attractive, extremely well dressed or perhaps ill at ease), whereas in other situations bystanders may

Figure 2.1 Layout used by Groff, Baron and Moore

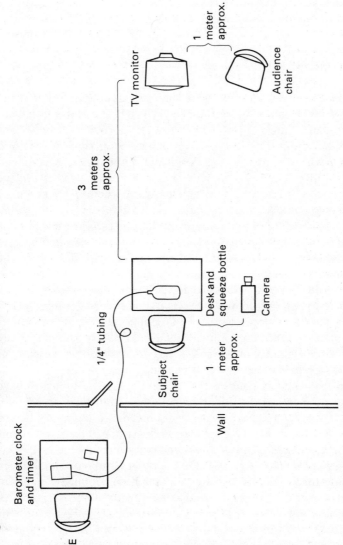

Source: Groff *et al.* (1983). Reprinted with permission of Academic Press. All rights reserved.
Note: Door in wall closed during experiment.

be so ordinary that little distraction occurs. Even evaluation pressure may produce 'internal' distraction if individuals are distracted from the task by worrying about how well they are doing. These variations may explain why social facilitation results are sometimes inconsistent from study to study.

Drive theory on trial

All the theories discussed above share the assumption that social conditions produce drive/arousal which then facilitates dominant responding. Lately, however, a number of writers have raised questions about this view (Manstead and Semin 1980; Carver and Scheier 1981; Glaser 1982; Bond and Titus 1983; Moore and Baron 1983; Geen 1989). One reason for these doubts are the results from those studies which measure whether physiological arousal (e.g. blood pressure, pulse, skin conductance) is increased by the presence of others. Moore and Baron (1983) reviewed some 29 tests of the notion that audiences or co-actors elevated arousal and found that it did so in eleven such tests and did not in the remaining eighteen. Using a different analysis strategy, Bond and Titus (1983) found evidence that audiences increased physiological activity during complex tasks, but not during simple tasks. These data are supplemented by Cacioppo et al.'s (1990) report that mere presence does not elevate arousal. Such data are hardly congruent with Zajonc's (1965) argument that the presence of others increases the individual's general arousal or drive level.[1] An additional cause of doubt is that in certain studies, audiences have failed to increase dominant responding. Manstead and Semin (1980), for example, conducted five substudies using four different tasks and found no evidence that audiences heightened dominant responses. Glaser (1982) lists some sixty-one instances of such failures occurring since 1965. On the other hand, you should keep in mind that well over 200 studies have been conducted on social facilitation over the years, and consequently some variation in results are to be expected. Indeed, in their extensive review of both published and unpublished work covering over 20 000 subjects, Bond and Titus (1983) found 'on average' reasonable evidence of social facilitation on simple tasks and social impairment on complex tasks. Nevertheless, the inconsistencies in this database have encouraged social facilitation researchers to consider non-drive explanations for social facilitation. In the next section, we will discuss several examples.

Self-awareness theory

This position (Duval and Wicklund 1972; Carver and Scheier 1981), holds that social facilitation occurs because audiences or co-actors heighten self-consciousness. This increased self-awareness is presumed to make us more aware of any discrepancies between our own performance and some idealized standard, which in turn leads us to improve our performance. Although this theory does not formally refer to the concept of drive, you should note that it does assume the self-aware individual will 'try harder' to perform well. This idea comes quite close to the notion that our 'drive' to perform is higher when others are present. Social impairment occurs on difficult tasks presumably because if self-aware people see that they are not gaining on their goal, they withdraw psychologically or physically from the task. That is, their motivation (drive?) drops and they 'stop trying' to excel. Presumably, this occurs more among self-conscious subjects because they pay closer attention to how well they are performing.

In order to test self-awareness theory, researchers have increased self-awareness using innovative manipulations such as having subjects work before a mirror. The effects of high self-awareness on performance are then compared to the effects of audiences. In several studies, both audiences and high self-awareness have been found to facilitate performance. Usually, the required task involves copying German prose as quickly as possible. For example, Carver and Scheier (1981) had forty undergraduates perform this task either before a mirror (high self-awareness) or while the experimenter watched closely (audience). Both conditions improved performance.

Theories of self-presentation and self-perception

Several writers argue that audiences and co-actors affect performance by increasing our concerns about projecting a positive self-image to onlookers. Whereas Carver and Scheier's self-awareness view emphasizes the need to 'feel good about oneself', self-presentational views (e.g. Bond 1982) stress the need to 'look good to others'. According to Bond, social impairment occurs on difficult tasks because initial failures produce embarrassment, which then disrupts performance. Several findings are consistent with this view. Bond and Titus (1983) observed that in general, social conditions are far more likely to provoke arousal on complex tasks. They believe that this reflects the embarrassment that they feel is likely on these tasks.

The self-presentation view and the self-awareness view share some of the same limitations. First, they both propose two separate explanations to account for facilitation and impairment, whereas drive theory requires only one. As a result, these theories violate the *law of parsimony*, in that they suggest a complicated process where a less complex one would suffice. Secondly, neither seems to apply easily to the animal or 'mere presence' results. However, it does seem plausible that self-consciousness and self-presentation affect performance in social situations. The challenge for future research is to document this process more carefully.

Attentional theories

Yet another alternative to the drive/arousal view of social facilitation are theories that emphasize how the presence of others affects information processing and attention. For example, overload can occur because the organism is trying to attend to more things (such as the task and the audience) than he or she has the capacity to process. How does the overload notion account for social facilitation? The key fact is that when we are bombarded with attentional demands, our focus of attention actually shrinks (e.g. Geen 1976, 1980a). Under such conditions, individuals attend to a narrower range of stimuli. This can lead to facilitation of performance in cases where a task requires us to process only a very few stimuli. A narrow focus allows an individual to 'screen out' irrelevant stimuli and concentrate on the key task features. In contrast, a narrow focus will impair performance if the task requires the individual to attend to a wide range of cues for here the narrow focus will screen out cues that are essential to the task.

Manstead and Semin (1980) suggest a related notion, arguing that task facilitation effects occur primarily on tasks that have become more or less automatic. On such tasks performance only requires that the performer process a narrow range of cues. Manstead and Semin (1980) reason that under these circumstances the presence of others will improve performance by increasing attention to task-related cues and by making subjects more aware of minor errors. On non-automatic tasks, however, a narrow attentional focus screens out needed cues. This perspective suggests that social facilitation effects may be limited to tasks where the correct response is more than just 'dominant', but instead more or less 'second nature' to the performer. Despite some preliminary findings that support the idea that audiences lead to a narrowing in attentional perspective (Bruning et al. 1968; Geen 1976), the research, to date, is sparse. The attraction of this view is that it nicely integrates a good number of the theoretical perspectives we have already discussed. Social uncertainty, self-consciousness and attentional conflict all are states that should provoke overload because they are likely to absorb attention (Geen 1989). It remains to be seen whether this overload view will be supported by the research that is conducted in the years to come.

Summary

After some 90 years of research on social facilitation several conclusions can be drawn. In most cases, having others around us appears to facilitate simple tasks and impair performance on complex ones (Bond and Titus 1983). These phenomena have been observed across a wide range of species and tasks. Most researchers believe that evaluation and competition enhance such effects. However, in a number of 'mere presence' studies, social facilitation has occurred when evaluation and competition appear to have been kept low. Such 'mere presence' effects, however, do not always occur. In some situations, social facilitation only has been found when competition, evaluation, distraction or careful scrutiny from others exists (e.g. Groff et al., 1983; Worringham and Messick 1983). Inconsistencies such as these have prompted a number of theoretical explanations in an attempt to integrate existing findings. Certain theories argue that when we are near others, our drive and arousal is stronger, thereby strengthening our dominant responses. Despite a large number of behavioral findings that support this view, studies that employ physiological measures (e.g. heart rate, skin conductance) do *not* consistently show higher levels of physiological activity (i.e. high arousal) when audiences and co-actors are present. This suggests that some revision of a strict arousal view may be necessary. A second group of theories emphasize self-consciousness and subject's concerns over self-image. Here too, the data are mixed, suggesting that these factors probably influence social facilitation effects, but do not completely explain the full range of data associated with the social facilitation area.

A third theoretical direction holds that attentional mechanisms are responsible for social facilitation phenomena. Attentional theories are appealing. They can explain a good deal of conflicting data and provide a means of integrating many of the theories that already exist. Unfortunately, there is not a great deal of relevant evidence regarding such views and so, for the moment, they must be regarded no more than that of a promising direction for future work.

Note

1 In the early theories of drive (e.g. Spence 1956), states of heightened drive were not equated with physiological arousal. For this reason some have argued that the physiological data is irrelevant to Zajonc's assertions regarding drive (Sanders 1981). Zajonc (1965), however, in his classic paper, did not draw a distinction between drive and arousal often using the terms interchangeably. Clearly, his views draw heavily from those who argue that arousal and drive should have similar effects on behavior (cf. Moore and Baron 1983, footnote 5). As such, we feel the physiological data are quite crucial to the 'drive' view of social facilitation.

Suggestions for further reading

Baron, R. S. (1986). Distraction-conflict theory. Progress and problems. In L. Berkowitz (ed.) *Advances in Experimental Social Psychology*, vol. 19, pp. 1–40. New York: Academic Press.

Bond, C. F. and Titus, L. J. (1983). Social facilitation: A meta-analysis of 241 studies. *Psychological Bulletin*, 94, 265–92.

Geen, R. G. (1989). Alternative conceptions of social facilitation. In P. Paulus (ed.) *Psychology of Group Influence*; 2nd edn. Hillsdale, NJ: Erlbaum.

Zajonc, R. B. (1980). Compresence. In P. Paulus (ed.) *Psychology of Group Influence*, pp. 35–60. Hillsdale, NJ: Erlbaum.

3 / INDIVIDUAL VERSUS GROUP PERFORMANCE

In the previous chapter we were concerned with the effects of the presence of others on individual performance. However, there is usually more to being in a group than just being in one another's presence. This is particularly true for groups which are trying to accomplish something – complete a laboratory report, plan a party, elect a candidate, etc. Members of such task groups typically interact with and influence one another, perceive themselves to be a group with a shared objective and a shared fate.

In this chapter we examine the ways in which individual and group performances are related. One important theme in our discussion will be that the link between individual and group performance cannot be understood without careful attention to the nature of the task. Here we will focus on what McGrath (1984) calls *cooperative tasks*. For such tasks, group members have a shared interest in working together toward some group goal. Such tasks also have some standard for evaluating performance.

Early research

In many ways, early research on group performance paralleled early research on social facilitation. In both instances, rather simple questions were posed initially. For group performance, that simple question was, 'which is more productive, groups or individuals?' One well-known study in this tradition was done by Shaw (1932). In a classroom setting, both individuals and four-person groups attempted to a series of intellectual puzzles. On one puzzle, three married couples are trying to cross a river. There is a boat available, but it can hold only three passengers. However, there were additional constraints (which reflected the sex and marital norms of the day). First, only the husbands can row and secondly, no husband will allow his wife to be in the presence of any of the other husbands unless he is also present. (If you have trouble solving the problem, the answer is provided at the end of the chapter.) This is an example of what Lorge *et al.* (1958) call a *eureka task*. If a correct solution for a eureka task is proposed, it should be clear immediately (or, at most, only after a quick confirmation check) that it is indeed correct. The 'husbands and wives' problem turned out to be fairly difficult for individuals in Shaw's study; only 3 out of 21 were able to solve the problem correctly. However, the majority of groups (viz. 3 out of 5) solved the problem. Shaw obtained similar results for the other puzzles she examined. Why did groups do better than individuals? Shaw's observation of the groups suggested to her that it was largely because of certain unique advantages for the groups – group members could catch one another's errors and reject incorrect solutions. This sounds plausible, but as we shall soon see, may be incorrect.

Shaw's basic finding summarizes the pattern obtained in numerous early comparisons of groups and individuals, not only for problem solving tasks, but also for production, learning and memory tasks. Although there were exceptions to the rule and the differences were not always large, groups generally learned faster, made fewer errors, recalled better, were more productive with a higher quality product than individuals (for reviews, see Davis 1969; Laughlin 1980). However, there was one way in which groups were typically inferior to individuals – the productivity per person. For example, if instead of simply comparing groups and individuals on the time needed for a solution (which tends to favor groups in most studies), we compare the number of *person-minutes* required (i.e. solution time × size of the group), then groups usually required more person-minutes. At least on a practical level, where an employer's payroll ultimately depends on the number of person-minutes required to complete some task, this could be an important advantage of individual performance. In summary, groups were generally more *effective* than individuals, while individuals were usually more *efficient* than groups.

Task, resources, and potential: Steiner's model of group performance

If you think for long about the simple question, 'which is more productive, individuals or groups?', you are likely to arrive at the typical common answer to any such overly simple question – 'it depends'. It clearly depends upon how capable the group members are at the task. Groups with incapable members may often underperform a skilled individual (e.g. a skilled lumberjack could undoubtedly cut, trim, split, and load more timber on his own than any given group of, say, 3 psychology professors). Less obviously, it also depends upon the kind of task one is considering. Certainly, if the task is one which allows group members to pool their efforts (e.g. pulling on a rope in a tug-of-war), groups should do better than individuals (with comparable abilities). But one can also think of tasks for which the reverse should be true. For example, tasks which require extremely precise coordination of action (e.g. splitting a diamond, driving a car) will probably be performed better by an individual than by a group. A well-trained individual can carefully control and coordinate his/her actions better than a group, which has more limited capacities for close coordination of member action. If this is correct, then the general conclusions which have emerged from the early study of individual *v.* group performance (tending to favor groups) may have as much or more to do with the types of tasks which were selected for study than with any general superiority of groups.

But where does this leave us when we have to decide whether or not to assign a job to individuals or groups? Steiner (1966, 1972) has proposed a model that helped reduce much of this confusion. The central concept in Steiner's model is the notion of a group's *potential productivity*, the group's maximum possible level of productivity at a task. He suggests that this depends on two factors – *member resources* and *task demands*. Let's consider each of these factors.

Member resources '. . . include all the relevant knowledge, abilities, skills, or tools possessed by the individual(s) who is attempting to perform the task' (Steiner 1972, p. 7). What makes a particular resource relevant, of course, depends on the task – physical strength is a resource at a tug-of-war, but not at an anagram task. A task's demands encompass several task features, the most basic of these being the task performance criterion –

what aspect of performance is being measured. Asking a group to read a page as fast as possible with no concern for comprehension is a fundamentally different task than asking it to read for maximal comprehension. Steiner suggests that if one knows a group's resources and the demands of its task, one can estimate the group's potential productivity. For example, if you knew how hard each of four members of a tug-of-war team could pull the rope individually, one could estimate the team's potential as the simple sum of those pulls. It would be rare, though, for a group to achieve its potential. Like machines which can never achieve 100 per cent efficiency, we would expect groups likewise to fall short of their potential. Steiner called this shortfall *process loss* and proposed that Actual productivity = Potential productivity – Process loss. Process loss reflects a group's failure to act in the most productive way possible. Steiner suggested that there are two general sources of process loss. *Coordination losses* occur when group members do not organize their efforts optimally. For example, if members of the tug-of-war team pull at different times, the force that the group exerts on the rope is diminished. When group members fail to be optimally motivated, *motivation losses* result. So, if members of the tug-of-war team did not try as hard when working together as when working alone, motivation losses would contribute to process loss.

With this simple equation, Steiner shifted attention away from the old, simple question, 'are groups more productive than individuals?' Since actual group productivity depends upon many factors (member resources, task demands, group processes), it became clear that there could be no general answer. Instead, Steiner posed new, more interesting questions – are groups as productive as they can be and if not, why not? In one form or another, those questions will concern us through the remainder of this and the next chapter.

Steiner also provided another useful tool for tackling these questions – a task classification or taxonomy. Steiner argues persuasively that the task is crucial for any analysis of group performance. However, is every task unique, or are there certain basic task features which enable us to classify tasks in meaningful and useful ways? Steiner suggested three such features. One is whether the task can or cannot be subdivided into subtasks, each of which may be performed by different individuals. Tasks which can, he termed *divisible*; those which cannot are *unitary*. The nature of the performance criterion offers a second feature. *Maximizing* tasks make success a function of how much or how rapidly something is done; our familiar tug-of-war task is a good example. *Optimizing* tasks make success a function of achieving some correct or optimal solution; the 'husbands and wives' problem is an example.

The final task feature identified by Steiner concerns how task demands link individual resources to potential group productivity. He identifies four types of unitary tasks. In a *disjunctive* task, the group must select the answer or contributions of a single member. That being the case, it should select the best or most proficient member's contribution. The 'husband and wives' problem is a unitary, disjunctive task; only one answer can be given and the group should select the answer of its most capable member. In a *conjunctive* task, the group's level of productivity is necessarily that of the least capable member. A good example of a conjunct-ive task is a mountain-climbing team connected to one another by ropes; the team can go no faster than its slowest member. In an *additive* task, the group product is the sum of group member contributions. The tug-of-war task is clearly an additive task. Finally, in *discretionary tasks*, group members may combine individual inputs in any manner they choose. For example, in a blues band, the group could combine the contributions of the various musicians in any way it liked from performance to per-formance.

To better understand this task taxonomy, imagine three track teams each containing four runners competing in the 400 m run. Suppose that the runners finishing times are as follows: Team A – 46 s, 47 s, 47 s and 49 s; Team B – 44 s, 45 s, 49 s and 53 s; and Team C – 45 s, 45 s, 46 s and 51 s. Which team wins the event? It depends on how team performance is defined – that is, on the demands of the groups' task. If the winning team is the team of the first runner to cross the finish line (disjunctive task demands), then Team B wins. However, if every member of the team must cross the finish line before the team has finished the race (conjunctive task demands), then Team A is the winner. And if the team score is the simple sum of the times of its four runners (additive task demands), then Team C has the best (i.e. lowest) score.

Clearly, many real tasks do not fit neatly into this taxonomy, but often complex, divisible group tasks can be broken down into parts which can be identified with one of Steiner's task types.

More importantly, Steiner's taxonomy has proved to be a useful guide for much basic research on fundamental processes in task performing groups.

To illustrate the application of Steiner's ideas, consider the 'husbands and wives' problem used by Shaw (1932). To determine a group's potential productivity, one needs to specify the task's demands. First, since the goal is to come up with the unique correct answer, this is an optimizing task. Secondly, since the task cannot be subdivided (e.g. you can't assign the first group member the job of getting Husband 1 across, the second, Wife 1, etc.), the task is unitary. It would also appear to be disjunctive; in theory, if any group member is capable of solving the problem correctly, the group should likewise be capable of solving the problem. What is the group's potential productivity? One can intuitively see that groups have the potential of being more productive than individuals; a random sample of four persons (a group) seems more likely to include at least one person who can solve the problem than a sample of only one person (an individual). Shaw found that 3/21 or 14.3 per cent of individuals could solve the problem. Others (Taylor 1954; Lorge and Solomon 1955) have shown that with this rate of individual solution, the probability of randomly composing a four-person group that contains at least one solver is 0.46. This figure is not significantly different than the actual rate of success Shaw observed in her four-person groups (viz. 3/5 or 0.60). This kind of analysis leads us to rather different conclusions than those reached by Shaw. She thought the superiority of her groups was largely due to better error checking in groups. However, Taylor's, and Lorge and Solomon's analyses suggests that one might attribute the superiority of her groups entirely to their greater likelihood of containing at least one solver (i.e. to the greater resources the group possessed) rather than to any cooperative social process like error checking.

However, as noted above, groups do not generally operate without process loss. Most studies which have made the comparison find that groups fall below their potential (i.e. that there is considerable process loss; see Davis 1969; Steiner 1972; Laughlin 1980, for reviews). A good example, which nicely illustrates how such comparisons of potential and actual group productivity can teach us something about group performance is Davis and Restle's (1963) study. They considered intellective problems similar to

Shaw's (1932), but rather than focusing solely on whether a solution was reached, they focused on how long it took individuals and groups to reach a solution. The basic idea was similar to the Taylor/Lorge and Solomon 'best member' approach. First, estimate how fast individual solvers reach their solution. Then estimate the speed of group solution under the assumption that the group should solve at the speed of its fastest solver. Davis and Restle (1963) found that groups were consistently slower than one would expect given this model. Thus, there was some process loss, but what might the source of this process loss be? Davis and Restle (Restle and Davis 1962; Davis and Restle 1963) suggested that perhaps these groups were too egalitarian; that is, every member might seek or be allotted part of the group's interaction time, even when they had little to offer (e.g. they might not be able to solve the problem). If you have ever been in a meeting where you and everyone else politely waited while some dimwit carefully elaborated on an obviously silly proposal, you have witnessed this process in action. Davis and Restle modified their original 'hierarchical' model, which assumed the groups could operate as fast as the best member, by assuming that the rate of progress a solver could make was inversely related to the number of non-solvers in the group. This modified, 'equalitarian' model of potential productivity fit the groups' actual productivity speed-of-solution data very well. Rather than simply concluding that groups were more productive than individuals, Restle and Davis's analysis gave more direct insight into the sources of their groups' effectiveness (and ineffectiveness).

Steiner's model implies that there exists a single, unique potential productivity baseline which constitutes an upper boundary on group performance. This may be true for certain simple tasks, but in many instances, there may even be more than one way of defining a group's potential productivity. For example, it makes sense to assume that a group can do no better than its most capable member at the 'husbands and wives' problem, but what if Shaw was right; what if groups can catch and correct errors in ways that individuals cannot? Groups might not only solve the problem if they contain at least one solver, they might also not pursue or submit an incorrect solution if there is at least one member who can recognize that it is incorrect.

Or consider a simple analogies task, like those you have probably seen on tests of verbal ability – 'is it true that A is to B as

C is to D?' How might you define a group's potential productivity in terms of the resources (vocabularies, verbal reasoning abilities) its members possess? You could think of this as a disjunctive task and assume that the group should get the correct answer if any group member is correct. (It has been shown, by the way, that groups usually fall short of this baseline; see, for example, Laughlin *et al.* 1975, 1976.) However, this task may also be considered divisible. A four-person group may contain no person who knows the meaning of all four words (A, B, C and D), yet the group may still obtain the correct answer if the meaning of each word is known by at least one member.

Steiner's analysis also implicitly assumes that individuals cannot be any more motivated in groups than they are when working individually, but at least theoretically, people may have higher motivation levels in some group settings (Hackman and Morris 1975). That is, it is possible that groups exhibit *motivation gains* as well as motivation losses. Social facilitation research suggests one feature of group settings (viz. the presence of others) which can enhance motivation. The point of this discussion is that there may be more than one reasonable way of defining a group's potential; and there are many more possible theoretical baselines which embody certain types of process loss (as the Davis and Restle study illustrates). Each such baseline makes different assumptions about how a group functions and by comparing different baselines against actual group behavior, we can get a better idea of which set of assumptions are psychologically reasonable and which are not.

The experimental analysis of process loss

We have been discussing one way of analyzing and understanding group process losses – through testing the goodness-of-fit of theoretical models. Another approach is first to identify an instance of process loss and then to analyze it experimentally. That is, one can determine whether certain variables or processes contribute to the process loss by carefully varying or assessing the conditions of group performance and seeing whether the level of process loss is affected. Below we describe a number of such analyses.

Group member characteristics

A series of older studies was reinterpreted by Steiner (1972) using this approach. All of the studies utilized the 'horse trader problem' which asks, 'A man bought a horse for $60 and sold it for $70. Then he bought it back for $80 and sold it for $90. How much money did he make in the horse business?' (Maier and Solem 1952). This is a unitary, optimizing and disjunctive task. Any group containing a solver should be able to come up with the correct answer (which is $20). Not surprisingly for this type of task, a group is more likely to correctly solve the problem than a single individual, but what is more surprising is that many groups that potentially could solve the problem do not. For example, in Maier and Solem's (1952) original study, less than 80 per cent of the groups that contained at least one person who had correctly solved the problem while working individually ended up solving the problem. Why?

Part of the answer may be that it is not enough that a group member can solve a problem. She or he must share that solution with the rest of the group and it must then be accepted by the group. Many factors, unrelated to the quality of one's ideas, can interfere with these steps in the group problem solving process. For example, group members who can solve the problem, but who have low status in the group may be less willing or able to present their solution. Furthermore, that solution may be under-valued by the rest of the group because of their low status. As we saw in a previous chapter, Torrance's (1954b) study with bomber crews dramatically illustrated this process. Only 6 per cent of solving pilots failed to persuade their crew they were correct. For tailgunners the figure was 37 per cent.

Another factor which seems likely to affect solvers' behavior is their confidence in their solution. The less confidence you have in your solution (even if it might be a correct solution), the less likely you are to propose, let alone defend, that solution in the group. Johnson and Torcivia (1967) had students work on the horse trader problem individually. They reached solutions and indicated their confidence in those solutions. Then dyads (i.e. two-person groups) consisting of one solver and one non-solver were composed. Potentially, all these dyads should have solved, but only 72 per cent did so. As suggested above, the relative confidence of the two members in their solution was strongly related to whether the group solved. When the solver was more confident than the non-solver, the group solved 94 per cent of the time, but when it was the non-solver who was more confident, the group only solved 29 per cent of the time (cf. Hinsz 1990).

Of course, unless the task is a eureka task, just presenting a solution to the group may not be enough to lead the group to accept it. It must usually be defended – its rationale must be presented, arguments against it must be refuted, the incorrectness of alternative solutions must be pointed out, etc. This cannot be done without taking a vigorous part in group discussion of the problem. Thus, all else being equal, we would expect greater process loss when a solver said little than when she or he said much. A subset of the groups studied by Thomas and Fink (1961) address this question. In each of these 18 groups there was only one solver. Potentially, every group could solve, but only six actually did, but in every one of these six groups, it was the solver who was the most talkative member of the group. A non-solver was the most talkative member in eleven of the twelve groups that failed. So we see that groups sometimes fall short of their potential because the most capable member in the group is not always the most confident, talkative or high status member.

Brainstorming

Other sources of process loss are constraints or distractions arising directly from the process of interaction in groups. A good example is the process loss occurring in brainstorming groups. Brainstorming is a group performance technique designed to facilitate creative thinking (Osborn 1957). Group members are instructed to generate as many ideas as possible, to build on others' ideas when possible and not to criticize any ideas. The group task of generating as many creative ideas as possible does not fit simply into Steiner's task taxonomy. The task of coming up with any particular idea is disjunctive – as long as one member has the idea, the group should, too. However, the task of accumulating such ideas is additive – the more (unique) uses a member generates, the better the group's performance. An average n-person group's potential productivity (in terms of the *number* of ideas) should be equal to the performance of a *nominal group* (i.e. the total number of unique ideas that n separate individuals can generate). Osborn (1957) suggested that brainstorming groups can even exceed this potential: '... the average person can think up twice as many ideas when working with a group than when working alone' (p. 229).

However, nearly all the studies that have made this comparison have found that actual brainstorming groups usually produce fewer (sometimes less than 50 per cent as many) ideas as nominal groups (Lamm and Trommsdorff 1973; Diehl and Stroebe 1987). Although there seem to be several reasons for this process loss, the main reason appears to be *production blocking*: only one group member can talk at any one time in a brainstorming group. Diehl and Stroebe (1987) showed, for example, that four individuals who verbally generated ideas in isolation, but who could only speak whenever another person in the 'group' was not speaking performed as poorly as an actual, interacting four-person group. Both performed far less well than four-person nominal groups where there was no production blocking. It is unclear at this point exactly why this is true. It may be hard to think of or remember ideas while waiting for a turn to talk, or one may feel less responsibility to contribute an idea if other group members are already doing so.

Group size and performance

In a way, the study of group size is just an extension of the old 'individual *v.* group' comparison, except now the comparison is between smaller and larger groups. So it is not surprising that early research on group size, like the individual *v.* group research, often paid little attention to task features and did not define potential productivity. Thomas and Fink (1963) reviewed this early work. Although a few studies found no effect of group size on group performance, the majority of studies did. In a study which competes with Triplett (1898) for the distinction of being the first experiment in social psychology (Kravitz and Martin 1986), Ringelmann (1913) obtained typical results. Ringelmann had individuals and groups of 2, 3 or 8 males pull on a rope as hard as possible. The average force (in kilograms) was: individuals – 63 kg; two-person group – 118 kg; three-person group – 160 kg; eight-person group – 248 kg. Clearly, group performance increased with group size, but the rate of increase was negatively accelerated; addition of new members to the group had diminishing returns on productivity. That is, the addition of another person to the group increased group productivity, but the size of that increase was less than the increase due to the last person added to the group. Similar results have been observed for groups working on intellectual puzzles (Taylor and Faust 1952), creativity tasks (Gibb 1951), perceptual judgments and complex reasoning (Ziller 1957).

Steiner's (1972) model suggests that in order to understand the effect of group size on actual productivity, one needs to understand the effect of group size on potential productivity and on process loss, and these both require careful attention to task demands. Group size should have very different effects for different tasks. For example, consider a disjunctive task like the 'husbands and wives' puzzle. Potential productivity for such a task depends on the probability of having a solver. As Lorge and Solomon (1955) have shown, for disjunctive tasks (e.g. intellective puzzles, complex reasoning), the probability of the group containing at least one solver and, hence, the group's potential productivity, is an increasing, negatively accelerated function of group size.

However, if the group is working on a conjunctive task (e.g. a tethered climbing team), larger groups should generally have a lower potential productivity. The larger the group, the better the chances of containing a low ability, non-solving group member. However, if the group is performing an additive task, like a tug-of-war, potential productivity ought to increase linearly in group size. In principle, a randomly-composed four-person team ought to be able to do twice as much as a randomly-composed two-person team. The moral should be clear – how well large *v.* small groups *can* perform depends very much upon the nature of the group's task.

The relationship between group size and group process loss is less clear. Steiner (1972) speculated that, for most tasks, coordination losses increase with group size and often do so in an accelerating manner. The number of ways in which a group can organize itself (e.g. divide responsibilities, combine contributions, coordinate efforts) increase rapidly as a group gets larger. For example, in a tug-of-war task with n-person groups, the total number of pairings of members who must coordinate their efforts (i.e. pull at the same time and in the same direction) increases very rapidly with group size [specifically there are $n(n-2)/2$ such pairings; Steiner, 1972]. Again, task demands are crucial. For some tasks, coordination problems do not increase with size (e.g. group members working simultaneously, but independently on anagrams). For other tasks, coordination problems quickly become severe as the group gets larger (e.g. a human-pyramid crossing a tightrope).

For such high coordination tasks we might expect coordination losses to increase faster with group size than potential productivity does; this would mean that actual productivity should actually drop as the group gets larger. This was nicely demonstrated in a study by Kelley et al. (1965), which simulated an important group task – evacuating a burning building. Group members were placed in separate booths. Each booth contained a switch. By pressing this switch for 3 seconds, one could escape an electric shock. However, there was a catch – if more than one person pressed their switch at the same time, no one could escape (just as an exit may be blocked if too many people try to squeeze through at once). Signal lights in each booth indicated whether or not others were pressing their switches. Clearly, group members had to co-ordinate their actions for everyone to escape. Groups were all given ample time to escape – 6 seconds per member, so potential productivity was uniformly high for groups of every size. How-ever, Kelley et al. (1965, Study 2) found that actual productivity dropped as the group size increased; for example, in a four-person group the number of persons per second escaping was 0.16, while this figure was 0.04 in a seven-person group. Since potential pro-ductivity was constant across group sizes, this means that process loss (most likely coordination loss) increased with group size for this task.

Steiner (1972) also speculates that in many task settings motiv-ation losses may also increase with group size. For example, when the reward for successful group performance is fixed, adding more people to the group clearly reduces each member's share and, thus, the incentive to exert effort on the group's behalf. We will consider several other sources of motivation loss in the next chapter.

Recall that Davis and Restle (1963) found that groups did not solve disjunctive intellective puzzles as quickly as the hierar-chical (i.e. 'best member') model would predict, but that the equalitarian model (which linked solvers' rate of progress to the proportion of solvers in the group) predicted group solution times well. Bray et al. (1978) obtained similar results in situations com-parable to those examined by Davis and Restle (small groups considering fairly challenging puzzles), but when the problems became easier or the groups became larger, groups took longer to solve the problems than either of these models predicted. A new model was needed, one which provided for an even slower rate of progress than the 'equalitarian' model.

What might slow down such groups? One could think of several possibilities: maybe there is a certain amount of time needed to organize a group which is unnecessary for individuals (Bales and Strodtbeck 1951), or perhaps non-solvers act as even more of a drag on solvers' progress than the equalitarian model assumes. Bray *et al.* (1978) suggested another possibility. Stephan and Mishler (1952) found that the proportion of active speakers in discussion groups declined with group size. Perhaps the proportion of active participants in task groups also drops as group size increases. Even though there may be ten persons in the group, if only a few people are actively trying to solve the problem, the group's *functional size* could be much smaller and, as we've already noted, smaller groups would be expected to solve more slowly. In fact, Bray *et al.* (1978) found that, in most instances, groups were solving about as fast as the fastest solver in 'groups' of one or two persons. When ten-person groups are functioning like individuals, there clearly is considerable process loss occurring. This could reflect coordination losses, such as the production blocking noted earlier for brainstorming groups. For example, if group interaction simply consisted of one group member at a time thinking out loud about the puzzle, it could be distracting and interfere with anyone else's thinking. In such a case, the group would function like a single individual. Alternatively, it could reflect increasing motivation losses in larger groups. Research to be considered in the following chapter bolsters this possibility.

Summary

Early research comparing individual performance with group performance generally favored groups – groups tend to be more accurate, faster and more productive, although often less efficient. Steiner's analysis of this question stressed the importance of task demands and suggested that clearer insights into group processes resulted from comparing groups' actual productivity with their potential productivity. Such comparisons suggest that groups routinely fall short of this potential. They also suggest several sources of group process loss. For example, when the most capable members of a problem-solving group are not confident, have low status, or are not talkative, the group is likely to under-utilize its resources. The inability of everyone in an interacting group to talk and think at the same time can likewise impede optimal group performance. Such process losses also tend to increase as the group gets larger. This means that a larger group's functional size may often be much smaller than its actual size. As we gain knowledge about such group process losses, we may be better able to minimize them and, thereby, help task groups achieve their full potential.

Solution to the husbands and wives problem
Let's denote the three couples as H_1–W_1, H_2–W_2 and H_3–W_3. H_1 rows across the river with his wife, W_1. He leaves her on the other side and rows back. Then he picks up the other two husbands, H_2 and H_3, and rows with them across the river. H_1 gets out and the other two husbands row back. They pick up W_2, leaving W_3 behind, and all (i.e. H_2, W_2, and H_3) row across. H_2 and W_2 get out of the boat. H_3 rows back, picks up his wife, W_3, and then returns with her.

Suggestions for further reading

Davis, J. H. (1969). *Group Performance*. Reading, MA: Addison-Wesley. An excellent introduction to the topic.
Steiner, I. D. (1972). *Group Process and Productivity*. New York: Academic Press. A scholarly and incisive analysis of the psychology of task groups.

4 / GROUP MOTIVATION LOSSES

During the 1989 college basketball season, a player from Ohio State University, Jay Burson, continued to play in a game after he had suffered a serious injury (viz. a broken neck). We can all probably think of other situations where people like Jay Burson double their efforts or place themselves in great jeopardy because of their feelings of devotion or loyalty to others in their group. However, most of the research to date has focused on how group settings can lower motivation. The primary reason for this is that some fascinating early studies of motivation loss captured many social psychologists' attention. Those studies raised interesting new questions: What psychological processes cause group motivation losses? How do they depend upon member, group and task features? How can they be reduced? In this chapter we examine some of the initial, preliminary answers to these questions for three distinct types of group motivation loss.

Social loafing

In the last chapter we discussed Ringelmann's (1913) early study which obtained a nearly linear decline in the average pull per member as the size of a rope-pulling team increased. If there had been no process loss, of course, the pull per member should have remained constant across group sizes. Both Ringelmann (1913) and Steiner (1972) speculated that the resultant process loss was probably due to the greater coordination difficulties arising in larger groups. Several of Steiner's colleagues at the University of

Massachusetts, Amherst (Ingham *et al.* 1974) decided to find out. Their plan was simple – to estimate motivation losses, first eliminate all coordination losses. Their means of achieving this were elegant – to eliminate group coordination loss, eliminate the group. As in Ringelmann's classic study, several persons were in the laboratory and on different trials, anywhere from 1 to 6 pulled on a rope as hard as possible. The key difference was that in Ingham *et al.*'s study, seven of the persons were confederates of the experimenter. Whenever the true subject was working, it was contrived that he was always ahead of any other persons on the rope, closest to the gauge which measured performance. Every person was also blindfolded, allegedly to eliminate distraction. During these trials, the confederates did not pull on the rope; in effect there was no group, only the performance of an individual who believed he was part of a group. Ingham *et al.* found that as the apparent group size increased, performance fell; this was particularly evident for the smallest group sizes (i.e. one to three persons). Thus, the Ringelmann effect appeared to be at least partially due to motivation losses: as the group got larger, people tended to pull less hard.

A few years later, Latané *et al.* (1979a) replicated this result with a new task – cheering as loud as possible. The experimental approach was similar – on key trials, a subject thought that she/he was cheering as part of a group, but in reality, only she/he was cheering. As both Ringelmann and Ingham *et al.* had found, individual motivation declined with apparent group size. Latané *et al.* called this motivation loss *social loafing*. They speculated that it might be a common 'social disease' doing widespread harm in many collective performance contexts. For example, they speculated that the low efficiency of the Soviet agricultural collective or 'kolkhoz' might reflect such social loafing.

Subsequent research has confirmed that the social loafing effect is genuine and reliable (Jackson and Williams 1986). It is not restricted to motor tasks like rope-pulling or cheering; it can also occur when groups are performing cognitive or perceptual tasks (e.g. Petty *et al.* 1980; Szymanski and Harkins 1987). It has also been demonstrated in many different cultures, including India (Weiner *et al.* 1981), Japan (Williams and Williams 1984) and Taiwan (Gabrenya *et al.* 1981). However, research has also suggested that the effect may not be nearly as universal a feature of group (as opposed to individual) performance as originally suspected. For example, it can be eliminated by introducing into the performance setting any of several factors known to enhance motivation. For example, social loafing is eliminated if the task is sufficiently involving (Brickner *et al.* 1986), attractive (Zaccaro 1984) or intrinsically interesting (Petty *et al.* 1985) to group members; if group cohesion is sufficiently high (Williams 1981); or if the group sets performance goals (Brickner 1987). In general, then, social loafing seems more likely to occur when there is no strong incentive to perform the task for individuals or for groups.

Research has also revealed the underlying cause of the social loafing effect (Kerr and Bruun 1981; Williams *et al.* 1981). When one is part of a group performing a rope-pulling or cheering task, one may feel less identifiable. These are additive tasks which combine all member contributions to produce a single group product. Thus, there is no way of identifying any individual member's contribution. So, if one chooses to reduce one's effort at such a task (perhaps because it was fatiguing, uninteresting or unrewarding), no one could tell. This anonymity would be enhanced somewhat by increasing the group size, since the more inputs there were to the group product, the more difficult it would be to attribute any process loss to any particular member. However, because the biggest difference in anonymity occurs between working alone (when one is fully identifiable) and working in a dyad (when one is no longer personally identifiable), this explanation also suggests that the biggest drop in effort should occur as one moves from individuals to dyads, with ever smaller drops in effort as group size increases. As noted above, the original social loafing studies obtained just this pattern. (You will also note these data correspond nicely to the prediction of social impact theory; Chapter 5.) As the number of targets of influences goes up, the social impact of task demands are 'diluted' and this effect grows weaker as the group grows in size. There is a straightforward way to do a more direct test of the identifiability explanation. One can alter the task so that subjects believe that every group member's contribution *can* be identified. So, for example, Williams *et al.* examined two variations of the cheering task. In one, the version originally used by Latané *et al.* (1979a), people sat in a circle around a single microphone. When groups cheered, only an overall sound level could be measured and each person's contribution was non-identifiable. For this task version, Williams *et al.* observed the usual social loafing effect; member effort declined with group size at a negatively accelerated rate. However, in the other version of the task, each person had his/her own individual microphone on a headset. No matter what the group size, a sound level reading could be taken for each person. For this task version, there was no social loafing effect. [Kerr and Bruun (1981) obtained the same result for a completely different task, pumping air.]

This result reillustrates what should now be a familiar theme – task features are crucial in analyzing group performance. The social loafing effect turned out not to be a universal social (i.e. group) problem. Rather, it is a problem which can only arise for certain group tasks – those tasks which combine member contributions so that no individual member's performance can be identified, what Davis (1969) terms an *information reducing* task. However, at tasks for which individual member contributions are always identifiable (*information conserving* tasks), there is no social loafing effect.

Actually, we have been a little imprecise about the basis for the social loafing effect. It seems not to be identifiability *per se*, but rather the possibility of evaluation that identifiability makes possible (Harkins 1987; Harkins and Szymanski 1987b). That is, even if my contribution to the group product can be identified, I might still loaf if I felt that no one could or would evaluate my performance. This was demonstrated in a clever study by Harkins and Jackson (1985). The task was to generate as many uses for an object as possible. Half of the people were led to feel identifiable; the experimenter would collect each group member's ideas separately. The other half were not identifiable; all group members' ideas were placed in a single receptacle, making personal identification impossible. When people thought that everyone in the group was generating uses for the same object, the usual social loafing effect was obtained – people generated fewer uses for the object in the non-identifiable condition. However, when people thought that every person generated uses for a unique object, so that person-to-person comparison and evaluation was not meaningful, loafing occurred even when everyone was fully identifiable. It was the possibility for evaluation, not identifiability, which was crucial for producing social loafing. In subsequent work, Harkins and his colleagues have shown that it is not just evaluation of personal performance by someone outside the group (e.g. the experimenter, a supervisor) which concerns and motivates a group member. Rather, the possibility of evaluation by other group members or even by oneself (Harkins and Szymanski 1987b; Szymanski and

Harkins 1987) has similar motivating effects. Furthermore, an opportunity for group members to evaluate the group (but not individual members') performance can likewise motivate group members to work (Harkins and Szymanski 1989). Thus, the social loafing effect seems to be restricted to a fairly narrow range of group task settings where evaluation of member or group performance by anyone is unlikely.

At first blush, there would appear to be a contradiction between social loafing and social facilitation effects. We learned earlier that having co-actors present facilitates performance, at least at simple, well-learned tasks (like rope-pulling or cheering). Yet in this chapter, we have seen that people work less hard and, therefore, accomplish less when working together than when working alone at such tasks. However, having learned how group processes depend so much on the demands of the group's task, we should quickly observe, 'But the tasks are not the same. In the social loafing setting one works together with others, while one works for only oneself in the social facilitation setting.' However, is it this difference in task demands which holds the key to the apparent contradiction, and if so, why? Harkins (1987; Harkins and Szymanski 1987a) has examined these questions. He notes that Cottrell's learned-drive theory of social facilitation gives a central role to the evaluation implicit in others' presence, at least for humans. (Incidently, none of the other viable theories of social facilitation would dispute the powerful impact that evaluative pressures can have on drive or on distraction, and hence, on performance.) Harkins' own work suggests that evaluation also underlies the social loafing effect. The difference between the two settings is the effect that the others have on the possibility of evaluation. In a social facilitation setting, the (mere) presence of others *increases* the likelihood of evaluation since here one's performance can be compared to that of others. In the social loafing setting (viz. group performance at an information reducing task), having co-workers *decreases* the likelihood of evaluation (since one cannot be sure who did what). The key point is that being in a 'social' as opposed to an individual setting does not have a single, simple effect on performance; depending upon task demands, it can have quite opposite effects.

If Harkins is right, if social loafing is really only a kind of inversion of social facilitation, with a single basic process – the concern with evaluation – underlying each, we would expect 'social' (i.e. group) conditions to have exactly the opposite effects in the two settings. We have already seen that this is true for simple tasks, but would it also be true for complex tasks? Would working together at a complex, poorly-learned, information-reducing task lower evaluation apprehension (and presumably drive) and, therefore, lead to better individual (and group) performance (remember high drive impairs performance on complex tasks)? That is, can social loafing actually improve group performance? Jackson and Williams (1985) explored this possibility. Subjects worked on a complex computer maze and were led to believe that their scores would be combined with a partner so that neither's score could be identified. Under these conditions, which usually produce social loafing, performance was actually better than when subjects worked alongside a co-actor. So even if certain group settings do encourage loafing, the effect on performance is not necessarily negative.

Free riding

When one works alone, success or failure rests entirely on one's own shoulders. However, when one works in a group, the responsibility for the group's success or failure is often shared among group members. So, for example, if one considers a collection of bystanders at an emergency to be a group, the responsibility for helping appears to be diffused among group members, such that the larger the group, the less likely it is that any particular individual will provide help (Darley and Latané 1968; Latané and Nida 1981).

Similarly, for certain group tasks there also exists the possibility that others in the group can and will do most or all of the work necessary for the group to succeed. If I share an apartment with others, I can enjoy the benefits of a clean apartment as long as someone (not necessarily me) cleans the place up. If I am working in a group on an intellectual puzzle like the 'husbands and wives' problem, as long as there is someone in the group able to solve the problem, I could exert no effort at all and still be part of a successful group. As this last example illustrates, this is especially likely for disjunctive tasks, where the group can succeed if only a single member succeeds.

It seems reasonable that we would be less willing to exert ourselves when such possibilities exist to *free ride* (Olson 1965), that is, to benefit from the task efforts of other group members. Kerr

(1983; Kerr and Bruun 1983) has suggested that group members are sensitive to the *dispensability* of their efforts. When they perceive their contributions to be dispensable, such that group success (or for that matter, failure) depend very little upon whether or not they exert effort, and when that effort is costly, they are less likely to exert themselves on the group's behalf. This was demonstrated in an experiment (Kerr 1983) in which subjects worked in isolation either as part of a dyad or as an individual performer. The task was to pump air using a rubber sphygmograph bulb. If a subject reached a certain performance threshold on a trial, she/he succeeded. For individuals, this meant a $0.25 cash reward per trial (and a potential $2.25 pay-off for the nine trials in the study). The group task was defined disjunctively; if either group member succeeded, the dyad succeeded and both members would receive $0.25. Regardless of condition, the subject received accurate feedback on his/her own performance after each trial. However, in the dyads, the feedback on the partner's performance was false and designed to encourage free riding. After each and every trial, the subject learned that his partner had succeeded. It should have soon become evident to the dyad member that he could free ride on his partner's efforts, since the partner was willing and able to do the unpleasant work required to ensure the dyad's success. Indeed, dyad members worked significantly less hard than the individual control subjects.

It should be emphasized that this motivation loss was different from the social loafing effects discussed above. As we have shown, social loafing effects depended upon low identifiability and, hence, low evaluation potential. However, in the experiments demonstrating free riding (Kerr 1983; Kerr and Bruun 1983), *every* group member's performance was individually monitored by the experimenter and fully identifiable. Research clearly shows that the original social loafing effect is eliminated under such conditions (Kerr and Bruun 1981; Williams *et al.* 1981). The opportunity to free ride – to get something for nothing – is not quite the same thing as the opportunity to socially loaf – to 'hide in the crowd'. Although both processes link social conditions (e.g. group size, group task demands) to the instrumentality of task effort, they are concerned with somewhat different outcomes – reductions of effort have a less direct impact on the chances of *group success* when free riding is possible; reductions of effort have less direct impact on the chances of receiving *salient personal and social evaluations* when social loafing is viable. [It should also probably be noted that the term 'social loafing' has been widely equated with what Steiner (1972) termed group motivation losses – i.e. lower effort by group members than by individual performers. When the term 'social loafing' is used in this more generic sense, free riding may reasonably be considered to be a type of 'social loafing'.]

Like social facilitation and social loafing (and nearly every other group performance phenomenon), the extent of free riding depends on task demands. For example, we might expect less free riding at an additive task, where group performance depends on every group member's contribution, than at a disjunctive task, where only one member's contribution counts. What is important is how dispensable the group member feels and this judgment can depend on many factors, including task demands, group structure and member resources. Consider, for example, the effect that self-perceived task ability might play. If your group is working on the disjunctive 'husband and wives' problem, the less capable you felt at the task, the more dispensable your efforts would seem; 'there's bound to be someone more capable than me who can solve this problem for the group'. However, if the task was conjunctive, so that it was the least capable member's performance that defined the group score, exactly the opposite relationship should hold – it would be the high ability member who believes that it is unlikely that his/her performance will affect the group's score. Thus, perceived ability should (and does: Kerr and Bruun 1983) have exactly opposite effects on perceived dispensability and effort for disjunctive and conjunctive tasks.

A feature of the group which seems very likely to affect perceived dispensability is the group's size. Generally, as our group gets larger and larger, we are less likely to see our own personal contribution to the group as being important to the group's chances of success (Olson 1965; Kerr 1989). Again, this will depend on the nature of the task. All other things (e.g. member ability) being equal, the larger the group, the more likely it is that there will be someone both more able than you *and* less able than you. Thus, for both disjunctive and conjunctive tasks, one should [and does (Harkins and Petty 1982; Kerr and Bruun 1983)] reduce one's efforts and free ride more as group size increases. However, with an additive task, one's own contribution will always affect the group product regardless of group size, so group size should not [and does not (Kerr and Bruun 1983)] affect free riding.

Earlier we learned that social loafing depends upon a key task feature – whether individual contributions can be identified (and thereby evaluated). Identifiability also turns out to be relevant to free riding, but in a somewhat different way. Harkins and Petty (1982, Experiment 3) gave group members a vigilance task (viz. to watch for dots flashing on a computer screen). In one condition, each group member had his/her own portion of the screen to monitor; she/he bore complete responsibility for detecting the dots that flashed in that portion. In another condition, all group members monitored the same portion of the screen; they shared the responsibility for detecting the dots that flashed there. The former task is essentially additive and gives little opportunity for free riding. However, the latter task is essentially disjunctive (if any member saw the dot, the group would get credit) and presents an opportunity to free ride. The interesting thing, though, is that this opportunity was only taken when subjects thought their individual performances could not be personally identified. When everyone could be identified, people took little [actually, in contrast to the Kerr (1983) study, described earlier, practically no] advantage of the opportunity to free ride. Thus, not only does identifiability underlie or mediate social loafing, it alters or moderates free riding.

Why? Probably, because free riding violates a number of familiar and salient social norms. Although a free rider might be saving him/herself work and may not even be hurting the group's chances of success, by not doing his/her best at a group task, she/he may break certain social rules or norms and thereby risk social sanction. If group members are anonymous, though, there is no way of telling who has violated the norm. This effectively removes the threat of social sanction for norm violation and leaves one free to free ride. Several norms might be involved. First, Tajfel (1970) suggested that there may be a 'generic ingroup norm' that prescribes that a group member act to benefit one's group; free riding would certainly violate this norm. Secondly, if other group members are working hard and you benefit from that hard work, your failure to work hard too would violate the norm of reciprocity, which prescribes that for a benefit received an equivalent benefit should eventually be returned (Gouldner 1960). Finally, if you free ride on others, but then share equally in the rewards of group success, the equity norm would be violated. The equity norm prescribes that ratios of inputs (e.g. effort) to outcomes (e.g. one's share of group reward) should be equal across comparable individuals (e.g. group members; Adams 1965). In the next section, we see how violations of the equity norm can give rise to another type of group motivation loss.

Inequity-based motivation losses

How might you react if you discovered that a group member was free riding on your efforts; that is, was reducing his/her efforts, allowing others to 'carry' the group and then was receiving the same rewards as every group member? For example, the group could be two people sharing an apartment whose task was to keep the apartment clean. How would you react to an apartment-mate who never made any attempt to help keep the apartment clean, yet regularly enjoyed the benefits of your cleaning? As we noted above, this free riding behavior violates several social norms and you would be likely to first remind the free rider of the norms and if necessary, begin to apply social sanctions (e.g. express your irritation, ask him/her to move out).

For the problem we are considering here, equity theory (Adams 1965; Walster et al. 1978) suggests another solution. If my free riding partner has lower inputs (i.e. less effort), but gets the same outcomes (e.g. same reward), one way in which equity could be restored would be for me to reduce my inputs, too (e.g. reduce my effort). For example, I might simply refuse to clean the apartment. Earlier, we discussed a study by Kerr (1983) in which free riding was demonstrated. It required dyads to pump air in a disjunctive task (success by either person ensured group success and reward). In another condition in that study, subjects first learned during practice trials that both they and their partner were quite capable of succeeding at the task. The subjects then received false feedback about their partner's performance following each of a series of performance trials which suggested that the partner was free-riding – namely, the partner failed consistently. Under the disjunctive task demands, the partner still received the same $0.25 reward every time the group succeeded through the subject's efforts. As equity theory predicts, subjects reduced their own efforts rather than carry this free rider. Drawing on the terminology of *social dilemmas* (which we consider in more detail in Chapter 7), Kerr (1983) christened this the *sucker effect*; subjects chose to reduce their own effort (and thereby, their own rewards) rather than 'play the sucker' and be exploited by a free riding partner.

There is also some evidence that we apply a 'means rule' when evaluating a person's inputs for equity calculations (Brown 1987). For example, a $100 charitable contribution will be viewed as a more generous gift when it comes from a poor person than when it comes from a rich one (Gergen *et al.* 1975). Thus, when deciding whether things are equitable or fair, we take more into account than our partner's objective level of performance – we also take into account his/her means to be productive (e.g. ability, skills). In another condition of Kerr's (1983) study, the partner again consistently failed. However, in this condition, the practice trial performance indicated that the partner had very low task ability. Under these conditions, subjects maintained high performance, willingly 'carrying' the failing partner. Apparently, one does not feel like a sucker when carrying a partner who cannot succeed (but does when the partner can, but will not work).

The sucker effect is but one of a family of group motivation-loss effects which stem from the equity norm. In each case, there is an inequity among group members which can be removed effectively by reducing one's efforts and, thereby, lowering one's level of inputs. For example, if you are much more qualified than a co-worker, you are likely to feel inequitably treated if you receive exactly the same pay. Several studies (e.g. Clark 1958; Kessler and Wiener 1972) have shown that people sometimes resolve this inequity by reducing their effort; presumably, this makes their total input level (including both qualifications and effort) more comparable to the co-workers. A more obvious case is one in which co-workers receive different levels of pay for doing the same job. Since 1977, many companies and unions have negotiated a new type of labor contract, the two-tiered wage plan. Under such plans, newly hired employees receive a lower rate of pay for performing the same job as older employees. When there is high employee turnover, high employment growth and current wages are high relative to the wages prevailing in the entire labor market, such plans can dramatically reduce labor costs and increase the competitiveness of a firm (Cappelli and Sherer 1990). In essence, such plans allow current employees (who are the ones who ratify labor contracts) to make concessions in wages, job security, work rules, etc., which will not affect them, but rather will affect only future employees (who, of course, have no voice in the matter). In some versions of these plans, the separation into two employee tiers is permanent; newly hired employees can never 'catch up' with comparable older employees. The more common form of such plans, though, allows new employees eventually to gain parity with older employees. Such plans have been gaining in popularity in the US and have been touted as a way of making industries with high labor costs more competitive and able to survive in a world economy with relatively low labor costs.

Although two-tiered systems may make economic sense, and may offer a workable way of negotiating lower operating costs, they also raise the possibility of inequity-based motivation losses. If two workers do precisely the same job, but one, because she/he was more recently hired, is paid less than the other, the resulting inequity may lower the newer worker's willingness to work hard. A number of press reports (e.g. 'The revolutionary wage deal . . .', *Business Week* 1983; 'The double standard . . .', *Business Week* 1985), based largely on interviews with workers and management, have suggested that there is widespread dissatisfaction among new workers with such pay plans. There has been relatively little systematic research on the question, however. If you ask workers who operate within a two-tiered system, there is evidence (Premeaux *et al.* 1986) that recently hired workers have more negative attitudes toward a two-tiered system than older workers; for example, they believe that new workers will be less productive, there will be more friction between old and new workers, and eventually all workers will have lower wages under a two-tiered system. There is also evidence (Martin and Peterson 1987) that newer workers in a *permanent* two-tiered system see it as less equitable than older workers.

On the other hand, there is also some evidence that two-tiered systems need not undermine new-workers' morale. Under certain conditions, new workers can have equal or even higher levels of pay satisfaction, commitment to the company, confidence of job security, etc., than older workers (Cappelli and Sherer 1990). When will this happen? Probably when new workers enter the job with lower pay expectations than older workers, when most of one's co-workers are also working on the lower tier and, most importantly, when the two tiers will eventually merge (Martin and Peterson 1987; Cappelli and Sherer 1990). The inequity of unequal pay for equal work may need to be salient and to seem permanent before workers feel particularly unhappy about a two-tiered system. Whether such unhappiness actually results in lower effort and productivity remains to be demonstrated.

We have been careful to say that group members only 'sometimes' reduce effort in the face of inequity because in most real group task situations there are many different types of outcomes and other inputs besides effort. It is not necessary that adjustment of effort be the only or the most likely means of restoring equity. So, for example, an underpaid worker might reduce the quality rather than the quantity of his/her work to restore equity (e.g. Evan and Simmons 1969). Alternatively, an underpaid worker could simply quit rather than work on at reduced levels of effort (e.g. Valenzi and Andrews 1971). Furthermore, equity may also be restored by distorting reality (Walster *et al.* 1978); in some instances, it may be more feasible to alter one's perceptions (e.g. I get paid more, but I work harder) than one's actual inputs or outcomes (e.g. Gergen *et al.* 1974). People seem likely to use the means of equity restoration which is most convenient and least costly (Adams 1965); whether this involves motivation or effort reduction is likely to depend upon many features of the task and the individual.

It should also be evident that, at times, inequity may be reduced through *increases* in effort. For example, if one is overpaid relative to others in the group, one way to restore equity would be to increase one's effort – one would feel deserving of the higher pay if one actually did work harder (Goodman and Friedman 1971; Pritchard *et al.* 1972). If one is less qualified than others in the group, one might compensate for lack of qualifications by working harder (Adams and Rosenbaum 1962; Adams 1963). Thus, as far as motivation in groups is concerned, the equity norm is a two-edged sword that can produce motivation gains as well as motivation losses.

Summary

The early studies of Ingham *et al.* (1974) and Latané *et al.* (1979a) gave rise to speculation that groups might be generally demotivating. For example, Latané *et al.* included a cartoon picturing hundreds of thousands of ancient Egyptian workers straining mightily on ropes to inch a pyramid block forward. The work foreman explains to an onlooker, 'Many hands make light the work'. The notion of social loafing gives a new meaning to these words – having many hands available (i.e. group performance settings) can lead us to make light of the work (to reduce our effort). We understand better now that there is nothing inherently demotivating about groups. Rather, only under certain very specific conditions will group members be less motivated than individual performers. Under other conditions, group settings can even produce higher levels of motivation (Kerr and MacCoun 1984; Stroebe 1990; Williams and Karan 1991). It seems likely that motivation gains occur, for example, in team sports and combat units where factors such as contagious excitement, strong norms favoring maximal effort, and intense feelings of loyalty and obligation arise. In this chapter, we have focused on some of the *de*motivating conditions arising in groups. These include:

(1) when being in the group makes identification and evaluation less likely (social loafing);
(2) when being in the group creates opportunities that other group members may do the necessary work (free riding);
(3) when being in the group suggests that there are others who are not doing their fair share of the work (sucker effect).

Undoubtedly there are other, as yet unstudied aspects of groups which also encourage reduced task effort. However, if the effects we do know about are any guide, it seems likely that these motivation losses can also be reduced or prevented through proper modifications of the task situation. Group motivation losses follow from well understood psychological principles, are limited in their occurrence and can be effectively remedied. Many hands can, but do not necessarily, make light the work.

Suggestions for further reading

Kravitz, D. A. and Martin, B. (1986). Ringelmann rediscovered: The original article. *Journal of Personality and Social Psychology*, 50, 936–41. Interest in group motivation traces back to the beginnings of scientific social psychology. This paper identifies Ringelmann's classic study as the discipline's first experiment.

Latané, B., Williams, K. D. and Harkins, S. G. (1979). Social loafing. *Psychology Today*, 13, 104–10. A discussion of some of the early findings and implications of work on this topic.

5 / SOCIAL INFLUENCE AND CONFORMITY

The belief that our actions reflect our preferences, attitudes and values (e.g. that I drink a particular brand of beer solely because I like it), is so common in our daily experience that we hardly stop to think about it. This tendency for individuals to see themselves and others as being in command, as the cause of their actions, is such a compelling feature of human experience that psychologists have coined the phrase *fundamental attribution error* to describe it. We routinely underestimate the contribution that the circumstances or the situation a person is in makes to that person's actions. Instead, we tend to believe that the causes of our actions are internal, that people act the way they do because that is the nature of their character. Yet, when even a new student of cultural anthropology examines and compares indigenous cultures, the degree to which this belief is a myth is obvious. What can account for the sharp contrast between the similarity of behavior, custom and belief within a culture, and the striking diversity between cultures? A likely answer is that we are influenced by those around us. The perception that our actions are internally caused can, at best, be only a partial truth.

A study conducted over 50 years ago at a small women's liberal arts college in Bennington, Vermont illustrates the operation of social influence in a natural setting (Newcomb 1943). Newcomb observed that students at Bennington, who came from politically conservative homes, became increasingly more liberal over their 4 years at college. The reason was that the norms at the college were heavily influenced by the liberal views of the faculty who strongly favored the social reforms championed by President Franklin

Roosevelt. New students soon saw that the more advanced, important and popular students echoed the faculty views. Slowly, they adopted such views as their own. Newcomb documented that such change was closely associated with various forms of social reward such as being included in popular social groups and important extracurricular activities. In this chapter, we will examine processes and theories of social influence that underlie some of the phenomena illustrated by this study.

Social comparison theory

In contrast to our commonsensical emphasis on self as the cause of one's actions, social psychology calls attention to external events as causes of behavior. Perhaps most prominent among such external stimuli are other people. Leon Festinger's theory of social comparison processes (Festinger 1954) is one influential attempt to understand the effects of others on our own thinking. As we note in Chapter 1, his starting point was that for many of the issues that concern us, there are no right answers, no objective or physical source of certainty. Whether a unified Germany will increase or decrease the economic and military stability of Europe, or whether Van Gogh or Picasso is the greater artist is not easily answered. Like many questions, there are good reasons for each of two opposing positions. Thus, with such uncertain questions, if one wishes to assess whether one's opinion 'seems right' one option is to check the 'social reality' (Chapter 1), i.e. to see if there is some social consensus regarding the correct view. In short, our belief about the right answer or the correct view will often depend on the people with whom we talk and their positions in our group. If group opinion corroborates our view, our confidence in that view increases (Orive 1988).

Social comparison can have another conceptually distinct effect, however, in addition to providing information. Festinger argued that groups prefer to be in agreement. Thus, when social comparison results in disagreement, various attempts are made to resolve matters. Festinger observed that group members will first try to persuade each other, but if this fails, rejection of group deviates will result. This was illustrated in a classic study by Schachter (1951), where groups discussed the case history of a young delinquent named Johnny Rocco. The group's chore was to decide on a treatment for Mr Rocco. Schachter had confederates planted in the discussion who purposely disagreed with the group's judgment. Despite the fact that the others directed a disproportionate amount of attention and commentary to the deviate, he remained unconvinced. At the end of the session, this deviate received lower ratings of desirability than others and was more likely to be chosen by the group for the unpopular job of handling group correspondence. Schachter *et al.* (1954) replicated this procedure in seven European countries, observing school boys as they discussed the desirability of model airplanes they anticipated building as a group. In each group there was a deviate. In every country, the rated desirability of the confederate/deviate was lower than average. We now know that such rejection occurs even when groups are not under pressure to reach complete consensus (Miller *et al.* 1987). Apparently, holding a different opinion is enough to trigger dislike even when it does not directly block group goals. Indeed, in one notable study, Freedman and Doob (1968) simply led subjects to believe that one of them had a personality profile that differed from the rest. Later in the procedure, the group was required to select someone to receive electric shock. Somewhat disturbingly, the deviate was disproportionately selected for this duty, indicating that just being different led to negative consequences even in the absence of any opinion disagreement.

Why does disagreement and deviation from group norms so often lead to rejection and abuse? Three answers seem plausible:

1 On occasion, group consensus (and conformity) will be necessary for groups to reach crucial goals. Here dissent will be threatening to group members and counter-productive and, therefore, likely to evoke irritation and social sanctions.

2 Disagreeing with a clear majority is often insulting to the majority ('You guys are all wrong. What dummies!').

3 Finally, when deviates disagree with a majority, this disagreement will often increase uncertainty among people who would otherwise have the security of social consensus for their views. Thus, deviates undermine 'social reality'. Here, too, abuse of deviates seems understandable. This punishment of deviates is one major force that increases our tendency to conform to group norms. This issue is discussed further in the next section.

Conformity

One of the more dramatic examples of being socially influenced by the opinions, behaviors and performances of those around us is illustrated by conformity research. Sherif's study of the auto-kinetic effect, described in Chapter 1, was an early classic. In this study, even when subjects' heads are locked into a stationary position with a head clamp, and they are told that the dot of light in the dark room is, in fact, stationary, they nevertheless see it as moving (Sherif 1935). More important, however, when each member of a group is making judgments about the distance the pinpoint of light moves on each trial, each person continues to be influenced by the judgments of the others. This produces an idiosyncratic convergence in the judgments of each particular group that distinguishes it from other groups. This effect is well repli-cated and powerful. One study by Rohrer *et al.* (1954) retested individual subjects a year after their original exposure to the group norm and found evidence that the original norm still affected subject's judgments. In a slightly different version of this study, Jacobs and Campbell (1961) slowly rotated group members out of a group, replacing them with new group members. Original norms were manipulated through the use of confederates. This study and several others which followed (MacNeil and Sherif 1976) indicated that norms such as these could continue to affect the judgments of group members for up to eight 'generations' after the departure of original group members and confederates. Thus, the norm in a sense acquired a 'life of its own'.

From the preceding paragraphs, we have seen that two forces, one based on group power (potential rejection and punishment) and the other based on trust in group opinion, can be causes of social influence. The first, *normative* social influence, refers to in-fluence caused by the implicit rewards and punishments controlled by the group, whereas the second, *informational* social influence, refers generally to the tendency to rely upon social definitions of reality, especially those based on consensus (Deutsch and Gerard 1955).

For the incoming freshmen at Bennington College, an individual who found herself among strangers at a developmental stage in her life when intellectual and conceptual horizons were rapidly expanding, both types of influence must have operated strongly to exert pressure toward conformity to the liberal political views that characterized the campus milieu. At one level, these beliefs and the information that was associated with them simply concerned the laws of economics, political science and sociology. In addition, however, if a student endorsed these views, it affected the approval and disapproval that would be received from others on campus. In turn, this approval or disapproval governed one's social status on the campus. In short, both informational and normative pressures produced conformity at Bennington College.

Conformity in Sherif's autokinetic situation probably is primarily due to just one of these two processes. Subjects, literally, are in the dark and lack any physical standard against which to compare the position of the dot of light. Because they are uncertain, they are easily influenced by others' ideas and responses. In short, conformity here seems strongly affected by informational social influence. Although ambiguity clearly does increase conformity, there is good reason to argue that it is not absolutely necessary. In another classic study of conformity effects, Solomon Asch (1956) asked groups of students at Haverford College to estimate which of three comparison lines matched a fourth 'test' line. The subject offered his estimates after hearing the responses of several other students who (unknown to him) were confederates. The group judged a large number of stimulus sets and on two-thirds of these (the 'critical' trials) the confederates systematically agreed on a clearly incorrect match. What did the subjects do when faced with this collective madness? Despite the blatant incorrectness of the group choice, subjects conformed with this norm on over one-third of all critical trials. In fact, 76 per cent of subjects conformed with at least one of these blatantly incorrect group judgments despite the fact that, even after they publically agreed with the group, most subjects stated that the 'group choice' did not look 'correct' to them. Thus, it would appear that normative (v. informational) pressures were largely responsible for the social influence observed in this study.

Social scientists tend to emphasize the fact that conformity processes can often produce irrational or erroneous judgments on individuals. Although this is true, we should not lose sight of the fact that conformity pressure for the most part serves crucial societal functions. As we noted in Chapter 1, conformity pressure insures social regularity and predictability that is essential for coordinated and efficient group action. Conformity pressure also provides one means of controlling group members, thereby increasing the likelihood that they will consider group interests as well as their own. This form of social control affects a wide range of behaviors, but is particularly crucial for public spirited actions such as water and energy conservation, not driving while intoxicated, providing aid to the unfortunate and conducting one's daily affairs with integrity. Consequently, it is not surprising that human groups place a good deal of emphasis on being able to elicit conformity from group members. In many cases, such conformity will be essential to group survival.

At present, conformity effects have been reported across such a wide range of judgments and subject groups that it represents one of the most substantiated and fundamental phenomena in social psychology. For example, conformity has been observed on auditory judgments, esthetic preferences, visual judgments and case history decisions, just to name a few. Indeed, our reactions to everything from wine to politics is susceptible to conformity pressure. Asch's early studies, however, indicated that conformity effects will not invariably occur when majorities pressure deviates. In one study (Asch 1955), conformity dropped substantially (i.e. to 10 per cent) if two naive subjects faced the incorrect majority. It dropped even further if the other deviate gave a clearly correct response. In short, conformity effects are undermined when the deviate finds that she or he is not alone in disagreeing with the majority. Indeed, Wilder and Allen (1977) found this to be true in an Asch-like situation even when the two 'deviates' disagreed with each other so long as they also disagreed with the majority. Thus, if a few brave souls are willing to stand up to a group majority, group pressure can be seriously weakened. As we have seen, however, being the person who takes the first step along this path can be perilous.

Another key finding in Asch's early work was that conformity increased as the size of the majority increased. This occurred, however, only up to a point. When the majority contained approximately three members, conformity leveled off (Asch 1955). This result has been replicated a good number of times (cf. Tanford and Penrod 1984). At least in part, these data stem from the fact that after the majority contains over three members, subjects begin to suspect that some of the majority members are just going along with the group to avoid trouble (see below) and do not really share the majority view. Wilder (1977) demonstrated that when subjects were sure members of the majority were unaware of each other's views (and, therefore, independent of each other), majorities of size six caused more conformity than those of size three, at least on certain judgments (e.g. how much a damage award should be). A second reason why conformity increases only slightly after majority size increases past three is that as group size grows, each person added to the majority is noticed less. This phenomenon is discussed below in the section on social impact theory.

These well known findings represent just a small portion of what we have learned about conformity over the years. Other critical results are as follows.

People conform more when:

1 The judgment or opinion issue is difficult (Deutsch and Gerard 1955): social comparison needs are stronger under uncertainty.
2 They face a unanimous group consensus (Asch 1956; Wilder and Allen 1977): all those people can't be wrong and isolated deviates are most likely to be rejected and punished.
3 They value or admire the group (Back 1951): rejection from one's friends is particularly threatening.
4 Their conformity or deviation will be easily identifiable (and therefore subject to social rewards and punishments; Deutsch and Gerard 1955)
5 They are scared (Darley 1966): fear increases dependency needs by undermining confidence.

People conform less when:

1 They have great confidence in their expertise on the issue: informational social influence is low.
2 They have high social status (Harvey and Consalvi 1960);
3 They are strongly committed to their initial view (Deutsch and Gerard 1955)
4 They do not like or respect the source of social influence (Hogg and Turner 1987).

In addition to these findings, in several early studies women were found to conform more than men. A careful review by Eagly (1978) of some sixty-one (face-to-face) conformity studies, however, revealed that in the majority of studies, men and women conformed at equal levels. In a substantial minority of studies, however ($n = 23$), sex differences did exist and when they did, women were far more likely to conform than men. This was due, in part, to testing conformity with materials on which men are more confident (sports as opposed to fashion). A second factor is that men are more concerned with appearing independent from others. Males do not conform less than women under private conditions. It is only under public conditions that males tend to resist social influence more than women (Eagly *et al.* 1981). A third factor, undoubtedly has to do with the fact that, historically, women were socialized to maintain social harmony in groups. Often this involved assuming a deferential and submissive role. This of course, would make them more vulnerable to conformity pressure. Interestingly, Eagly (1978) found far more evidence of greater female conformity in those studies done earliest. It would appear then, that changes in women's socialization is changing their susceptibility to social influence.

Most writers attribute conformity effects to informational and normative social influence. These forces can operate jointly or independently. Thus, you could be completely certain that you are right and the group is wrong (no informational social influence) and still conform because you have a great need to be accepted by the group (high normative social influence). This type of social influence, generally known as *compliance*, refers to situations where one adheres to a group norm despite harboring strong private reservations about its legitimacy (as in Asch 1956). In contrast, *internalization* describes a situation where conformity reflects privately accepting the group norm as an accurate depiction of reality. As this implies, compliance primarily results from normative social influence while internalization reflects the operation of informational social influence. As such, compliance is likely to persist only as long as normative pressure is present. Internalized change, however, is thought to be far more lasting. Both normative and informational social influence will be effected by the number and power of those attempting to exert influence. This is dealt with explicitly by the theory of social impact (e.g. Latané 1981).

Social impact theory

It is a well-accepted fact within social psychology that the judgments, attitudes and behavior of others influence our own judgments, attitudes and behavior. There is far less agreement, however, about how such influence operates. The simplest assumption is that influence will increase as a function of the number of others who exhibit a particular behavior, or express a particular opinion. Latané and his colleagues developed a model of social influence that incorporates this notion (Latané 1981). It states that influence is a multiplicative combination of the effects of three major factors: the number of influence sources; their immediacy to the influence target; and the strength of the source.

An analogy will help illustrate the model. In a totally dark room a sheet of white paper, like everything else in the room, appears black. Consider the impact of light on the sheet of white paper. How white or grey might the sheet of paper be were it at the opposite end of a large room? If many bulbs (sources), each with high wattage (strength), were close to the sheet (immediacy), it would appear quite white. If instead, the only source of light were a single bulb of 15 W located at your end of the room, the sheet of paper would appear rather grey. Because the three variables in the model combine multiplicatively, as any one of them approaches zero the total impact of all three will also approach zero. Latané also noted what we might call the 'Law of Diminishing Social Impact'. Just as an increase in weekly allowance of $1 means little to the rich boy who gets $50 a week, the effect of adding ten people to an audience of 1000 would not affect a speaker who has a stuttering problem as much as would adding ten to an audience of five. In short, early additions in group size (when size is small) will have much more impact than later additions (when size is already large).

Corresponding to the multiplicative effect of different sources of influence, Latané also proposed that the presence of multiple targets divides impact. We could name this the 'Law of Diluted Social Impact'. Thus, were you able to arrange to have an audience with the Pope in which you were the only person present, the experience would be more impactful than if there were 10 or 100 others present. These principles of social impact would appear to apply to both normative and informational social influences. Regardless of whether a group is trying to influence a deviate with power or credibility, the strength (status, knowledge, power), number and immediacy of influencing agents should have noticeable effects on the success of the attempt. Although our concern here centers on conformity effects, Latané has applied his model to an array of social situations, including in addition to conformity, bystander intervention in emergencies and the experience of stage fright, among others. Here are some basic findings:

1 Conformity effects – the impact of a group norm on individuals: when more people comprise the group consensus (i.e. multiple sources of influence exist) conformity increases, but each added group member produces less and less conformity (the Law of Diminished Social Impact).

2 Stage fright – the impact of an audience on a speaker: large audiences produce more stage fright (because multiple sources of influence exist), but each added audience member produces less and less of an increase (Law of Diminished Social Impact). Solo performers have more fright than non-solo performers (the Law of Diluted Social Impact).

3 Emergencies – the impact of a victim on bystanders: the probability that you will help an accident victim goes down as the number of other bystanders increases (the Law of Diluted Social Impact). Each added bystander depresses aid less than the one before (Law of Diminished Impact).

4 Tipping – the impact of a server on patrons: the tip you will give to a waiter or waitress will be lower if there are many other patrons at your table (the Law of Diluted Social Impact).

Milgram's studies of obedience

Milgram's obedience experiments (see Chapter 1) illustrates these features of social impact theory. You will remember that in the basic Milgram paradigm, a teacher (the subject) was ordered to shock a learner (a confederate) located in the next room each time the confederate made a series of mistakes. When compared with this basic form of Milgram's study, other versions illustrate some of the principles of social impact theory (Brown 1988). In the basic version, there are two sources of impact on the teacher: the experimenter, whose high status makes him a strong source of influence, and the learner, whose strength of influence is initially less than the experimenter's. The experimenter also has an advantage over the learner in terms of immediacy. He is standing next to the subject, overseeing the experiment, whereas the learner is out of sight in the adjacent room. In one condition, however, the experimenter gave instructions and answered queries by phone and, in the condition with least impact, he left the teacher free to select shock levels. In these conditions only 20 and 2 per cent of subjects, respectively, continued to shock right up to the limit of 450 V.

The learner's immediacy was also varied. Obedience rates of over 60 per cent were dramatically reduced by allowing visible as well as auditory contact with the learner. Compared to the baseline condition in which 63 per cent shocked the learner to the limit, sight of the learner reduced compliance to 40 per cent. Adding other targets of social influence to the setting should further reduce the experimenter's impact. In one version of the experiment, two additional confederates collaborated with the teacher. All three were assigned aspects of the teaching role. In this setting, in comparison to the standard version of the experiment, there are three times as many targets of influence standing against the experimenter, the balance of influence shifts dramatically toward the learner. In this study, the two confederates refuse to be obedient. When the second teacher quit, 25 out of 40 subjects immediately joined the two rebels. In contrast to the standard version in which 63 per cent continued to the limit, only 10 per cent of the subjects in this condition ignored the rebellion of their peers and continued to comply with the experimenter's instruction right up to the highest level of shock. In short, when there is social support for resistance or rebellion, the voice of moral concern can be heard more clearly.

Groupthink

The frequent failure of individuals to express their own individual view after hearing others offer a differing opinion, is not merely a curious laboratory finding. Its seriousness in real life is illustrated by an analysis of many important national policy decisions. One example was the decision made by President Kennedy and his national security advisors in the 1960s to proceed with a CIA plan for an invasion of Fidel Castro's Cuba (at the Bay of Pigs), using anti-Castro exiles as a strike force. The invasion was to be supported with US air and naval cover. In retrospect, the Bay of Pigs plan was a fiasco. The invasion failed, resulting not only in much useless loss of life, but also in national embarrassment for the United States. Moreover, from the outset there were serious moral and practical reasons to doubt its wisdom (e.g. it seemed doubtful that US involvement could really be hidden and there was strong reason to question the assumption that Mr Castro's troops were not loyal). The question, then, is why Kennedy and his advisors overlooked these considerations and authorized the action. According to Janis (1972), the answer has to do with a phenomenon he called groupthink.

Janis (1972) invoked the term *groupthink* to refer to a kind of pathology that often occurs in group decision making, a pathology that arguably contributed to high stakes foreign policy disasters such as the Bay of Pigs invasion, Argentina's decision to initiate the war in the Falkland Islands or Lyndon Johnson's escalation of the Vietnam war. By groupthink, Janis referred to situations in which leadership style, group cohesion and crisis combine to suppress dissent within groups to such a degree that group members end up supporting policies (norms) that are extraordinarily ill-considered. Janis believes that groupthink occurs, in part, because in highly cohesive groups the opinions of the other (well-respected) individuals are particularly credible. (My Lord! That is John F. Kennedy saying that! *He* can't be wrong!) In addition, no one is eager to rock the boat by deviating since the prospect of rejection by such a group would be very disheartening.

The problem is exacerbated if the group leader adopts a directive style by championing a particular course of action because this then becomes established as the favored group norm. This was one of Kennedy's great errors in the Bay of Pigs decision. A crisis atmosphere contributes to the problem by leading the group to push for a rapid consensus thereby stifling dissent. For example, Bobby Kennedy pressured a cabinet member to withdraw his objections due to the President's need for support. In short, what results is an illusion of consensus in which each member assumes that he or she alone has doubts about the emerging group decision. Because other group members are viewed as being both powerful and wise in these groups, each member keeps objections to her/himself. By not disrupting the group consensus, the individual accomplishes two things. He or she allows the group to 'solve' a threatening and demanding problem, thereby reducing any personal stress and uncertainty created by the decision (all these people can't be wrong) (Callaway *et al.* 1985), and he or she remains in the group's good graces as well. The result of this process is that:

(1) dissent becomes inhibited;
(2) the group tends to feel it is invulnerable and morally correct;
(3) doubts are 'explained away';
(4) the enemy is disparaged as weak, stupid or immoral and;
(5) a false sense of consensus exists.

For example, in the late 1960s, President Johnson and his advisors were able to delude themselves into thinking that the opposition to the Vietnam War in the US was due to a small minority of misfits, weirdos and political extremists, when in fact it was a widespread reaction that eventually made it impossible for him to run for a second term as president.

Laboratory research on groupthink has been sparse. In this research, manipulations of high cohesion (e.g. letting friends participate in the study together) have generally not produced the poor discussion quality Janis' theory predicts (e.g. Flowers 1977; Leana 1985). In fairness, however, these laboratory manipulations do not produce the extremely high level of in-group feeling that characterizes the policy making groups in which Janis is interested. On the other hand, the laboratory work does indicate a good deal of support for the notion that directive leadership results in low quality group problem solving (e.g. Flowers 1977). Added to this, Janis offers a careful historical analysis to substantiate his various hypotheses. While we must be careful of such an approach since we cannot be certain that contradictory examples have not been overlooked (Longley and Pruitt 1980), there is little doubt among social scientists that groupthink is a process that often produces poor group decisions. A quantitative content analysis of public statements made by key decision makers showed that, for policy decisions that Janis had categorized as exemplifying groupthink, decision-makers' perceptions of the issues were much more simplistic than was true for decisions that Janis categorized as non-groupthink (Tetlock 1979). Moreover, in a recent content analysis of historical international decisions, Herek *et al.* (1987) report a negative correlation between the number of groupthink symptoms and the quality of the decision; the greater the groupthink, the more negative was the outcome of the decision. A third study using an historical analysis suggests that at least two key groupthink decisions discussed by Janis were characterized by compliance processes that overrode decision-makers' serious reservations regarding the group's decision (McCauley 1989). McCauley's analysis also suggests that particularly crucial factors in the groupthink process are directive leadership (stating the leader's views early), homogeneity among group members and insulation of the group from outside influence.

For those who wish to avoid this trap the message is clear:

(1) foster open discussion of all alternatives;
(2) consider 'worse case' scenarios and create contingency plans;
(3) caution leaders not to champion any one plan early in discussion;
(4) have group ideas reviewed by outside experts and devil's advocates (Janis 1972; McCauley 1989).

Group polarization

The groupthink phenomenon illustrates how an emerging group norm (often one suggested by the group leader) can bias the content of discussion by suppressing dissent. Group polarization focuses on a related process whereby group discussion tends to intensify group opinion, producing more extreme judgments among group members than existed before discussion.

Initially, researchers felt that group discussion would have a mellowing influence on hotheads and extremists within the group. Group discussion was expected to produce more moderate decisions than individual decision-making. Research soon made it apparent, however, that group discussion typically had just the opposite effect. Stoner (1961) was the first to report that group discussion led to riskier decisions on risk problems than did individual decision-making. Similar results have since been reported on a wide range of decision judgments. For example, group discussion led French students in the late 1960s to increase their disapproval of the US (Moscovici and Zavalloni 1969). Similarly, Myers and Bishop (1970) found that in the US, discussion intensified racial attitudes – liberals becoming more tolerant and 'traditionalists' becoming less tolerant following group discussion. Numerous other researchers have found very similar effects on other judgment and attitude dimensions. For example, group discussion also intensifies attitudes related to feminism, equality, underage drinking and guilt or innocence of a defendant (cf. Myers and Lamm 1976). Moreover, as noted by Dion et al. (1970), these effects occur in different countries (e.g., England, France, Israel, Germany, US, and Canada) using a wide variety of subjects (e.g. grade school children, industrial supervisors).

Most theorists agree, however, that this *group polarization* effect does not occur invariably. One major requirement is that group members must basically agree, at least in a general sense, about what side of the issue they favor. For example, groups become riskier after discussion only when most members feel (before discussion) that taking some kind of risk in the setting is sensible. In this sense, group polarization represents the intensification of a pre-existing initial group preference. The primary sources of this effect are the joint operations of two previously discussed social influence processes, normative and informational influence. If there is a pre-existing group preference (or norm) favoring risk, normative influence will make group members reluctant to deviate from that norm. In this case, those who are relatively least committed to the group norm are likely to be seen as deviates. Knowing that most members advocate positions or recommendations between 6 and 8.5 on a 9-point risk taking scale has implications for what they are likely to think of me if I urge a very cautious position of 2. They are likely to reject or dismiss my views, and may even ridicule me. Thus, knowledge of group members' positions can, by itself, exert influence by initiating a subtle competition among group participants to be at least 'above average' regarding their adherence to any group norm. If the group favors risk, it is best to be above average on that dimension.

On the other hand, informational influence will also affect group members when they hear the arguments and reasons that other group members provide when discussing decision preferences. Continuing the preceding example, group members are likely to hear numerous reasons for a risky position from other group members. This, in turn, might persuade initially cautious individuals that their original position was ill-conceived and lead them to shift toward a riskier position.

For a number of years social psychologists debated which of the two basic influence processes was necessary and sufficient to produce the polarization effect (e.g. Sanders and Baron 1977). It is now clear that either process is sufficient and that neither is necessary. To document that normative influence alone (i.e. competitive pressure) is sufficient to produce polarization, researchers have used experimental tasks in which no persuasive arguments are exchanged (e.g. Baron and Roper 1976; Cotton and Baron 1980; Myers 1982). Blascovich *et al.* (1975), for example, found that betting became more extreme during group play in a blackjack card game even though players did not discuss their bets. To document the sufficiency of persuasive arguments, the opposite strategy has been used. Subjects hear the arguments offered by other subjects, but are somehow prevented from knowing precisely what position these fellow group members favor. As a result, social comparison based competition is difficult. Here, too, group polarization occurs (e.g. Burnstein and Vinokur 1973).

In the research that has addressed the relative contributions of these influence modes, persuasive arguments (informational influence) seem to have produced stronger polarization effects than has the competitive process triggered by knowledge of other positions (normative influence) *per se* (Isenberg 1986). As indicated, however, the degree to which normative and/or informational influence contributes to polarization effects will vary from one situation to the next. A number of factors are likely to affect their relative contribution.

Normative influence is more likely when the topic concerns values, tastes, and preferences as opposed to factual issues (Laughlin and Early 1982). In task-focused groups, as opposed to friendship groups, informational influence is more likely to predominate (Kaplan and Miller 1987). High attention to the task is thought to mediate such effects (Campbell and Fairey 1989). When the decision task is highly ego-involving, normative influence should exert more impact (Isenberg 1986). Stronger normative influence effects are also associated with greater ambiguity of the situation or the topic under discussion (Boster and Hale 1990). Normative effects should also be stronger whenever forces make group identity more salient and individual members' unique identities less salient (Isenberg 1986; Kaplan and Miller 1987).

Information sampling

In the last section we have seen that during group discussion a variety of factors may occasionally make group members more concerned with social approval (normative social influence) than with carefully evaluating the facts and logic provided by their peers (informational social influence). In addition to these factors, Burnstein and Vinokur (1977) suggest that two other key variables affect the impact of persuasive arguments: their quality and their novelty. Arguments in the discussion will only produce polarization when they are both compelling (logical, well thought out), and new to some of the group members. In short, our tendency to polarize should be stronger when we hear lots of new, persuasive arguments during discussion. Note, however, that according to Burnstein and Vinokur (1977), if during discussion all group members offer precisely the *same* reasons for their own judgments, little polarization will occur because these arguments would be 'old news' to everyone.

Burnstein and Vinokur's assumption that when we hear new information we are strongly affected by it seems most plausible and, indeed, has been supported by some of their own research. On the other hand, recent research on *information sampling theory* by Stasser, Titus and their associates (e.g. Stasser and Titus 1987) indicates that whatever its potential impact, often such novel information never gets expressed in discussion. This team of researchers report several studies indicating that group members have a strong tendency to discuss primarily the information that they share in common and to fail to mention important elements of information that are known only to single individuals within the group. This is thought to be particularly true when the shared information supports group members' initial preferences.

Suppose, for example, that a group of five politicians must choose between two candidates, Dan and Arlen. Suppose, further, that all five politicians share the same two positive beliefs about Dan (e.g. he's young and photogenic), while each politician holds a single, unique positive belief about Arlen (one believes he's hard working, another believes he's brilliant, etc.). Since each politician has twice as many positive beliefs about Dan as about Arlen, we would expect all five to favor Dan. However, if they pooled all their available information in a group discussion, they would have five positive beliefs about Arlen and only two about Dan, and as a group, should prefer Arlen. Stasser (1988) labels this state of affairs a hidden profile. It describes a situation in which the information held in common by group members favors a particular choice while the unshared information contradicts the choice.

What happens when groups discuss such profiles? If all information is discussed and considered equally during discussion, the rational group choice would be to prefer Arlen. However, in fact, Stasser and Titus' (1985) study suggests that such a group would actually prefer Dan to Arlen. Groups do not seem to pool unshared information efficiently, but rather dwell on shared information. In support of this interpretation, it has been shown that subjects recall fewer unshared arguments from the discussion (Stasser and

Titus 1985, 1987). Moreover, analysis of tape-recorded discussions document that unshared arguments are less likely to be expressed (Stasser *et al.* 1989a). In short, hidden profiles lead to biased information sampling during group discussion. Sometimes, as in the purely hypothetical example we just considered, this can lead to very poor group decisions. Stasser and Titus (1987) argue that this bias for shared information is most likely to occur when it supports the general sentiment within the group and when there is a relatively large number of 'shared' facts among members to discuss. In other words, if there is hardly anything to talk about, even unshared and unpopular views may get expressed during discussion. Stasser *et al.* (1989a) also reported that this bias was more pronounced in six-person groups than in three-person groups. Whereas, overall, 46 per cent of shared information was mentioned in contrast to only 18 per cent of unshared information, this difference was even larger in six-person groups.

Why might *hidden profiles* lead to this selective bias in information sampling? One obvious explanation is that normative group influence (i.e. fear of group rejection and desires for social approval) make group members reluctant to offer unique and unshared views that contradict emerging group consensus. If true, this would represent a case in which normative social influence biases the process of informational social influence by determining what information gets exchanged. Although this matter is not yet resolved, information sampling bias seems to be a robust effect. In one particular condition, Stasser *et al.* (1989a) gave instructions intended to curb it. Group members were asked to avoid stating their initial preferences and were encouraged to review all relevant facts. Groups discussed the candidate problem for 30 minutes. These instructions did increase the amount of discussion that occurred, but the discussion again primarily favored those facts initially shared by group members (67 per cent of all shared facts were discussed in contrast to 23 per cent of unshared facts). Although Burnstein and Vinokur may be correct assuming that novel (i.e. unshared) information is very persuasive when it is presented in discussion, Stasser and Titus' (1985, 1987) data indicate that group members seem reluctant to introduce such ideas unless they detect some signs of social support for their unique ideas.

The effect of real consequences

Over three hundred studies have examined the group polarization phenomenon using a wide range of judgments and subject populations. Relatively few of them, however, have studied decisions or judgments that have real and immediate consequences for the decision-maker. For instance, subjects generally are asked to make a series of hypothetical decisions in which they advise non-existent persons how much risk they should take (e.g. what would the odds of success at a new job have to be before you would advise Mr/Ms Make Believe to leave his/her present job for a new opportunity).

Given the powerful generality of the group polarization phenomenon, one might expect similar effects for both hypothetical and real decisions, but this has not always proven to be true. Several studies on gambling behavior illustrate this complexity. The most common finding from early work on hypothetical decisions is that group discussion elevates risk taking. Thus, we should expect group interaction to elevate gambling behavior. This indeed occurred in several studies conducted by Blascovich, Ginsberg and their associates (e.g. Blascovich *et al.* 1975). These researchers found that subjects bet more money playing blackjack if they discussed or otherwise knew the bets of fellow players. What complicates matters is that two race track studies find just the opposite. McCauley *et al.* (1973), and Knox and Safford (1976) recruited bettors at a race track by offering to pay for their next $2 bet. The subjects' task was to decide which horse to bet on. This allowed the researchers to assess risk taking by noting the betting odds of the horse the subjects selected. In both studies, bettors tended to make *less* risky selections if they decided via group discussion rather than individually.

How can we resolve this inconsistency? A key procedural difference may be responsible for these contradictory outcomes. In the race track research, the group decision was to be *binding* on each group member in that the group's unanimous decision would determine what all group members bet. Here individual group members may have been reluctant to vote for or advocate a risky option in the group since it might force someone who couldn't afford it to lose their money.

In contrast, the blackjack research did not require a binding unanimous decision. As a result, group members could advocate risk without feeling that they were coercing others. In short, when groups make decisions that have binding, costly implications for all group members, the tendency to avoid coercion of those with less resources into committing more than they can afford may limit and even reverse group polarization effects.

Other research supports this view. Group discussion increased the willingness of college students to donate student fees to a (hypothetical) fund for Bengali refugees that was unlikely to be established by their student government (Baron *et al.* 1974). This corroborated other studies in which group discussion enhanced generosity on hypothetical issues (Schroeder 1973; Muehleman *et al.* 1976). When these same students were asked to make actual personal donations to an already existing Bengali relief fund, however, group discussion to full binding consensus reduced donations below subjects' initial individual contributions. Thus, when group decisions had real and immediate costs for group members, they were reluctant to advocate a decision that would force others to incur them.

Minority and majority influence

Until recently, research on social influence focused almost exclusively on how individuals were affected by group majorities. In the 1970s, however, several researchers essentially turned the tables. If social influence always was directed from majorities to deviates, they asked, why was there ever any social change or innovation? Why did ideas about music, hairstyle, clothing and politics change? Why weren't we all still listening to nothing but Mozart (or jungle drums for that matter)? Why didn't we all still believe the world was flat? Obviously, majorities were not always successful in influencing deviates. Obviously minorities, at least on occasion, could very dramatically influence majorities. The first theorist to champion this (minority) position was Serge Moscovici who conducted a number of studies of color perception (e.g. Moscovici *et al.* 1969). In this research, Moscovici and his collaborators observed that when minorities (actually two confederates) offered unusual color judgments (labeling blue as green), they were more likely to affect subjects' private beliefs than when majorities offered these judgments. To be sure, individuals were more likely to agree publicly with the majority than with the minority, but in private sessions (away from the group) their beliefs were influenced most by minorities (cf. Moscovici 1980).

These results were conceptually replicated in a series of studies. Maass and Clark (1983), for example, had subjects read passages on gay rights in which minority and majority positions were obvious. Subjects then indicated how they themselves felt in these issues. In some cases this was done quite anonymously, but in other cases, subjects expected their responses to be made known to the others at their session. Regardless of whether the minority favored gay rights (in some sessions) or opposed it (in other sessions), individuals tended to agree with the minority (and, therefore, oppose the majority view) when their opinion was to be kept private. In public conditions, however, just the opposite occurred. In brief, these data provide good evidence that minorities can have substantial influence on opinions and judgments under specified conditions. Other studies have found minority influence on tasks as varied as jury deliberation of an injury case (Wolf 1979), attitudes towards abortion (Maass *et al.* 1982) and attitudes towards foreigners (Mugny 1975).

The after-image study

A major contention of Moscovici and his associates is that minority influence is particularly effective at producing internalized change in beliefs. How can one be sure, however, that such change has really occurred? Subjects may say that 'a blue slide looks green' after hearing a minority say so, but how can we be sure they truly believe it? Perhaps they are trying to please the experimenter or show that they are creative and open-minded. Moscovici and Personnaz (1980) designed a particularly ingenious study to address this issue. This study relied on the fact that just after seeing a bright color slide in a dark room we tend to see the complementary color as an afterimage. Specifically, a green slide should evoke a red/purple after-image whereas a blue slide should evoke a yellow/orange after-image. Moreover, very few people know this fact. Consequently, Moscovici and Personnaz reasoned that if minority influence really was leading people to 'see' blue slides as being green, they should be more likely to see a red/purple after-image than people exposed to a majority. In addition, such a response would be unlikely to represent deliberate falsification by the subject (e.g. compliance) since most subjects have no idea of what after-images are caused by the various colors. The data from several of Moscovici and Personnaz' experiments were very encouraging. For example, in one, subjects examined five blue slides. Before offering their own description of each, they heard a confederate describe the slide as green. This caused very little overt compliance. Only 5 per cent of subjects said the slide was green. However, when this confederate was described as a minority, subjects were more likely to report seeing the red/purple after-image (that would be triggered by truly seeing a green slide) than when the confederate was part of a majority.

This remarkable result is particularly impressive when one considers that after-images are caused by the pattern of stimulation of rods and cones in the retina. Thus, these data imply that minority influence actually led the eye to respond to the blue stimulus as if it were a green stimulus. Astounding! Astonishing! Implausible? And unfortunately not well replicated. At least two teams of researchers have conducted very close replications of Moscovici and Personnaz' work and have failed to corroborate their original findings (Doms and van Avermaet 1980; Sorrentino et al. 1980). As a result, these data cannot be viewed as very compelling evidence that minorities are superior to majorities in producing internalized conversion. Nevertheless, the research represents a highly creative attempt to deal with an extremely slippery issue; i.e. proving that a particular instance of social influence primarily reflects internalized belief change as opposed to some subtle form of compliance. Subsequent research, however, leaves little doubt that minorities can be an important source of social influence, particularly when the target person's opinions are stated outside of the group's presence (cf. Moscovici and Mugny 1983; Brown 1988).

Variables affecting minority influence

The most effective form of minority influence occurs when the minority is comprised of more than one individual and they are in basic agreement. For example, Moscovici and Lage (1976) found that a minority of one exerted non-significant influence over color judgments when the minority asserted that blue was green, but that when two minority individuals made this judgment, minority influence was evident in both public and private responses of the majority. The result is actually not that hard to explain. A minority of only one can be dismissed by the majority as either a lunatic or a moron, but this reaction is harder to support when several people serve as the minority. Research on minority influence has also suggested that the minority should hold their position consistently over time in order to maximize their influence. Research by Mugny and Papastamou (1976), however, suggests that this consistency should avoid the appearance of rigidity and refusal to compromise. These researchers varied whether messages from minorities (on the topic of pollution) used flexible, moderate language or a more doctrinaire style. Only the former was effective in influencing listeners. In short, there is a good deal of support for the notion that minorities can influence majorities, but there do seem to be some crucial limits to this phenomenon.

The two-process model

The study of majority and minority factions within groups has raised the question of whether minority influence differs from majority influence. Two-process theorists (e.g. Moscovici 1980) argue that minorities and majorities tend to elicit distinct influence effects. The distinction corresponds to that between compliance on the one hand and conversion (or internalized attitude change) on the other. Put differently, it corresponds to normative versus informational influence. Moscovici (e.g. 1980) argues that because of their numerical advantage and implicit power, majorities induce compliance, but no true change of belief. In contrast, minorities allegedly draw attention to the arguments that underlie or support their position. When the contents of their arguments become attended to, this in turn presumably acts to change the attitudes of others. Thus, majorities are said to elicit compliance whereas minorities induce attitude change (Moscovici 1980).

One factor that contributes to the persuasive power of minorities is the fact that by sticking to their opinions in the face of majority opposition (and often times ridicule), they demonstrate their sincerity and commitment. Here are people who are so convinced and concerned that they are willing to risk the costs of assuming the role of group deviate. A second reason why minorities, more than majorities, might draw attention to themselves has to do with the structural feature that defines the majority/minority distinction. Minority, by definition means less frequent. That which is novel or numerically infrequent stands out (Duval and Wicklund 1972). Thus, a minority directs attention toward its members (and their arguments) as a consequence of its category distinctiveness (Wilder 1986). For these reasons, Moscovici (1980) and his associates argue that minorities are more likely than majorities to produce permanent attitude change.

The answer to the question of whether minority influence qualitatively differs from majority influence requires a clear understanding of what is meant by distinct processes. There are several interpretations and they give different answers.

Outcomes

First, one can ask whether minorities and majorities produce different outcomes. With respect to the distinction between compliance and internalized belief change, a number of reviews suggest that the answer is yes (e.g. Maass and Clark 1984). The majority is said to induce compliance more readily than the minority, whereas when the minority succeeds in exerting influence its effects appear on delayed and indirect measures of belief, and not merely on those administered in the presence of the majority members (e.g. Maass et al. 1987).

As indicated, despite the fact that research does support this distinction in outcome, there is also good evidence that majorities can produce attitude change as well as compliance. Similarly, anecdotal data suggest instances in which a minority can elicit compliance, as when terrorists force an exchange of an imprisoned compatriot by threatening the life of a citizen abducted from the country that has jailed him. Thus, undermining the claimed distinction between minority and majority, there seems to be no intrinsic reason why both majorities and minorities cannot each produce each type of influence. Of course, what is possible may not occur with equal frequency. Although each is capable of producing either mode of influence, it also may be that they typically do not do so as often, thereby lending support for the distinction between minority and majority influence.

Behavior

A related possibility is that each subgroup differs in the way it behaves during its persuasive efforts. Here, the focus is on process rather than outcome. Do minority subgroups, as observed naturalistically, typically emit behavior patterns during the group discussion that differ from those of the majority? Moscovici (1980) argues that in order to have any impact the minority must consistently and persistently present its position, that it must not waiver or compromise. As noted above, Moscovici is referring to consistency both over time and across individuals. The minority members should agree among themselves and remain steadfast over time. The majority, having more power, as a result of its numerical superiority, feels that it can always impose its will, and consequently need not behave dogmatically. Without compromising its ability to prevail, it can behave in a more conciliatory and compromising manner, and display some largesse toward the minority.

In contrast, because its position is the unpopular one, the minority, more typically than the majority, may buttress its expressed desires with well thought-out reasons. The unpopularity of typical minority positions may often generate instances where they must be defended, resulting in more elaborated, novel, and well-practiced arguments. In contrast, the normative power of the majority undercuts its need to give explanations for its wishes. Those holding the majority view, rarely having been asked previously to explain their views, may lack expertise and practice in doing so effectively. Note, however, that were they motivated to do so, the majority, merely by virtue of the greater resources implicit in its numerical advantage, should ordinarily have a greater capacity to contribute new arguments to the pool, be more likely to have an articulate spokesperson, etc. Thus, when the minority does exhibit persuasive superiority, it may typically reflect motivational factors that have overcome the resource advantage ordinarily implicit in majority status. This suggests that persuasive advantage for the minority is most likely not on novel topics, but rather, on issues for which they have exhibited prior commitment, on issues on which they are highly involved. It is on these latter types of issues that the effects of prior thought, practice and expertise will appear (Kerr, in press). Interestingly, these are the types of issues on which their involvement makes minority members most resistant to persuasion and least likely to comply with majority pressure (Johnson and Eagly 1989).

Again, although such differences in behavior patterns as described above naturally may be correlated with minority or majority status, they may not be intrinsic or necessary consequences. For instance, one can readily think of cases for which majority as well as minority members are likely to have well practiced and well thought-out arguments. Likewise, the greater attentional focus allegedly elicited by the minority may not be a necessary consequence of minority status. It may be important to distinguish between the initial perceptual attention to an unusual stimulus (a person uttering a distinctive view) and the careful processing of that person's supporting arguments (Mackie 1987). Nor are the conditions that control differential attention to each well understood. Despite the substantial evidence supporting attentional focus toward that which is distinctive, some evidence supports greater attention to a majority than a minority source (Tesser *et al.* 1983), and despite some evidence of better recall of minority message content (Moscovici 1980) other data shows better recall of majority messages (Maass and Clark 1983; Mackie 1987).

Discriminative construct validity

A third way of considering the issue of whether distinct processes underlie minority and majority influence is to cast the question in the framework of criteria for construct validity. One requirement for construct validity is that a scientific concept should exhibit lawful relationships to other constructs. For many years, physical anthropologists made detailed measurements of the *cephalic index*, the ratio of head width to head length. These measurements could be made reliably and, moreover, distinct racial/ethnic groups were shown to have cephalic-index ratios that distinguished them from other racial ethnic groups. Is the cephalic index an important scientific construct? No, because research never disclosed relationships between it and other variables.

A second criterion concerns discriminant validity. Even when a concept is shown to have empirical relationships with other variables, those relationships must be distinct from the relationships found for other, seemingly similar, concepts. If not, they are not distinct concepts. Applying this criterion to the potential distinction between minority and majority influence, one must ask whether the relationships found between variables when the minority is the influence source differ from the relationships between the same variables when one examines, instead, the influence of the majority. If each of an array of variables has the same direction of effect on minority and majority influence, by the criterion of discriminant construct validity there is no reason to conceptualize the two as distinct.

For example, if as Moscovici argues, minorities produce influence through their arguments while majorities produce influence solely as a function of their power, manipulating variables such as verbal threat and argument quality should have very different effects in majorities and minorities. Verbal threat from a minority (towards a majority) could well lower the minority's influence since it usually has less power than majorities. Thus, such threats would produce resentment rather than fear. Threats from majorities, however, should increase influence if Moscovici's two-process view is correct. Similarly, increasing the quality of the majority's arguments should have no effect on minorities since minorities presumably are focusing only on the majority's power. Increasing the quality of the minorities' arguments, however, should increase their influence substantially.

Taking this approach to the question of mono v. dual influence processes, one could examine the full array of variables that are likely to affect influence processes within group discussions. These might include time pressure to make a quick decision, extremity of the position advocated by the faction, size of the faction, power and status of the source within the faction, whether the topic under consideration is value-orientated as opposed to factual, etc. According to a recent review, examination of the effect of various independent variables on minority and majority influence shows little evidence of any difference in the direction of effect as a consequence of minority/majority status (Kruglanski and Mackie 1990). It does not seem to matter whether influence is directed at minorities or instead stems from minorities. Thus, from the perspective of *discriminant construct validity*, there is, as yet, little basis for viewing minority/majority influence as distinct processes. This appears to be a research area that will receive a good deal of attention in the near future.

Intense indoctrination

As we have seen, the study of social influence raises a number of interesting theoretical questions for academic researchers. Social influence processes, however, can have powerful and important real life implications as well. This is seen quite dramatically in instances of intense indoctrination. In Chapter 1, we referred to Patty Hearst's abduction by the Symbionese Liberation Army. What was most startling about this incident was that, within weeks of her kidnapping, Ms Hearst had joined forces with her captors, participating in both a bank robbery and a shoot-out at a sporting goods store. A year later at her eventual capture she proclaimed her occupation as 'urban guerilla'. Somehow the SLA had transformed Patty Hearst from a student into a revolutionary in a matter of weeks. This 'accomplishment' seems somewhat less surprising, however, when one considers the psychological principles underlying such cases of intense indoctrination and the social influence process to which Ms Hearst was exposed (Hearst 1982) – a process in which initial compliance slowly becomes transformed into internalized belief change.

If one examines classic cases of intense indoctrination, such as the 'brainwashing' of western civilians by Chinese Communists in the early 1950s (Lifton 1961) or the treatment of political dissidents by the Soviet KGB in the 1930s and 1940s (Hinkle and Wolff 1956), a common pattern becomes evident. The indoctrination takes place in stages. The first can be called the *softening up stage*. This is marked by a variety of disorientating and stressful procedures commonly involving isolation from one's friends and family, inadequate sleep and nutrition, overstimulation (e.g. overwork) and various emotional manipulations (e.g. fear). Patty Hearst, for example, was held handcuffed in a dark closet for 4 weeks while being repeatedly threatened with death. In other cases, indoctrinees find themselves away from home in a dizzying round of activities, lectures, games, prayers, meetings and work, often leaving them scant time for sleep or private reflection.

This stage is followed by the *compliance stage* in which the recruit tentatively 'tries out' some of the behavior requested by the group, more or less going through the motions or paying lip service to many of their demands. Often this is viewed as a period of exploration by the recruit to see what such compliance nets him or her. In other cases, individuals comply out of politeness or from a desire to not make a scene. In Ms Hearst's case, her initial decision to 'join' the SLA was only a simple ruse on her part to appease a group that was threatening to murder her (Hearst 1982). In this stage, indoctrinees may change their appearance and may 'try out' various novel behavior patterns (e.g. meditation, martial arts drill, learning a new doctrine). This stage is not hard to understand. People are responding to threat, curiosity or deeply ingrained norms of politeness. It is in the *internalization stage* that things become interesting, in that the compliance transforms itself into privately held belief change.

Here, the recruit or indoctrinee begins to consider the possibility that the group is correct in its world view. In most cases of compliance, occurring outside of intense indoctrination, individuals conform due to some noticeable threat or inducement. Once this pressure is removed, the compliance ends. In intense indoctrination, however, a variety of subtle pressures serve to prolong the behavior and these pressures often lead to actual belief change. How can we explain this process? First, conformity pressure is likely to be quite strong. Because of the experiences in the softening up stage, the individual will often be confused, exhausted or scared. These conditions lower self-confidence and leave the indoctrinee more dependent on others. Darley (1966), for example, found greater conformity when subjects were frightened by the prospect of up-coming shock. Additionally, by separating the recruit from her/his friends and family, the indoctrinating group denies the recruit access to allies who might bolster her/his original views. As a result, the indoctrinating group becomes a more powerful influencing agent, especially since they will generally be united. If there is one lesson from the conformity research it is that we underestimate how susceptible we are to social influence when everyone around us agrees on a given point. This is true not just because group judgment is credible. As we have learned, groups are a key source of approval. In these cases of intense indoctrination, the group is the only source of immediate approval. This dramatically increases their power, for we generally underestimate the extent to which we depend upon positive relationships with others to maintain our self-esteem and sense of well-being.

A second cause of internalization is that the stress of the softening up period undoubtedly leaves us less capable of carefully considering the wisdom (or lack of same) of the arguments and doctrine of the indoctrinating group. Using such techniques, cults have persuaded their members of beliefs that seem absolutely bizarre to outsiders. For example, one small religious sect active in the US in the 1970s convinced members that in order to transcend 'needs of the flesh', they should try to restrain themselves from bathing, touching other people and even wearing glasses (Martin and Young 1979). Another religious sect preaches that the urge to sleep more than 4 or 5 hours a day is pressure from the devil. In short, stress reduces our attentional capacity, thereby leaving us more susceptible than usual to flawed and illogical arguments and doctrine; our ability to counterargue is impaired.

A third mechanism that provokes private belief change is the individual's need for identity. Mass movements provide us with larger than life goals and a sense of purpose that transcends the insignificant of our own lives. The dedicated follower can feel special, selfless and a part of history. Thus, many of the major existential dilemmas that plague modern man evaporate once one totally accepts an indoctrinating group's message.

The final and perhaps most crucial mechanism producing internalization, however, involves cognitive dissonance phenomena. Put simply, we have a strong tendency to justify our behavior. This tendency is particularly strong when our behavior has been costly and unusual. One straightforward means of justifying an unusual action (e.g. Patty Hearst's participation in the Hibernia Bank Robbery) is to think of reasons why the action was sensible, correct or necessary. This, in turn, will often lead the individual to embrace the group's cause and doctrine. (I robbed that bank to finance and publicize a needed revolution.) From this perspective, it is not surprising that indoctrination procedures generally require indoctrinees to engage in increasingly public self-criticisms and attacks on their 'old' pregroup associates. Indeed, Ms Hearst was required early in her indoctrination to make radio announcements critical of her family. The public nature of these confessions increases their cost which, in turn, heightens the dissonance the indoctrinee feels. A large number of studies verify that cognitive dissonance procedures such as these are a powerful means of producing attitude change (Aronson 1968) and there seems little doubt that they play a major role in intense indoctrination. Moreover, this process can produce a 'one step at a time' pattern of escalating commitment in which initial compliance triggers private belief change which then leaves the indoctrinee susceptible to even more extreme requests from the group. This is a phenomenon known as the *foot in the door* effect.

The final phase of intense indoctrination can be described as the *consolidation* stage. In this stage, the recruit solidifies his or her newly acquired allegiance to the group by making various costly behavioral commitments that are hard to undo (e.g. donating one's personal possessions to the group; recruiting new members, etc.). This final stage of indoctrination is marked by totally accepting group doctrine and policy, with little critical examination. The primary reaction of the recruit to negative information about the group is denial and rationalization. Doctrine is accepted on the basis of absolute faith. At this point, it takes extremely dramatic evidence to shake the faith of the believers. This almost total acceptance of doctrine on faith probably occurs because group members find it quite effortful to agonize continually over whether or not the group's ideology is correct, justified, etc. The believer can avoid this painful process by simply deciding at some point that the group doctrine is correct and henceforth, *anything* the group requires or argues is accepted on faith as being justified and true. In a sense, the group member has adopted a biased perspective so that he or she can avoid confronting any doubts. For this reason the indoctrinee who has reached the consolidation stage will be highly resistent to persuasion from those outside the group.

Summary

Conformity is a pervasive and useful social process, sometimes operating without our awareness, and at other times being instrumental behavior to garner others' approval. Its opposite, resistance to influence, usually requires social support of other like-minded protestors. Social impact theory, which emphasizes the number of influence sources, the strength of each source, and its immediacy, accounts for social influence effects in a wide array of settings and was shown to apply to Milgram's studies of obedience. We distinguished between two distinct modes of social influence: normative and informational influence. We examined their operation in group discussion, including Janis' analysis of the operation of groupthink in high-level national policy decisions. Research on information sampling theory suggests that normative influence affects the functioning of informational influence by biasing the selection of information that group members present to the group.

Consideration of factions or subgroups within a group discussion raised the issue of whether minority influence differs from majority influence – the former eliciting compliance, the latter producing true belief change. While there is some support for this dual process view, the issue is far from closed. At least one research strategy, the examination of discriminant construct validity, suggests that the same basic processes are involved in both minority and majority influence.

Aside from these theoretical issues, social influence phenomena can have powerful effects on behavior and beliefs, as instances of intense indoctrination amply demonstrate. Such indoctrination can be viewed as a process having a number of stages and involving a number of interlinking social dynamics including conformity effects, cognitive dissonance phenomena and impoverished message processing.

Suggestions for further reading

Deutsch, M. and Gerard, H. B. (1955). A study of normative and informational social influence upon individual judgment. *Journal of Abnormal and Social Psychology*, 51, 629–36.

Janis, I. L. (1972). *Victims of Groupthink*. Boston: Houghton Mifflin.

Latané, B. (1981). The psychology of social impact. *American Psychologist*, 36, 343–56.

Maass, A. and Clark, R. D. (1983). Internalization versus compliance: Differential processes underlying minority influence and conformity. *European Journal of Social Psychology*, 13, 197–215.

Stasser, G. and Titus, W. (1985). Pooling of unshared information in group decision making: Biased information sampling during group discussion. *Journal of Personality and Social Psychology*, 48, 1467–8.

Wilder, D. A. and Allen, V. L. (1977). Social support, extreme social support and conformity. *Representative Research in Social Psychology*, 8, 33–41.

6 / GROUP DECISION MAKING

At one time or another you have probably been part of a decision-making group. It might have been a rather formal affair, such as a committee or club meeting with a formal agenda and rules of procedure. More likely it was an informal setting, such as a group of friends trying to decide what movie to see. A lot goes on in decision-making groups – many viewpoints are expressed; discussion may shift from topic to topic suddenly and without apparent reason; genuine persuasion may occur, but so may capitulation to social pressure; common political processes (e.g. compromise, logrolling, coalition formation) may be observed; people form impressions of one another. It is to this rather complex, but fascinating topic that we now turn our attention.

Group decision making is not only a fascinating topic, it is an important one as well. We entrust groups to make many of our most important decisions. The US Congress declares war (in principle, if not in practice), boards of directors make business decisions which can affect thousands of workers, the US Supreme Court decides whether and when women may end their pregnancies, and juries, sometimes literally, make life-or-death decisions.

In this chapter we will not attempt to consider in detail all of the complex psychological processes involved in group decision making. For example, we will not be concerned here with how groups generate decision alternatives (a key issue in the group problem-solving process), but will rather be concerned with how groups choose among a set of well specified and known alternatives. Unlike group problem solving or group performance tasks, we will not assume that there always is a clear standard for evaluating a group's decision. That is, although we can usually tell which group has solved a problem fastest or been the most productive, often there will be no way of evaluating the quality of a group's decision. Sometimes group choices are entirely subjective (e.g. a group judging a beauty contest); sometimes there is just no way of telling whether or not the group has made a valid choice (e.g. a jury's choice between conviction or acquittal).

Nearly every decision-making group must achieve some level of agreement or consensus among group members to define a group choice. This required degree of consensus is called the group's *decision rule*. A good example is the familiar majority-rules criterion used in most elections; another example is the unanimity rule used by most juries (see Miller 1989). Decision rules may be explicit and formal (e.g. the voting rule specified in an organization's bylaws) or implicit and informal (e.g. a chairperson's intuitive assessment that sufficient agreement exists in a meeting to consider the matter at hand settled). Such decision rules are one of several important aspects of group decision-making *procedures*. Other aspects include:

(1) the voting rules that govern how individual preferences may be expressed and pooled (e.g. vote for your favorite option *v.* rank order all options);
(2) the group's formal agenda (e.g. sometimes the order in which issues are taken up affect the decisions reached).

However, we will restrict our attention here to the typical, small, face-to-face, decision-making group which has a rather simple agenda (viz. a single decision to make) and a simple, usually informal voting rule (e.g. direct polling of first preferences).

In this chapter we will be primarily concerned with understanding the process by which a group moves from initial disagreement (i.e. failure to satisfy its decision rule) to agreement (i.e. satisfaction of the operative decision rule). Viewed in this light, group decision making is fundamentally concerned with social influence processes, the topic of the last chapter.

The traditional approach to the study of group decision making might be called the *social communication* approach. It assumes that the best way to analyze how a group reaches its decision is to listen to what the group members say to one another. Typical questions posed by someone taking this approach might include 'who talks to whom?'; 'who says what?'; 'do others agree or disagree?' This approach has yielded much useful knowledge (e.g. Bales and Strodtbeck 1951; Strodtbeck and Mann 1956; Bales 1958). For example, it seems clear from this type of analysis that groups often develop two kinds of leaders; those that focus on task demands, and those that attend to the feelings and social needs of group members. Another interesting finding is that those who take on leadership roles tend to have very high rates of participation in the group (Sorrentino and Boutillier 1975; Mullen *et al.* 1989).

However, in this chapter we will focus on a rather different approach to investigating the group decision-making process. It has been termed the *social combination* approach (Laughlin 1980; Davis 1982). Its basic unit of analysis is not a spoken thought or argument, but rather the actual preferences of the group members. Someone taking this approach might ask 'how much support does each alternative have at the beginning of group deliberation?'; 'are there regular patterns in the way preferences change?'; 'can I predict what the group's decision will be if I know the members' preferences?' This approach is called the social combination approach because it tries to specify how group members combine what they bring to the group (e.g. their personal preferences) into a single group product (e.g. a group decision).

Social combination approaches to group decision making

The basic idea of the social combination approach is to find some recipe or rule or function for translating what group members bring to the group's task (e.g. their abilities, motivations) into what the group actually accomplishes (e.g. the group level of performance). A social combination approach to group decision making asks, 'Is there a way of relating the preferences of individual group members (the input) to the final preference of the entire group (the output)?' The most ambitious attempts to answer this question have employed Davis' (1973) *social decision scheme* or SDS model. (See Smoke and Zajonc 1962, or Hastie *et al.* 1983, for other interesting social combination models.) Before describing the SDS model, we should perhaps warn the incurably math-phobic reader that a good understanding of this approach will require the use of some mathematics. The good news is that the required math is not too hard to follow if you familiarize yourself with the terminology and work through the description of the model carefully, step by step. More importantly, the basic ideas behind the math are fairly simple.

The SDS model assumes that groups of a fixed size, r, must choose among a set of n alternatives, A_1, A_2, $A_3 \ldots A_n$. A simple illustration is a six-person jury that has to choose between a 'guilty' and 'not guilty' verdict: thus, $r = 6$, $n = 2$ and (A_1, A_2) = (guilty, not guilty). The SDS model does not try to predict the final decision of any particular group, but rather the overall *distribution* of group decisions, denoted as $(P_1, P_2, P_3 \ldots P_n)$. For example, if 65 per cent of the six-person juries, considering the same case, decided that the defendant was guilty, then the distribution of group decisions would just be (P_1, P_2) = (65 per cent guilty, 35 per cent not guilty). The input for the SDS model is not the corresponding distribution of *individual* preferences (denoted p_1, p_2, $p_3 \ldots p_n$), but rather all the possible ways that the r members of the group could be distributed across the n decision alternatives. For the example we have been considering, there are seven such 'splits', which are displayed on the left side of Table 6.1. If each individual juror starts deliberation preferring either a guilty or not guilty verdict, then each six-person jury must begin deliberation with one of these seven splits. In fact, for any particular trial, one could estimate just what percentage of juries would begin deliberation with each possible split. A simple way to do this is to poll each jury before it begins deliberation. [Alternatively, one could poll a sample of individual jurors to estimate the overall distribution of *juror* verdict preference (p_1, p_2), and then, using some basic probability theory, one could calculate the probability of occurrence of each possible split in randomly composed juries.]

The challenge of the SDS model is to link group member input (viz. starting splits) to group output (group decisions). As noted above, the SDS model does this probabilistically. It does not assume that all groups starting from the same place (i.e. with the same starting split) end up in the same place (i.e. reach the same group decision). Rather, the model tries to identify d_{ij}, the probability that a group starting with the ith split will eventually decide on the jth decision alternative. If we allow that another possible jury 'decision' is to reach no decision at all (i.e. to be hung), then in the jury example we have been considering, there are 21 such values (7 possible splits × three jury decision

Table 6.1   Some illustrative social decision schemes

Initial splits		Final jury verdict										
		(a) Majority/hung otherwise			(b) Zeisel and Diamond (1978)			(c) Proportionality		(d) Kerr and MacCoun (1985)		
G	NG	G	NG	H	G	NG	H	G	NG	G	NG	H
6	0	1.0	0.0	0.0	1.0	0.0	0.0	1.0	0.0	1.0	0.0	0.0
5	1	1.0	0.0	0.0	0.95	0.02	0.01	0.83	0.17	0.81	0.0	0.19
4	2	1.0	0.0	0.0	0.83	0.13	0.04	0.67	0.33	0.31	0.26	0.42
3	3	0.0	0.0	1.0	0.42	0.46	0.12	0.50	0.50	0.11	0.46	0.43
2	4	0.0	1.0	0.0	0.12	0.85	0.03	0.33	0.67	0.00	0.84	0.16
1	5	0.0	1.0	0.0	0.02	0.97	0.01	0.17	0.83	0.00	0.89	0.11
0	6	0.0	1.0	0.0	0.0	1.0	0.0	0.0	1.0	0.00	1.0	0.00

alternatives). These values can be conveniently arrayed in a box or matrix form, as illustrated in panel (a) of Table 6.1. As you can see, this particular D matrix or *social decision scheme* is a way of expressing the simple idea that initial majorities will ultimately prevail in the jury. For example, if the jury begins deliberation with four jurors favoring conviction and two favoring acquittal (the third row), this decision scheme matrix predicts that the jury will eventually convict with certainty (i.e. with probability d_{21} = 1.0), and has no possibility of either acquitting or hanging (i.e. d_{22} = 0.0 and d_{23} = 0.0). When the jury begins deliberation with a majority favoring acquittal (see the last three rows of the matrix), this social decision scheme predicts jury acquittal with certainty. Remember that a social decision scheme has to make a prediction for *every* possible initial split; what happens when there is no initial majority [i.e. when the jury is initially split evenly (three guilty, three not guilty) as in the middle row of the matrix]? In this particular matrix, it is predicted that such a jury will not be able to reach any ageement – that is, the jury is certain to be hung (d_{43} = 1.0).

We will be discussing the other matrices in panels (b), (c) and (d) of Table 6.1 in a moment, but their presence should suggest to you that there are many other conceivable decision schemes besides the simple 'initial majority wins' idea summarized by matrix (a). The whole idea of the SDS approach is to identify useful D matrices – useful in the sense that they can reveal patterns which illuminate the process of group decision making. A couple of general ways of doing this have been proposed (Kerr *et al.* 1979). One way is to estimate *D* directly. For any particular group decision task, one might simply count how often groups move from each possible starting split to each possible final group decision. This has been attempted, for example, with jury decision making. Zeisel and Diamond (1978) interviewed actual jurors after their trials to learn their verdict preferences at the start of deliberation. Knowing the juries' final verdicts, Zeisel and Diamond were then able to construct the estimated *D* for jury deliberation presented in panel (b) of Table 6.1. Take a careful look at this matrix. As you can see, it is a variation on the first decision scheme we considered. Kalven, Zeisel and Diamond's results suggest that although initial majorities do not always, but usually prevail in juries, minorities very occasionally may also prevail. (Apparently, Henry Fonda's accomplishment of reversing a large majority's position in the film, *Twelve Angry Men*, is not complete fiction.) The *D* matrix also suggests, unsurprisingly, that the more even the initial split, the more likely it is that the jury will be unable to satisfy its decision rule (i.e. that the jury will be hung).

A second way of identifying useful *D* matrices is to start with an idea or theory of how group's reach consensus, and to translate it into a social decision scheme. For example, if you believe that all group members contribute equally to discussion and that the probability that a group adopts a position is simply equal to the *proportion* of all arguments expressed which are in favor of that position, then a proportionality *D* matrix like the one presented in the (c) panel of Table 6.1 should accurately summarize group decision making and predict group decisions. Alternatively, suppose you theorized that numerically larger majorities are usually able to persuade or pressure minorities into submission, and that the group would only have trouble reaching agreement if there was considerable intitial disagreement. Davis *et al.* (1975) suggested several *D* matrices for describing jury decision making which incorporated these assumptions. Of these, a *D* which held that an initial two-thirds majority would always prevail and that the jury was likely to be hung otherwise [embodied by the now-familiar panel (a) of Table 6.1] predicted their simulated juries' decisions best. As one can see, in most regards, it parallels the *D* obtained by Zeisel and Diamond [panel (b)]. The most glaring difference is the much higher rate of predicted hung juries in Davis *et al.*'s *D* (in the middle row). This may be explained by the fact that deliberation time was limited in Davis *et al.*'s simulated juries, but not in Zeisel and Diamond's real juries; sharply divided simulated juries are less able to reach agreement before available time runs out (Kerr 1981).

Jury decision making

As we have seen, one group to which the social combination approach has been applied is the jury. Juries are particularly fascinating decision-making groups. They routinely make decisions with very extremely important consequences – at times, literally life-or-death decisions. Juries also have attracted considerable research interest because they lend themselves nicely to experimental study. Their decision alternatives are explicit and usually small in number (e.g. guilty *v.* not guilty). Furthermore, unlike many other important real-world decision-making groups (e.g. boards of directors, legislative committees), juries are typically composed of a few unacquainted lay persons who have no further contact after reaching their decisions. In these regards, typical laboratory groups of strangers may nicely simulate actual juries (Bray and Kerr 1982).

Jury size and decision rule

Another reason for special interest in the jury is that over the past few decades, courts have raised basic psychological questions about jury behavior. For example, early in the 1970s the US Supreme Court had to decide whether departures from the jury's traditional size and decision rule (viz. twelve persons and a unanimity rule) were proscribed by the US Constitution. The majority of the Court held that they were not (Williams *v.* Florida, 1970; Johnson *v.* Louisiana, 1972); states could constitutionally use juries which contained fewer than twelve persons and which followed a non-unanimous decision rule (e.g. simple majority).

The dissenting minority disagreed with the Court's decisions on several grounds. They rightly pointed out that smaller juries would be less representative of the local community. For example, suppose the local community contains an ethnic or racial minority group comprising 5 per cent of the total population. Although

46 per cent of all randomly composed twelve-person juries would contain at least one member of this minority, only 26 per cent of all six-person juries would do so. When representation of a minority group viewpoint bears on the jury's task (e.g. the defendant belongs to the minority group), such differences could be important. The Court's dissenting minority also argued that convicting someone under a non-unanimous rule meant that one or more jurors could remain unconvinced of the defendant's guilt; has a prosecutor really proved this defendant's guilt beyond any reasonable doubt when there are jurors who harbor doubts that they feel are reasonable? Furthermore, under a non-unanimous decision rule, once the decision rule has been satisfied, there is no necessity that juries continue to deliberate. It would even be possible, in principle, that a jury would have enough votes for conviction on its very first poll and would quit deliberation without listening to any of the opinions of the pro-acquittal minority.

The Court's majority dismissed these concerns. For example, they thought the majority would never simply outvote an unconvinced minority, but would continue to deliberate as long as necessary to give everyone his/her say and to reach unanimity if at all possible. (It is interesting to note that jurors are often minimally or wholly uncompensated for their time. The Court's theory suggests that jurors who might normally be earning $100 a day would voluntarily choose to listen, perhaps for days on end, to the views of someone whose judgment they question, while compensated for their time at the rate of, say, $10 per day.) An explicit assumption of the Court majority was that a jury's size and decision rule would not materially affect either the process or product of group decision making.

The initial studies (e.g. Bermant and Coppock 1973; Mills 1973; Davis *et al.* 1975; Nemeth 1977; Saks 1977) seemed to bear this opinion out – conviction rates did not seem to be affected by changes in jury size or decision rule. In addition, Davis *et al.* (1975) found that a single social decision scheme (viz. the two-thirds majority/hung otherwise D matrix) accurately predicted the verdicts of both six- and twelve-person juries, and juries operating under both a unanimity and a two-thirds-majority decision rule. Thus, there also appears to be little effect of size or decision rule on the process of decision making. However, it would have been premature to conclude that the Court's majority was correct. It is always possible that jury size or assigned rule might have an effect under conditions unexamined in those initial studies. One of the virtues of the SDS model is that once you have validated a social decision scheme under particular experimental conditions, you can also predict what decisions groups should make under new and unstudied conditions (e.g. for different group sizes, for cases producing different juror conviction rates). The SDS model allows one to do simulations or 'thought experiments' (Davis and Kerr 1986), in which one can explore the likely impact of many variables by extrapolating from what's known to what's unknown. Such thought experiments (Bray 1974; Davis *et al.* 1975) suggested that both jury size and assigned decision rule should exert effects on jury verdicts under certain conditions. Specifically, they suggested that the impact of these variables should be strongest for 'close' cases (i.e. ones for which the evidence for and against conviction was nearly equally balanced, producing a conviction rate near 50 per cent) and should be manifest primarily in the rate of hung juries.

As far as the effects of varying the assigned decision rule is concerned, this prediction is intuitively plausible for assigned decision rule. We would expect (and much research has confirmed, see Stasser *et al.* 1982), that juries are most likely to hang when they begin deliberation with large factions favoring both sides. Such initial splits are clearly more likely to occur for close cases than for lopsided ones (i.e. ones with conviction rates near 0 or 100 per cent). Furthermore, under a unanimity rule, to avoid a hung jury it is necessary that every single member of one of the opposing factions be converted to the other side. Under a rule of non-unanimity, it is not only more likely that the jury will begin deliberation satisfying the rule, but if this does not occur, fewer conversions will be required.

The reason for the corresponding predictions involving jury size is only slightly less apparent. You know that pollsters always want to get as large a sample as possible to estimate the overall opinion of a population. The smaller the sample, the more possible it is for the sample results to differ greatly from the population value. The same logic applies to the size of juries. In a maximally close case, half the individual jurors would convict and half would acquit (i.e. p (guilty) = 0.50). The conviction rate among jurors in a very small jury (as in a small polling sample) would be expected to depart more from this population value than in a larger jury. The smaller the jury, the less likely that the jury will also be evenly split and, therefore, the less likely the jury is to hang. It is interesting to note that these effects require no assumption of differences in the way in which different sized groups seek consensus; rather, they are direct consequences of sampling processes.

Armed with the results of such thought experiments, subsequent studies confirmed these predictions. Switching from a unanimous to a non-unanimous decision rule (Bray 1974; Kerr *et al.* 1976) or from twelve- to six-person juries (Kerr and MacCoun 1985) does not materially affect the ratio of convictions to acquittals, but such variations do decrease the rate of hung juries, especially for close cases. This is important because defendants consider a hung jury a relatively positive outcome. Because retrials are expensive, prosecutors will often drop charges or will plea bargain more flexibly following a hung jury.

The reaction of the Supreme Court to the research evidence on the effects of jury size and assigned rule has been disappointing. In one ruling (Ballew *v.* Georgia, 1978), after reviewing much theoretical and empirical evidence that indicated that jury size affects many aspects of jury functioning, the Court allowed its previous endorsement of six-person juries to stand, contenting itself with prohibiting jury size to drop lower than six persons in criminal trials. The Court has held (Burch *v.* Louisiana, 1979) that unanimity is necessary in juries as small as six, but at this time (1992) has not reconsidered this issue for larger juries. In this, as in many other areas (Saks and Baron 1980; Kerr 1986; Thompson 1989), the Court has ignored or misinterpreted relevant scientific evidence.

Juries' leniency bias

As we have seen, initial majorities usually prevail in juries. This pattern suggests that, as far as determining the final verdict is concerned, there is 'strength in numbers': numerically larger factions (e.g. majorities, pluralities) are more likely to prevail than their relative size would indicate (Stasser *et al.* 1989a). Several social influence processes are consistent with this conclusion. Larger factions should be able:

(1) to generate more arguments for their position (Hawkins 1962);
(2) to exert greater power to entice or coerce conformity to their expectations (Asch 1956; Latané 1981);

(3) to provide a more viable standard for defining social reality (Festinger 1954) than smaller factions.

Departures or exceptions to a rule (e.g. such as the 'strength in numbers' pattern) may be as informative about the nature of group decision making as the rule itself. For example, if a faction's power to win converts is related to its size, as a simple strength-in-numbers rule might suggest we might expect factions of equal size to have equal drawing power in groups. However, research on criminal jury behavior has revealed an exception to such a rule. It is nicely illustrated in the D obtained by Kerr and MacCoun (1985) and displayed in panel (d) of Table 6.1. As you can see, equal-sized factions did not have equal chances of prevailing. Juries that begin deliberation with equal splits (i.e. guilty 3, 3 not guilty) were not equally likely to convict and acquit; rather, they were much more likely to acquit than to convict. Similarly, a two-person minority advocating acquittal was much more likely to prevail (26 per cent of the time) than a two-person minority advocating conviction (which, in this study, never prevailed). This *leniency bias* has been observed in many studies (Stasser *et al.* 1982; MacCoun and Kerr 1988). It suggests that for close cases, juries would be less likely to convict than individual triers of fact (e.g. individual jurors or comparable judges). Interestingly, Kalven and Zeisel (1966) found that most disagreements about verdict between the trial judge and jury represent cases where the jury would acquit, but the judge would convict.

One possible explanation for this effect could be that the college students who comprise nearly all of the simulated juries examined in this research area are just more politically liberal and lenient; however, MacCoun and Kerr (1988) also observed a comparable leniency bias in both non-student and student mock juries. The leniency bias effect seems to be attributable to the standards of proof used in criminal trials. Jurors can make two kinds of errors – falsely convicting an innocent defendant or falsely acquitting a guilty one. Common law has long emphasized avoiding the former of these errors, even if it would increase the chances of committing the latter type of error. This is achieved through several means – instructing jurors to presume the defendant's innocence; placing the burden of altering this presumption on the prosecution; and by requiring proof of guilt beyond a reasonable doubt. This general prescription to give defendants the benefit of any doubts could make pro-acquittal advocates more persuasive. Similarly, Nemeth (1977) suggests that pro-acquittal jurors have the easier task. They need only plant one reasonable doubt in opponents' minds. However, pro-conviction faction members must eliminate all reasonable doubts from their opponents' minds.

MacCoun and Kerr (1988) tested this explanation by varying the standard of proof under which juries deliberated. All of their four-person mock juries began deliberation with equal splits (2 guilty, 2 not guilty). Half were instructed by the judge to apply the usual, reasonable doubt standard of proof. The rest of the juries were told to apply the 'preponderance of evidence' standard, which requires them to favor whichever side produces the stronger evidence. The latter standard is symmetrical, and should not give any advantage to either side. In the reasonable doubt condition, they found the usual effect – 74 per cent of all juries which reached a verdict acquitted the defendant. However, there was no leniency bias in the preponderance of evidence condition; their verdicts were split roughly equally between conviction and acquittal. The leniency bias appears to have its roots in demands of the group decision task.

SDS analysis of group performance

The SDS model was initially developed by Davis (1973) to analyze group decision making. However, it may also be applied to group problem solving. Instead of focusing on all the ways member preferences may be split or distributed, we may focus on all the possible ways members' task relevant resources (e.g. knowledge, abilities) are distributed in the group. For example, at a simple task like an anagram task, we might simply classify each group member as a solver or a non-solver. Thus, in a six-person group, there again would be seven possible splits, as listed in the left side of Table 6.2. The social decision scheme matrix D again summarizes what happens between the beginning and end of group interaction; here, the output is the distribution of groups that manage to solve and not solve the problem. Again, there are many possible social combination rules. In Chapter 3 on individual v. group performance, the Lorge–Solomon model was described; it predicts that a group will solve the problem if it contains at least one solver. This idea is translated into the 'truth wins' D matrix in Table 6.2.

Table 6.2 Social decision schemes and group problem-solving

		Group performance			
		(a) Truth wins		(b) Truth supported wins	
Initial splits					
S	NS	S	NS	S	NS
6	0	1.0	0.0	1.0	0.0
5	1	1.0	0.0	1.0	0.0
4	2	1.0	0.0	1.0	0.0
3	3	1.0	0.0	1.0	0.0
2	4	1.0	0.0	1.0	0.0
1	5	1.0	0.0	0.0	1.0
0	6	0.0	1.0	0.0	1.0

Note: S = solve; NS = not solve.

Again, the key issue is which of the many possible social decision schemes provides the most informative and predictively accurate description of how groups combine their members' inputs. In an extensive series of studies (see Laughlin 1980; Laughlin and Ellis 1986), Laughlin and his colleagues have compared the predictive ability of a number of possible D matrices for groups' performance at a number of different group problem-solving tasks. The best fitting D varied across tasks. More importantly, Laughlin noticed a pattern – the minimum size of a 'winning' faction seemed to depend on how *demonstrable* a correct answer was (Laughlin and Ellis 1986). There are many tasks that have an 'objective' criterion for evaluating group performance. Simple arithmetic problems are good examples of what Laughlin terms *intellective* problems. In principle, group performance on an intellective task should be predicted by the 'truth-wins' rule – having a single solver should guarantee the group's success. Of course, before truth can win, solvers need to be motivated to share their knowledge, and non-solvers must have the ability and motivation to recognize when a proposed answer is correct. When all these conditions are met, the correct response is fully demonstrable.

These conditions seem most likely to be met for simple mathematics or verbal intellective tasks. For example, Laughlin *et al.* (1976) had groups work on the Remote Associates Test (Mednick and Mednick 1967). A test item consists of three words; you have to think of another word which is associated with all three. For example, you might be given the words *cookie*, *heart*, and *sixteen*. The correct answer is *sweet*. With practically no effort our shared linquistic and sensory experience tell us that this is 'correct'; cookies are sweet, 'sweetheart' is a common term of endearment, and a sixteenth birthday is commonly called 'sweet sixteen'. Thus, we might expect the group to get the correct answer if even one group member knows it. This is exactly what Laughlin *et al.* (1976) found. Similarly, Laughlin and Ellis (1986) found that truth won in groups considering simple arithmetic problems. Moscovici's (e.g. 1985) work suggests that the power of a minority depends on its style of advocacy (viz. consistent, non-rigid) and its possessing at least some social support in the group. Here we see another route to minority influence – when the minority is advocating what can be persuasively shown to be the 'truth', even a minority of one can have considerable influence.

At the other extreme, there are tasks where there is no objective basis to evaluate group solutions/decisions. Trying to decide many ethical, political, esthetic or attitudinal issues represent what Laughlin terms *judgmental* tasks. At such tasks, since there is no objective (i.e. universally shared) basis for evaluation, potential group choices must, of necessity, be evaluated through social consensus. Consequently, the most accurate social decision schemes for such tasks should be ones for which there is considerable 'strength in numbers,' such as 'majority rule' decision schemes. Indeed, group decisions on judgmental tasks low on demonstrability (e.g. a group rating Billy Graham on a seven-point good–bad scale) seem to be best described by social decision schemes for which there is considerable strength in numbers (e.g. initial majority wins – averaging otherwise; Kerr *et al.* 1976).

Between these two extremes are tasks of intermediate demonstrability. Such tasks as verbal analogies (A is to B as C is to _____) and English vocabulary tasks seem to be 'quasi-intellective', and relatively high on demonstrability. There is high, although not complete agreement on the relevant conceptual system (i.e. the meaning of English words). Answers may be correct according to the dictionary, but they are often not obviously correct, especially to non-solvers. For such tasks, Laughlin (e.g. Laughlin *et al.* 1975, 1976) has shown that it is not enough to just be right, one needs some support in the group to guarantee group adoption of a correct answer. The 'truth-supported wins' decision scheme is pictured in panel (b) of Table 6.2.

How would we categorize the decision-making task of a jury? Jury decision making seems to be 'quasi-judgmental'. There is generally much disagreement about what the facts in a trial are and what those facts really mean. It is extremely rare that a particular verdict is demonstrably correct. Thus, we might expect juries to accept the position of strong majorities and, as we have seen, they usually do. However, there is fairly general agreement on one point – criminal defendants should be given the benefit of the doubt. In essence, when there is no clear majority to define the 'correct' verdict socially, an 'acquittal well supported wins' decision scheme seems to describe jury decision making accurately. In a sense, if we agree to give the defendant the benefit of the doubt and enough jurors express such doubts, acquittal is the 'correct' verdict.

Laughlin's research makes a point in the realm of group decision making that we have stressed repeatedly – group behavior depends strongly on the group's task. In the present case, we see that the demonstrability of a task determines which social decision scheme and, hence, which type of social influence processes occur in group decision making and problem solving.

Social communication and social combination: towards integration

Science is always caught between the desire for (and intuitive belief in) simple explanations and the apparent complexity of the natural world to be explained. So it is with group decision making. It would be nice if either the social communication or the social combination approach alone provided a complete understanding of how groups reach decisions. Each approach has independently contributed to our understanding. However, other research, much of it quite recent, is suggesting that the two approaches must be combined to achieve a full understanding of group decision making. It is not only true that member preferences and member comments both affect group outcomes, but they also affect one another.

A simple illustration is Hawkins' (1962) finding that there is a simple linear relationship between the size of a faction and that faction's share of jury deliberation. You can easily imagine two interesting extremes for such a relationship. At one extreme, opposing factions would simply trade arguments, so that the pro-conviction faction and the pro-acquittal faction would each have roughly half of the speaking time, regardless of the size of those factions. At the other extreme, each juror would take an equal share of deliberation. This would make a faction's share of deliberation equal to its relative size (e.g., a nine-person faction would take up roughly 75 per cent of a twelve-person jury's deliberation time). However, Hawkins found that the actual relationship fell in between these two extremes – larger factions took a larger share of deliberation, but less than their proportional share. This suggests an exchange of arguments between factions, but one in which larger factions give a bit more than they get.

The size of a faction (or of a group) also seems to affect which particular arguments are expressed, as we have already seen in Chapter 5. Stasser and his colleagues (Stasser and Titus 1985, 1987; Stasser et al. 1989b) have shown that information that is shared by several group members is much more likely to be voiced during group deliberation than information which is unshared. Furthermore, the larger the group (or faction), the stronger this tendency is.

Faction size not only seems to affect the amount and content of speech, it also seems to affect the way we speak. Kerr et al. (1987) led mock jurors to believe that their own verdict preference was favored by either a majority or a minority of the jury. They were then asked to serve as spokespersons for their faction. Jurors (especially male jurors) who thought they were in the minority sounded more nervous, were less likely to raise novel arguments and were less likely to identify personally with those arguments than jurors who thought they belonged to the majority. Part of the power of majorities may derive from their members' speech style.

There are also indications that the relative importance of what people say v. what they prefer can vary. When groups are considering an intellective task (like a jury deciding on how much money is required to pay for someone's medical expenses) group discussion tends to consist of the exchange of factual information (e.g. 'how much does a hospital room cost per day?'), but when the task is more judgmental (e.g. a jury deciding on punitive damages), group discussion focuses much more on non-factual, value judgments (e.g. 'how can you say that when we all disagree . . . ?') (Kaplan and Miller 1987). Also, group decision-making procedures which force members to take sides early and publicly (e.g. asking for a show of hands before beginning discussion) seem to alter the style of group deliberation from an exchange and weighing of information (*evidence-driven* deliberation) to a battle of antagonistic factions (*verdict-driven* deliberations; Hastie *et al.* 1983). One consequence of this change is that it is harder to get group members to compromise and agree on anything when they publicly identify with and become committed to a particular faction (Kerr and MacCoun 1985).

Finally, the impact of arguments depends upon whether they come from a majority than from a minority. Although some research (Maass and Clark 1984) suggests that minorities can sometimes have greater impact on private beliefs than majorities (see Chapter 5), other research indicates that both private (Mackie 1987) and public (Kerr *et al.* 1987) opinions move more toward the majority position than the minority position, even when the content of group discussion is held constant. Mackie (1987) has further shown that arguments attributed to a majority faction are better recalled and are more likely to stimulate consistent positive thoughts than the same arguments attributed to the minority in the group. Apparently, faction size not only affects what is said and how it is said, but how it is heard and interpreted. Such research clearly demonstrates that member preferences and member comments are complexly interrelated, and that both determine the path groups take to reach consensus.

Summary

Group decision making can be viewed as a process whereby groups move from initial disagreement to a sufficient level of agreement to satisfy some decision rule. This process can be analyzed in several ways. The traditional approach has been to analyze the content of communication in the group. An alternative approach is to relate individual member preferences to group preference through some type of social combination function. One example of such a function is a social decision scheme, D, which specifies for every possible initial distribution of individual preference the probability that the group will choose each possible decision alternative. The decision making of juries in criminal trials, for example, seems to be summarized by a D in which strong initial majorities nearly always ultimately prevail. When there is no strong initial majority in the jury, the jury is more likely to be hung. Furthermore, pro-acquittal factions are relatively more likely to prevail than comparable pro-conviction factions. Thought experiments and actual experiments have confirmed consequences of this social combination process – reducing the size of juries or not requiring unanimous agreement in juries reduces the likelihood of a hung jury, which constitutes a net disadvantage to defendants. Juries' leniency bias illustrates another principle – majorities to do not always prevail. For decision tasks with a demonstrably correct alternative, even a single correct member may be sufficient to insure that the group adopts that correct alternative.

It has become increasingly apparent that neither the social combination approach nor the social communication approach alone can fully describe how groups reach decisions. Not only does what members say to one another change group member preference, the levels of support for various positions in the group appear to affect what is said, how it is said, how it is heard and what effect it has on others. An integration of alternative approaches to group decision making holds the greatest promise for understanding this complex and important process.

Suggestions for further reading

Hans, V. and Vidmar, N. (1986). *Judging the Jury*. New York: Plenum Press. A wide-ranging and readable overview of the scientific study of the jury.

Stasser, G., Kerr, N.L. and Davis, J. H. (1989). Influence processes and consensus models in decision-making groups. In P. P. Paulus (ed.) *Psychology of Group Influence*, Chapter 9, 2nd edn. Hillsdale, NJ: Erlbaum. Provides a current overview of social decision scheme theory and research.

7 / SOCIAL DILEMMAS

A basic feature of group life is that group member's outcomes often depend not only upon his/her own actions, but also to some degree on the actions of others in the group. At times this *inter-dependence* among group members strongly encourages mutually beneficial behavior. For example, in order for an Olympic rowing team to have any chance of winning a highly-prized Olympic gold medal, every member must do his/her best. Such *pure cooperation* situations provide a set of behavioral choices (e.g. every team member rowing as hard as possible) which can simultaneously maximize every group member's outcomes (e.g. all win medals); personal and group interests coincide. At the opposite extreme, termed *pure competition* or *zero-sum* situations, any gain by one person necessarily entails an equivalent loss by another person. An example would be the interaction between a buyer and seller; any change in the purchase price necessarily means a gain by one party and an equivalent loss by the other party. Here, one's own and others' interests are opposed.

Between these two extremes lie a variety of interesting *mixed-motive* situations, so called because one must choose between behaviors which serve different motives – personal interest *v.* the interests of others or of the group as a whole. For example, when a buyer and seller must reach agreement on several points (e.g. price, warrantee, interest rate on loan) which they value differently, there exists the possibility of finding some agreement with which each is content, although neither obtains his/her most preferred outcome. Research on bargaining and negotiation examines how such agreements are sought and obtained (e.g. Pruitt 1981). Another example is the wrangling that goes on at political party conventions. Sometimes, in order to win a nomination or to determine the party's position on some issue, two or more candidates may join forces and end up sharing a valued prize (e.g. patronage jobs, political power) which each, of course, would rather have all to him/herself. Considerable research has also been devoted to studying such coalition formation processes (Stryker 1972; Kahan and Rapoport 1984).

Although groups face many interesting mixed-motive situations, in this chapter we will focus our attention on one particularly important type, the *social dilemma*. The ecologist Garrett Hardin (1968) provides a vivid and well-known illustration of a social dilemma. Suppose a community permitted any citizen to graze his herd on a commonly-held pasture (the 'commons' that students of US history will associate with battles of the American Revolutionary War). Each individual herdsman is motivated to add additional animals to his herd, since his profit grows as his herd increases. But the commons is finite; it cannot accommodate additional animals without limit. If the number of animals becomes too large, the commons will be overgrazed, there will be no grass for any animals, and all the herdsmen will be ruined. Therein lies the dilemma – the pursuit of personal self-interest by individual herdsmen produces collective disaster.

In any social dilemma, one has to make a behavioral choice. One has to choose between behavior which benefits the group and behavior which benefits oneself. In the simplest case, where there are only two possible behavioral choices, the first alternative is typically designated C (for the cooperative choice), while the latter is designated D (for the defecting choice) (Orbell and Dawes 1981). In social dilemmas, the defecting choice (e.g. adding more animals to the herd) will always (or usually [Liebrand 1983]) result in better personal outcomes, at least in the immediate future; that is, one will be personally better off by defecting than by cooperating. So, for example, no matter what other herdsmen do, increasing my own herd (D) increases my own profit. *But*, in a social dilemma, universal defection (everyone chooses D) results in a poorer outcome for everyone than universal cooperation (everyone choosing C): unrestrained pursuit of personal self-interest leads to collective disaster.

What makes social dilemmas so important? One reason is that they bear on some very fundamental questions about social life: Will humans always pursue their personal interest? If so, is this necessarily a bad thing for the group? Under what conditions will humans sacrifice personal interest for the common good? For example, advocates of *laissez-faire* economic theories often cite Adam Smith's (1976) argument that unrestrained pursuit of self-interest ultimately serves the welfare of the whole group (Orbell and Dawes 1981). The existence of social dilemmas challenges this viewpoint. Social dilemmas suggest (as have other political philosophers, e.g. Hobbes 1974) that unless some limits are put on the pursuit of personal goals, the entire society may suffer.

A second good reason for studying social dilemmas is that they are extremely common and have very important consequences. In Table 7.1 several examples are provided. As you can see, many important environmental, political, and social problems are social dilemmas. But social dilemmas do not only occur in very large groups or societies – small groups also routinely face social dilemmas. For example, in a previous chapter we considered the problem of keeping clean an apartment shared by a group. As long as there is some chance of somebody else cleaning the apartment, one saves time and effort by not doing any of the cleaning. But if everyone living in the apartment follows this reasoning, the apartment will never be cleaned.

The most popular experimental simulation of a social dilemma is the *Two-person Prisoner's Dilemma* (PD) game. It gets its name from the scenario defining the earliest version of the game (Luce and Raiffa 1957). Two prisoners, let's call them Jake and Elwood, are suspected of being accomplices in a crime. The police question them separately and urge them to confess. The deal offered to the prisoners is summarized in the top matrix of Figure 7.1. Each prisoner must choose whether to 'confess' (the defecting choice) or 'not confess' (the cooperative choice, in terms of the two-person group, not with respect to the police or to society) to the crime. The police deal makes the prisoners interdependent; Jake's fate depends not only on his own decision, but also upon Elwood's. If Elwood refuses to confess, but Jake does confess, providing the evidence necessary to convict Elwood, Elwood will receive the maximum 10-year sentence, while Jake will go free for 'turning state's evidence'. Elwood has the same opportunity. If neither confesses, the police will only be able to get convictions on a lesser charge resulting in a 1-year sentence for each. Finally, if both confess, both will be convicted and receive intermediate 5-year terms.

Figure 7.1   Two-person prisoner's dilemma games

Original prisoner's dilemma game

		Elwood's choice	
		Confess	Not confess
Jake's choice	Confess	5 years \ 5 years	0 years \ 10 years
	Not confess	0 years \ 10 years	1 year \ 1 year

Alternative prisoner's dilemma game

		Player B's choice	
		Choice D	Choice C
Player A's choice	Choice D	$1 \ $1	$0 \ $8
	Choice C	$8 \ $0	$3 \ $3

Generic prisoner's dilemma game where T > R > P > S

		Player B's choice	
		Choice D	Choice C
Player A's choice	Choice D	P \ P	S \ T
	Choice C	T \ S	R \ R

Note: Each cell of the matrix defines the outcomes of the two players choosing the alternatives indicated for that cell's row and column headings. The pay-off below the diagonal is received by the row player; the pay-off above the diagonal is received by the column player. (For the purposes of applying the inequalities of the bottom matrix to the original prisoner's dilemma game, remember that years in prison are disutilities; the larger the number, the worse the outcome. So after attaching negative signs to the entries of the top matrix, it too satisfies the inequalities.)

What would you do if you were in Jake's shoes? If Elwood confesses, you would be personally better off confessing (5-year sentence) than not (10-year sentence). Again, if Elwood does not confess, you would be personally better off confessing (0 years) than not (1 year). So no matter what he does, you would be better off confessing (which is why the police offered the deal). However, if Elwood in the other room comes to the same conclusion and decides that it is in his personal best interest to confess, we both end up worse off (5-year sentence) than if we both made the other, personally costly choice of not confessing. You are caught in a social dilemma. As Figure 7.1 suggests, you do not have to use the prisoner scenario to play the prisoner's dilemma game. All that is important is that the basic requirements for a social dilemma be met, i.e. the players' pay-offs satisfy the inequalities presented in the bottom matrix (Rapoport 1973).

Experimental research has produced several consistent findings which give us some insight into how people behave in social dilemmas. Below we sample a few of those findings (for more detailed reviews, see Pruitt and Kimmel 1977; Orbell and Dawes 1981; Stroebe and Frey 1982; Messick and Brewer 1983).

Cooperation in social dilemmas: motives and determinants

In almost every setting, behavior is multiply determined. That is, there are often many different motives underlying a particular behavioral choice. This is certainly true in social dilemmas (Messick 1984). The most obvious motive is *self-interest*; all other things being equal, you are likely to choose that alternative which yields the most positive tangible outcomes to you. However, that cannot be the only motive at work. If it was, people would rarely if ever cooperate in social dilemmas, because by definition, the defecting choice produces better objective outcomes in such situations, at least in the short term. Yet we know that people often do cooperate in social dilemmas like those listed in Table 7.1. Soldiers do fight, listeners do support their public radio stations, and (at least some) people do limit their consumption of scarce resources. Clearly, other motives also come into play.

Messick (1984) has suggested several such motives. One is the motive to solve the collective group problem – win the battle,

Table 7.1 Examples of social dilemmas

	Cooperative (C) choice	Defecting (D) choice	*Nature of the dilemma*
Commons dilemma	Conserve the resource	Consume the resource	It is rewarding to consume the resource (e.g. to keep your house heated to 70°F/21°C), but if everyone does, it may be exhausted
Population control	Have fewer children	Have more children	Large families may be personally better (e.g. by providing labor or old-age security), but over-population could lead to general misery
Public radio	Contribute	Do not contribute	Each listener saves money by not contributing, but if no one contributes, all are denied the benefit of the station
Free trade	Allow full access to your markets	Restrict access to your markets	One's own national industries will profit if other nations are denied access to local markets, but all nations suffer in a general trade war
Budget deficit	Give up personal entitlement, tax break, etc.	Cling to any entitlement, tax break, etc.	Each individual or special interest is personally better off if they retain their entitlement, but large and damaging budget deficits may result from too many such entitlements
Cartels (e.g. OPEC)	Restrain production	Produce as much as possible	The larger each producer's output, the larger his personal profit, but when everyone produces as much as possible, the price is driven down to all producers' detriment

Table 7.1   (Cont.)

	Cooperative (C) choice	Defecting (D) choice	Nature of the dilemma
Soldier's dilemma	Face the dangers of battle	Avoid the dangers of battle	Each soldier is personally better off by avoiding the battle, but if no soldier chooses to fight, the battle will certainly be lost and all may perish
Unionization	Join the union	Do not join the union	Each employee saves dues by not joining the union, but without member financial support the union (and its benefits) are lost

preserve the radio station, save the commons. When one focuses one's attention on and places a high *subjective value* or *utility* on outcomes which benefit the entire group, cooperative behavior becomes more likely. Another is the motive to comply with salient social norms; we may often cooperate because we are expected to. For example, Jake may refuse to confess and send Elwood off to prison because this would violate the strong street norm against informing ('ratting' or 'grassing') on a pal.

Many factors can be expected to influence such motives. These include features of the dilemma itself, the person making a C/D choice, the other person(s) in the dilemma, and the nature of the interactions and relationships among the group members. Let us consider each of these in greater detail.

Dilemma features

The most obvious factors affecting cooperation are the specific pay-offs offered in the dilemma. We would expect Jake to be more tempted to confess if, in addition to going free, he were to receive a $10 000 reward if his testimony resulted in Elwood's conviction. (Generally, in the generic PD game pictured in Figure 7.1, we would expect cooperation to increase as R or S increases and to decrease as T or P increases; Rapaport 1973.) Such predictions have been experimentally confirmed (e.g. Rapoport and Chammah 1965; Komorita *et al.* 1980).

It is not only important what the actual pay-offs for C and D choices are; it also matters how such choices are presented or framed (Kahneman and Tversky 1984). For example, half of Brewer and Kramer's (1986) subjects were allowed to *take* from 0 to 25 points (worth 2¢ apiece) from a shared replenishable resource pool. The rest of their subjects were first given 25 points and then had to choose how many to *give* to such a pool. Although the two versions of the task were functionally the same, with the same pay-off possibilities, subjects cooperated more (i.e. left more in the shared pool) under the 'take' frame than under the 'give' frame. Apparently, it was harder to give up resources one already had than to forgo equivalent resources never possessed (Kahneman and Tversky 1984; Thaler 1985).

Individual differences

If you have ever had to compose a group which would later confront social dilemmas together (e.g. you had to choose apartment mates), you probably discovered that there are real individual differences in willingness to cooperate (e.g. to help keep the apartment clean). Some people will rarely free ride, even though they could easily do so, and will even continue to cooperate (for a while, at least) in the face of other group members' free-riding behavior. Others are likely to defect at every opportunity.

What distinguishes a cooperating group member from a defecting one? One element seems to be the person's level of *trust*. Given the options, most people would recognize that mutual cooperation is preferable to mutual defection in a social dilemma, but it is rather risky to cooperate unless you can count on the rest of the group to cooperate as well. One needs to be confident 'that one will find what is desired from another, rather than what is feared' (Deutsch 1973), that is, one needs to trust one's partner. Of course, such trust could develop over the course of past interaction (e.g. Jake knows that Elwood never betrayed him all the other times they were arrested). However, some people seem to possess a 'depersonalized trust' (Brewer 1981), a belief that other people can generally be counted on to cooperate. Such 'high-trust' people have been found to be more likely to cooperate than 'low trust' individuals (Messick *et al.* 1983). Moreover, when placed in a commons dilemma where the resource pool is dwindling, low trust subjects increase the size of their harvests (getting theirs while the going is good), while high trust subjects decrease their harvests (persisting in the hope that others would see the need for mutual sacrifice to save the commons) (Messick *et al.* 1983; Brann and Foddy 1987).

There are also clear individual differences in the relative weight placed on one's own *v.* others' outcomes (Messick and McClintock 1968; McClintock 1972). Some people, termed *individualists* place no weight at all on others' outcomes; their behavior is governed completely by personal self-interest. Others, termed *cooperators*, weight both their own and others' outcomes, acting to optimize joint welfare. A precious few, termed *altruists*, put no weight on self-interest and complete weight on others' welfare. Finally, *competitors* strive to maximize the difference between their own and others' outcomes; their goal is to do better than others, even if that means getting somewhat less for themselves. With the possible exception of the altruist, you can probably think of particular individuals who hold each of these *social values*. It is not surprising that the greater value one tends to place on others' outcomes, the more likely one is to make cooperative choices in social dilemmas (Kuhlman and Marshello 1975; Liebrand and van Run 1985; Kramer *et al.* 1986).

However, such social motive differences seem to reflect more than the relative importance of own *v.* others' outcomes. A competitor seems to have different expectations of others and to place different interpretations on others' behavior than a cooperator. For example, *a propos* our earlier discussion of trust, competitors are less trusting than cooperators (Cunha 1985). Although nearly everyone sees defecting as worse than cooperative behavior, competitors draw this distinction less strongly than cooperators (Liebrand *et al.* 1986b). On the other hand, there is a tendency to see someone who sacrifices self-interest for collective welfare (i.e. chooses C) as weaker, more naive and less purposeful than someone who looks out for his/her own interest (i.e. chooses D). However, it is competitors who most strongly draw this distinction. Thus, cooperators seem more likely to evaluate others' behavior on moral grounds; competitors seem more likely to interpret a partner's behavior in terms of power (Liebrand *et al.*

1986b). Finally, both competitors and cooperators think that a smart person would choose as they would choose. That is, when asked to guess how another person would behave in a social dilemma, cooperators think that an intelligent person would cooperate more than an unintelligent one, while competitors expect that anyone with brains would defect (van Lange *et al.* 1990). Clearly, different social motives reflect profound differences in values, outlooks, and beliefs.

Others' choices

In many simulations of social dilemmas, subjects are asked not only to make a single C/D choice, but to make several such choices over repeated trials. One of the earliest questions examined was, how will the apparent behavior of the partner(s) affect the subject's behavior? We say 'apparent' because the experimenter could and usually did control the feedback subjects received; typically, this feedback did not correspond to the actual behavior of another player, but was preprogramed by the experimenter.

One pattern is clear in this research – if my partner always defects, I am almost certain to defect, too. In multiperson social dilemmas, people seem to imitate what their partners do (Schroeder *et al.* 1983; Messick *et al.* 1983); it is as if the partners' behavior establishes a norm for the group. However, in simple two-person situations, at least, things are not so simple. In these dilemmas, if the partner always chooses C, the majority of subjects will defect, exploiting the partner (Rubin and Brown 1975). Is there any way a partner can behave to encourage high rates of cooperation? One partner strategy does seem to work – the 'tit-for-tat' strategy (Axelrod 1984; Rapoport 1973). This is when my partner always mimics my last response; if I cooperate on one trial, s/he cooperates on the next trial.

We noted earlier that cooperative choices were influenced by several motives: self-interest, effective problem solving, conformity to norms. One norm which seems particularly relevant in the present context is the *norm of reciprocity* (Gouldner 1960). This powerful norm prescribes that for each benefit (or harm) received, an equivalent benefit (or harm) should eventually be returned. When my partner consistently defects, both self-interest and the reciprocity norm prescribe that I too defect. When my partner consistently cooperates, however, self-interest prescribes that I take advantage of him/her and defect, while the norm of reciprocity prescribes that I also cooperate. In the light of such competing forces, it is not surprising that a 100 per cent cooperative partner produces subject cooperation levels that are neither very high or very low. Nor should it surprise us that people especially concerned with their own welfare (e.g. those with individualistic or competitive social motives) lean toward exploiting such a situation, while those especially concerned with doing the moral, right thing (viz. those with a cooperative social motive; Liebrand *et al.* 1986b), are more likely to reciprocate a partner's uniform cooperation (Kuhlman and Marshello 1975).

Why then is the tit-for-tat strategy so effective. There are several possible reasons (e.g. see Axelrod 1984). One is self-interest. When my partner uses a tit-for-tat strategy, I cannot exploit him/her. If I choose D, so will she/he and we are both worse off than if we both choose C. Thus, the situation becomes one of either both choosing C or both choosing D, and in a social dilemma, mutual cooperation is always preferable. Another related reason is that the tit-for-tat strategy makes the reciprocity norm very salient. If my partner mimics my last response, I should soon come to realize that the best way to get my partner to cooperate with me is for me to cooperate with him/her.

Communication and commitment

Recall that Jake and Elwood were separated by the police and not allowed to talk with one another about their choices. Would it make any difference if they had been allowed to communicate? Many studies (e.g. Rapoport 1974; Dawes *et al.* 1977; van de Kragt *et al.* 1986) indicate that it would – that each would be more likely to make a cooperative choice (i.e. not confess) if they had been allowed to talk it over first. Although communication could encourage cooperation in several ways (e.g. by clarifying the nature of the dilemma; by enhancing feelings of group solidarity, Kramer and Brewer 1984), it now seems likely that another social norm underlies at least part of the effect of communication – the norm of commitment. This norm prescribes that you carry out those actions which you have promised or committed yourself to perform. There is some clear evidence that communication leads group members to make and keep promises to cooperate. For example, Braver and Wilson (1984) gave every member of a nine-person group $5 and then told them that if at least three members returned the money, each of the non-returning group members would get an additional $10. Groups were then allowed to discuss the problem. Every group ended up holding lottery to decide which three members should sacrifice their $5 for the others' sake. All decisions to keep or give up the money were made in private. Furthermore, each subject left the laboratory separately, so there was no possibility of interaction afterwards. Nevertheless, even though it meant surrendering $5 for no personal gain, 71 per cent of the group members selected in the lotteries observed their commitment and voluntarily returned their $5. Elsewhere (Orbell *et al.* 1988), it has been observed that high rates of promising to cooperate during group discussion are followed by high rates of actual cooperation, even when fellow group members have no way of checking whether such promises are kept.

Structural solutions to social dilemmas

The research reviewed above gives us some insight into the psychology of individual choice behavior in social dilemmas, but by and large, such research does not suggest direct ways to remedy uncooperativeness in such settings. For example, one could rarely restrict membership in real groups facing real social dilemmas to people with high depersonalized trust or with cooperative social motives. Nor could one plausibly lead real group members to believe that other group members will always operate under a tit-for-tat rule. Another approach to solving social dilemmas is to apply *structural solutions* (Messick and Brewer 1983). Such solutions 'eliminate or alter the pattern of incentives that characterize social dilemmas' (p. 29). The basic idea is to change the pattern of pay-offs so that defection is less attractive. Several such structural solutions are listed below.

Privatizing

One structural solution which can sometimes be used in shared resource pools is *privatizing*. One converts the commonly held resource to a privately held one. For example, the community might divide up the grazing commons into privately held, fenced plots. Now if the size of a citizen's herd exceeded the carrying capacity of his plot, only he would be affected adversely. Under these conditions, each herdsman would be motivated to use the resource responsibly. Research has confirmed the effectiveness of privatizing (Cass and Edney 1978: Messick and McClelland 1983). Unfortunately, there are many social dilemmas, including commons dilemmas, where this solution cannot be used. For example, certain commonly held resources cannot easily be divided and reserved for individual use (e.g. the air we breathe; shared fishing grounds).

Supplementary pay-offs/costs

We all routinely enjoy many public goods, commodities which, once provided, are available to all, regardless of whether they actually helped to provide them. Examples are police protection, public highways, public parks and national forests. Why do citizens pay the money needed to supply these public goods if they could enjoy them whether they pay (choice C) or not (choice D)? The answer is as inescapable as death. Unlike the experimental situations we have been considering, the taxes used to provide such public goods are not paid on a voluntary basis; there are very substantial penalties for failing to cooperate. An alternative to adding such costs for defection is adding extra incentives for cooperation. For example, during fund raising drives for public television in the US, viewers are offered not only continued use of the station (a public good), but also various 'premiums' (i.e. prizes) for contributing to its support.

Group size

A number of studies suggest that cooperation is more likely in smaller groups. This would suggest, for example, that smaller communities would be better able to provide needed public goods and preserve commonly held resources than larger communities. Why should this be so? Perhaps because reducing group size affects each of the basic processes we discussed earlier – maximizing self-interest, conforming to norms, trying to solve the group's problem effectively.

First, people may more easily identify with a small group than with a large, faceless collective. Kramer and Brewer (1986) have suggested and shown that a strong sense of belonging or *social identity* leads to cooperative behavior. They suggest that the more you feel part of the group, the less strongly you distinguish between your personal welfare and the group's welfare. If I value the group as I value myself, cooperation becomes an indirect form of self-interested behavior.

We have pointed out that groups can rely on formal rules (e.g. tax laws), informal local norms (e.g. a community standard for the proper herd size) or general norms (e.g. reciprocity) to encourage cooperative behavior. However, enforcement of any social norm requires two things:

(1) the ability to monitor behavior so that norm violations will be detected;
(2) that the social sanctions the group uses to punish norm violation be salient.

Reducing group size may enhance each of these. As we learned in our discussion of social loafing, it is often easier to monitor the behavior of members of small than of large groups; and if we generally feel a stronger attachment to smaller groups, their sanctions (e.g. rejection from the group) should also be more salient (Fox 1985).

Finally, when it comes to avoiding the tragedy of mutual defection, people may feel that their behavior has little impact in large groups (Olson 1965; Messick 1973). For example, whether or not I decide to become a supporting member of my local public radio station seems to matter far less if I live in a community with 1 000 000 listeners than a community of 1000 listeners. This belief seems to hold even if there is, in fact, no objective difference in how important our behavior is for smaller and larger groups (Kerr 1989). Even when our behavior really does have some effect on the group's fate, it tends to be much harder for us to discern that unique effect when the group is very large (Allison and Messick 1985).

Summary

We learned earlier that for most tasks, groups are potentially more productive than individuals, but we also learned that group settings can sometimes undermine individual effort (e.g. through social loafing or free riding). In this chapter we have seen another potential risk of group life – in social dilemmas, personally rewarding behavior can hurt the group (and can, therefore, hurt me as a member of the group). As this chapter has shown, much has been learned about behavior in social dilemmas. Of course, much more remains to be learned, but there may be an even larger challenge than extending the scientific study of social dilemmas. It is applying our knowledge to the solution of actual social dilemmas. Besides the usual problems of disseminating and applying social science research, this topic poses a special problem. When a group realizes that it faces a social dilemma and wants to do something about it, it suddenly faces a new social dilemma (Yamagishi 1986). Its choices are to contribute time, energy, knowledge, etc., to the solution of the original dilemma (C) or to do nothing (D). Everyone would prefer to let others solve the problem, but if everyone defects, the problem remains unsolved. Clearly, finding solutions to social dilemmas will be a very difficult and challenging task, but the grave consequences of ignoring these problems also suggest that is a vitally important task.

Suggestions for further reading

Hardin, G. (1968). The tragedy of the commons. *Science*, 162, 1243–8. A classic illustration of a social dilemma.

Orbell, M. and Dawes, R. M. (1981). Social dilemmas. In G. Stephenson and J. H. Davis (eds) *Progress in Applied Social Psychology*, Vol. 1. Chichester: Wiley. An excellent introduction to theory and research on social dilemmas.

8 / GROUP AGGRESSION AND INTERGROUP CONFLICT

On June 15, 1990, the Detroit Pistons won a second consecutive National Basketball Association title, beating Portland on the Trailblazer's court 92 to 90 in the final seconds. Throngs of Piston fans crowded into downtown Detroit in jubilant excitement, dancing on car roofs, waving fists and shirts, tossing and dribbling basketballs. The end of the celebration saw seven dead, twenty gunshot wounds officially recorded, hundreds hurt by gunfire, stabbings and fighting, and city streets littered with shards of glass from looting.

On August 23, 1989, Yusuf Hawkins, a 16-year-old black, ventured into the tightly knit Italian section of Bensonhurst, New York City, with a group of his friends to inspect a used car. A gang of whites, armed with baseball bats and other weapons, attacked them and when the melee was over Hawkins lay beaten and dead with two bullet wounds in his chest. Leader of the whites, Keith Mondello, and his friends had armed themselves that night because his former girlfriend had invited blacks and Hispanics to her birthday party. They mistook the Hawkins group for them. After several of the whites were arrested, a series of protest marches were led by black leader Reverend Al Sharpton, adding to the ensuing tension. Verdicts of *not guilty* 'would be telling us to burn the town down', he repeatedly explained. The first two Bensonhurst youths charged with the killing went on separate trials on April 16, 1990. A jury acquitted Mondello, 19, of murder and manslaughter. 'He did it, he did it', the Hawkins family shrieked in dismay while pointing to him in front of the jurors. Will New York City face race riots in the 1990s? Simple explanations will not account for these and similar instances of aggression. To understand them we must consider (a) specific features of group and intergroup settings that provoke hostility as well as (b) variables that contribute to individual aggression. Moreover, although violent actions readily capture our attention, more common than collective intergroup hostility and war is the bias or prejudice that characterizes the perceptions, judgments and evaluations of group members toward themselves, and toward those of other groups. The present chapter considers these two closely related topics: group aggression and intergroup conflict.

Group aggression

In our attempt to understand group aggression, it is instructive to first consider factors that affect aggression between individuals. Important among these are arousal, situational cues and modeling influences.

Arousal

Researchers generally agree that the psychological experience of arousal, which typically accompanies frustration and anger, contributes strongly to aggression (Berkowitz 1989). Other sources of psychological arousal, which commonsensically do not seem tightly linked to aggressive behavior, such as crowding, temperature, erotica and exercise, can also contribute.

In general, seemingly irrelevant arousal augments aggression when a person lacks clear information about its source and can readily misattribute it to an irritating or insulting event – as when subjects who were first angered and then pedaled an exercycle for 2½ minutes shocked the person who provoked them more than those who exercised, but had not been provoked. If instead, one (correctly) attributes residual arousal from exercise to the exercise, as one might when it is not followed by a rest period, it does not increase aggression (Zillmann et al. 1974). Similarly, arousing erotica (viewing a pornographic film) can increase angered subjects' aggressiveness (Donnerstein and Hallum 1978), but if not previously provoked, those exposed to it act no more aggressively than unexposed subjects (e.g. Cantor et al. 1978). The effects of misattributed extraneous arousal point to the importance of human interpretation (cognition) in understanding aggression. In crowd and intergroup settings, arousal will often be elevated by the excited actions and statements of the crowd. If it is interpreted as anger by crowd members, it will heighten aggression.

The weapons effect

In a classic experiment, subjects previously angered by an insulting provocateur administered a greater number of retaliatory shocks to him when a shotgun and a revolver (as opposed to badminton rackets or no objects at all) were lying on the table in front of them (Berkowitz and LePage 1967).[1] Thus, the presence of cues typically associated with aggressive behavior increased aggression. In a recent replication of this phenomenon, Carlson *et al.* (1990), found that the weapons effect was more pronounced when other cues associated with aggression (such as a low status victim) were present. In short, if you are surrounded by an armed angry group, the sight of their weapons should provide the conditions for a weapons effect. It seems likely that the weapons effect is due, in part, to the fact that weapons prime aggression related concepts and ideas. Thus, it may well be that any cues associated with aggression may elevate the propensity for violence. This would explain why for a member of a street gang, the mere sight of a rival gang can cue aggression.

Models

Conformity documents the powerful effect of others' behavior on an individual. Children who had been frustrated by having had special toys taken from them rarely exhibited angry talk or destructive play, probably because social norms constrain aggressive impulse, especially in a new situation. In contrast, those who, in a previous setting a short time before, had observed an adult viciously attack a large inflated plastic Bobo doll were much more likely to pick out the Bobo doll from the remaining toys and attack it. Moreover, the modeling was sometimes rather specific in that the children's comments and actions exactly paralleled those of the adult (Bandura *et al.* 1961). Thus, models not only provide instruction about what is appropriate or apparently good, but also about what specific actions are called for (Campbell, 1961).

Numerous studies of child abuse show a clear correlation between being abused and becoming an abuser (Gil 1970; Lefkowitz *et al.* 1977; Straus *et al.* 1979). Modeling probably accounts for much intergenerational transmission of behavior. There may be 1.5 million cases of child abuse in a year in the United States alone, with a quarter of mothers in one study spanking their children before they were even 6 months old (Korsch *et al.* 1965). Many of these child abusers are neither psychotic lunatics nor sadistic fiends. They are modeling behavior experienced from their own parents.

One additional feature of viewing aggressive models is physical arousal. Group aggression, almost invariably, is exciting and emotional for witnesses as well as participants. Indeed, as we have seen from the social facilitation literature (Chapter 2), several theorists argue that the simple presence of others in itself, can be arousing. This arousal can contribute to aggression in several ways. First, as we note above, such arousal will often be interpreted by participants (and therefore experienced) as anger which, of course, can serve to fuel aggressive behavior. Secondly, many theorists argue that strong emotional arousal impairs our ability to reason (e.g. Easterbrook 1959). As a consequence, we are more likely to be swayed by poor logic and/or emotional demagoguery when highly aroused. This too, can clearly elevate propensities for violence, especially when the reasons for restraint are subtle ones.

As indicated, in a new setting, people look for cues about what is appropriate. Models should also be able to reduce aggression. In one version of the teacher–learner paradigm (see Chapter 5), subjects were first insulted then witnessed their attacker receiving electric shocks from a third person serving in the teacher role. Compared to insulted subjects who had no opportunity to observe a model administering shocks, those who witnessed a temperate model deliver mild shocks subsequently used lower intensities themselves (Baron and Kepner 1970). The success of non-violent group protest relies strongly on leaders (models) who display saintly temperance in the face of strong provocation.

As implied in the discussion of modeling, the factors that affect aggression in interpersonal settings will often affect it more strongly in groups in that group settings possess other key features that augment competitiveness and aggression (Brown 1954). Some of these features are discussed in the sections which follow.

Within-group similarity—actual similarity

Others who are similar are more influential as models. A group's members typically are more similar to one another than are a random sample of persons. This is due to both mutual selection and mutual influence of group members on each other. When faced with some situational instigation – e.g. discovering that the park in which the group picnic was to be held is closed for repairs to the barbecue pits – those with very low thresholds for aggression may verbally display anger or destroy property and serve as models for others who are disappointed. Because fellow group members are likely to share your attitudes and values and confer moral appropriateness on actions taken, the aggressive behavior of in-group members is more likely to be modeled than that of a group of strangers.

Within-group similarity—assumed similarity

This is an additional factor which augments the real within-group similarity discussed just above. This is the pervasive tendency to exaggerate one's similarity to others (Marks and Miller 1987). This bias, discussed by Sir Francis Bacon in 1620, is now referred to as *social projection, assumed similarity* or the *false consensus effect*. In one procedure for studying this phenomenon, students were asked to walk around campus for 30 minutes wearing a sandwich board which said *Repent*. Those who agreed estimated that 63.5 per cent of their fellow students would do so, whereas those who refused expected 76 per cent to refuse (Ross, *et al.* 1977). One interpretation of this effect, called the selective exposure view, emphasizes the previous point – that people associate with others who are in fact similar to themselves. The resulting biased sample of experience creates an illusion of similarity that extends beyond one's circle of immediate acquaintances. According to this explanation, when asked what percentage of *other students* would wear the sign, one thinks of one's friends, and because they are similar to oneself in many ways, one assumes they are similar with respect to this particular issue, too. Making group membership salient increases this effect (Miller *et al.* 1991).

Your tendency to aggress, fueled by seeing other group members who share your values and interests already displaying aggressive behavior, will be further strengthened by your exaggeration of your similarity to them. Thus, the assumed similarity effect further augments existing modelling tendencies.

Group polarization

As we saw in Chapter 5, during group discussion, normative and informational influence can polarize the prevailing view. It should not be surprising that this same extremitizing effect occurs in the comparison of group to individual aggression. In two 'teacher-learner' aggression experiments Jaffe and Yinon (1983) gave subjects (the teachers) the opportunity to shock a learner who had previously insulted them. In these studies, university men and then unskilled workers retaliated in response to the learner's errors with increasingly higher levels of shock when making a group decision than when alone. After provocation, even when groups actively discuss options, they are more aggressive than individuals.

Groups and the reduction of social restraints: deindividuation

As we have seen, forces such as modeling, the sight of weapons and group polarization often heighten aggressive tendencies in group settings. However, group interaction can not only heighten aggressive impulses, but can also reduce inhibitions about expressing them.

Observers of nineteenth-century mass behavior (LeBon 1895; Tarde 1895) saw crowds as behaving more impulsively and irrationally than individuals. They thought that crowds undermine the constraint induced by social norms by leading people to ignore their own individuality – a process of *deindividuation*. In such a state one is presumed to be less susceptible to feelings of fear and guilt and less concerned with one's ordinary standards and the consequences of abandoning them. As we will see in Chapter 9, a substantial body of literature suggests that being with others (i.e. acting as part of a group) does reduce fear (e.g. Amoroso and

Walters 1969). Whether this fear reduction occurs due to conditioning, social comparison, or the fact that often people are truly safer when protected by groups, the result should be the same, namely less fear-induced inhibition of aggression. In a similar vein, people who aggress as part of a group can often absolve themselves of much of the guilt by attributing primary responsibility to others. (I only threw one rock in that riot. How much damage could that have caused? I'm not to blame for the fact that the town was destroyed.) A good deal of research indicates that individuals often *diffuse responsibility* in this manner when in group settings. Darley and Latane (1968), for example, found that bystanders acted less responsibly in a crisis if they thought other people were also present. In this study, when bystanders were part of a larger group they were less likely to aid a person feigning a seizure. The idea that, in group action, key restraints against aggression are lowered has much in common with the construct of deindividuation, which refers to the reduced fear and guilt that results simply because one becomes less self-conscious in groups.

Zimbardo (1969) developed a model that outlined the antecedents and consequences of a deindividuated state. Among the contributing factors were arousal, anonymity, diffused responsibility, being in a group and having a focus on the present. He argued that when individuals become deindividuated (by a combination of these circumstances) their inhibitions will be lowered, leading them to give way readily to impulsive antisocial behavior such as revelry, vandalism, violence or aggression.

Zimbardo emphasized anonymity as a key component and most deindividuation studies have manipulated it in one form or another, typically defining it as identifiability. In some studies identifiability is manipulated by having the experimenter record or not record the subject's name. Others manipulated identifiability to the victim, putting eye-blinds (as opposed to clear goggles) on the victim, having group members wear hoods or telling subjects that the victim would think it was the experimenter who administered shock.

Unfortunately, across the many studies, anonymity has no consistent effect, sometimes increasing (e.g. Donnerstein *et al.* 1972) and other times decreasing aggression (e.g. Baron 1970). However, many of the experimental studies differ in an important way from the crowd situation in Detroit mentioned at the start of this chapter, in that subjects were tested individually. Nevertheless, even when laboratory studies make subjects non-identifiable in a group setting, outcomes are inconsistent. Sometimes anonymity in a group setting augments aggression (e.g. Yaffe and Yinon 1979), but other times it decreases it (e.g. Diener, 1976).[2] This has led some to argue that lack of self-awareness, not anonymity *per se*, is critical to a deindividuated state (e.g. Diener 1980; Prentice-Dunn and Rogers, 1989).

In accord with this view, several manipulations that increase self-awareness (e.g. the presence of mirrors) have been found to reduce such antisocial behavior as cheating (Diener and Wallboom 1976), hostile aggression (Rule *et al.* 1975) and petty greed (Beaman *et al.* 1979). In the ingenious study by Beaman *et al.*, groups of costumed children were observed as they arrived at a home to request candy on Halloween. After requiring them to give their names at the door, the children were asked to take only one candy each and then left alone at the candy bowl. Increasing the children's self-awareness by placing a mirror by the candy bowl suppressed their illicit candy-taking. When the mirror was present, only 12 per cent took extra candy, whereas with no mirror in sight 34 per cent exceeded the limit of one candy each. In Diener and Wallboom's study (1976) 71 per cent of their subjects violated time limits on an IQ test under normal conditions, but only 7 per cent did so when made self-aware by working in front of a mirror and hearing their own voice. Size of the group may be another key variable related to self-awareness. Mullen (1986) has argued that the larger the group, the less self-aware is any particular member. In accord with the expectation of increased aggression when self-focus is reduced, he found that in 60 lynchings between the turn of the century and 1946, the larger the mob relative to the number of victims lynched, the more vicious and brutal was their murder of the victim (Mullen 1986). This was true controlling for severity or type of crime allegedly committed by the victim.

Emergent norm theory

Although, as seen, studies support the role of self-focus in reducing aggression, other studies concerned with Zimbardo's deindividuation model suggest that considerations other than self-awareness are important. For instance, in some studies that were concerned with an aggressor's identifiability, contradictory effects were found even within a single study. Wearing nurse-like gowns decreased aggression, whereas Ku Klux Klan outfits increased it (Johnson and Downing 1979). Rabbie *et al.* (1985) found that anonymity decreased the aggressiveness of males, but increased that of females. It seems unlikely that differences in self-awareness can account for such within-study differences. Rather, these outcomes suggest that interpretations of the situation are important. In contrast to Ku Klux Klan outfits, nurse uniforms bring to mind norms of helpfulness. Analogously, aggressive action is seen as normatively more appropriate for males than females (e.g. Eagly and Steffen 1986). Consequently, because people generally conform more to norms when observed, it makes sense that when identifiable, males would aggress more and females less. In short, each group, when identifiable, conforms more to the norms that define their gender-linked role.

Such findings suggest that social norms might play an important role in determining the aggressiveness of a crowd. In an alternative to the deindividuation model, Turner and Killian (1972) argue that an emergent norm develops in the crowd, much like the transmission of a rumor, to establish a shared view of the situation that may contradict other norms. Thus, a pro-aggression norm may develop despite the fact that in many situations aggression is antinormative. The stone throwing of the Intifada Palestinian Arabs in Israel occurs not because they are less responsive to norms, but instead, because it has become normative for that situation. Not all group members will enthusiastically adopt the new norm, but it will guide those who most strongly want approval. Consequently, in this model, individuals are more likely to exhibit behaviors in keeping with the emergent norm when identifiable by other group members. In accord with this view Rabbie and his associates found that aggression was more pronounced when aggression was made normatively appropriate and legitimate. For example a group's aggression towards a victim was greater if the victim had previously taken unfair advantage of group members in an experimental game. Under these circumstances aggression could be legitimized as justifiable retaliation (Rabbie and Horwitz 1982; Rabbie and Lodewijkx 1983).

Returning, for illustrative purposes, to the lynching data, several factors are at work. Obviously, a lynch mob gathers to aggress. A larger co-acting group provides more support and legitimacy for engaging in vicious behavior. Others' actions are not only modeled, but define aggression as appropriate – a normative effect. People feel better about themselves when a comparison to others shows they are better than average at meeting group norms. As each individual observes the brutal actions of others, increased brutality is required to exceed that which came before. A larger number of participants exacerbates this process. As previously suggested, ordinarily there is little self-focus when one is co-acting with a group of similar others (Mullen 1986).

Most important, however, is that a lynch mob is not merely a group process. It is also an intergroup process. The victim generally belongs to an outgroup. Ingroup–outgroup relations introduce additional important features. In terms of the deindividuation and emergent norm models, the former, with its emphasis on normlessness and lack of self-awareness, is likely to apply to situations like the Detroit outbursts. Such crowds, however, should not be thought of as solely or primarily displaying unregulated individualistic panic, stampede, or uncontrolled exuberant behavior. The latter view omits the fact that even the most rampant riots primarily contain sequences of rational and purposive individual and collective action (Berk 1974; McPhail 1991). Whenever there is intergroup conflict, however, as with the Bensonhurst murder and the Palestinian–Israeli conflict, or whenever a group celebration or a peaceful protest march deteriorates into an intergroup conflict, as when police brought in to control the crowd come to be viewed as an out-group, the emergent norm perspective is also likely to be applicable. In such situations a group identity can become highly salient. Consequently, conformity to the norms of one's group becomes important. Under these circumstances, that is, when one is identifiable in the presence of group members – as opposed to being unidentifiable and having no salient group membership – if aggression is the norm that one ascribes to one's group one will behave more aggressively (Spears et al. 1990).

There is little doubt that some of the most violent forms of group aggression are directed at other groups. This follows from a basic fact of social life; the human tendency to disparage, distrust and dislike groups other than our own. Analyzing the basis of such intergroup conflict and the cognitive biases it both generates and is based on, is of major interest to group researchers. The sections which follow examine this topic more closely.

Intergroup conflict and prejudice

Initial conceptions of intergroup conflict assumed that group hostility and aggression occurred primarily when groups were competing for scarce resources or otherwise had incompatible and mutually frustrating goals. In one classic field study, Sherif and his associates carefully manipulated events in a boys' summer camp to produce this form of competition between two groups of boys. Overt aggression and destruction of property was evident within days, culminating in food fights and fisticuffs on several occasions. Sherif and his team then introduced a series of 'superordinate' goals requiring the two groups to cooperate in order to achieve key rewards (e.g. food and water). Intergroup aggression diminished, replaced by intergroup friendship in a matter of days (Sherif *et al.* 1961).

The Minimal Group Paradigm

The dramatic results reported by Sherif *et al.* (1961) are consistent with the idea that incompatible goals contribute to intergroup conflict (i.e. dislike, distrust, hostility, etc.). Other research, however, suggests that such competition for resources may not be a necessary condition for such feelings. Tajfel and his associates (e.g. Tajfel 1982) found that British schoolboys tended to show in-group favoritism even when the groups in question were temporary and had little real meaning. For example, in one study, boys were 'grouped' on the basis of whether they over- or underestimated the number of dots on a slide. It is hard to imagine these groups being very important to subjects. Nevertheless, when asked to allocate money to the participants, the boys tended to over-compensate those of their own group and under-compensate those of the other group. Indeed, subjects seemed more intent on creating large payment differences between the two groups than on just getting as much for their group as they could. For example, they tended to reject options that would pay both groups extremely well. Here we see intergroup bias despite no history of incompatible goals or competition. The cause of this minimal group bias effect is still under debate. One contribution to it, however, is that these group labels simplify and order the environment, enabling people to react to others on the basis of their group membership rather than having to consider each on the basis of individual characteristics. An additional explanation of the bias is that over-rewarding their own group reflected subjects' needs for self-enhancement (if it's my group, it must be better; Tajfel and Turner 1979). As we will see below, mechanisms involving competition, cognitive simplification and self-enhancement are all thought to contribute to intergroup conflict.

In-group and out-group homogeneity

A major factor in intergroup bias and aggression is our tendency to view outgroup members as interchangeable, faceless, stereotypic caricatures. External threat (e.g. Lanzetta *et al.* 1954; Radloff and Helmrich 1968), group conflict or competition (e.g. Wilson and Wong 1968; Wilson 1971; Kahn and Ryen 1972), even strong task demands (e.g. Roth and Kubal 1975; Miller *et al.* 1985) can exacerbate this tendency. Under such circumstances our identification with our key reference groups increases. Members exaggerate their similarity to one another – the assumed similarity effect, thereby augmenting the group's cohesiveness (Stephan 1977; Simon and Brown 1987). Stronger distortion occurs with respect to out-group members. They are seen as homogeneous or interchange-able and their differentiation from the in-group is exaggerated (e.g. Judd and Park 1988). These processes undoubtedly stem in part from our tendency to rely on groups in times of stress (see Chapter 9), as well as our proclivity to see the world simplistically at such times. These processes build on more general aspects of perception and cognition. As indicated, to organize and deal with unfamiliar aspects of the world, humans simplify. One great aid in simplifying is to base one's decisions on broad categories (e.g. not hiring people who have not graduated from college). The more that stimuli in a given category are (or appear to be) similar, the more confident one can be in basing decisions solely on categorical information. Moreover, the more clearly categories differ from each other, the more useful categorically based de-cisions will be. Since people prefer to conserve attentional energy (especially so in times of stress), they try to construct and rely upon useful categories. As a result, people have a tendency to exaggerate:

(1) the extent to which stimuli can be grouped easily into categories;

(2) the extent to which these categories differ from each other.

This is seen in an experiment that required subjects to learn the spatial location of fourteen nonsense syllables (Figure 8.1a). Seven had a middle E, seven others a terminal X. Each was assigned a spatial location equidistant from the next adjacent one. The middle E syllables were mainly located on the left side of the continuum whereas the terminal X syllables were mainly on the right. However, three from each set perfectly overlapped at the three middle positions.

With successive randomly ordered presentations of the 14 nonsense syllables and feedback on the correctness of their guesses, subjects could eventually learn the exact locations of all fourteen. In the early stages of learning (after about twenty or thirty trials), however, the basic cognitive processes of over-simplification were in evidence. Subjects exaggerated the closeness of the locations of syllables within each category, as well as the difference between categories. Syllables in the three pairs with overlapping center positions were, respectively, displaced toward non-overlapping locations closely adjacent to others of their category (see Figure 8.1b). Tajfel and Wilkes (1963), report very similar data from a line estimation task. As subjects were exposed to a series of lines, it became apparent (in one condition) that all the lines labeled as A were shorter than those labeled as B. As subjects became familiar with this distinction they exaggerated the true extent of this difference and tended to overestimate how similar lines in each category (A or B) were to each other.

As noted, recent research indicates that we make the same type of errors when making judgments about people. For example, Quattrone and Jones (1980) found that after Rutgers students learned the opinion of one Princeton student, they were more willing to assume other Princeton students felt the same way than were Princeton students who received that same information. Similarly, Park and Rothbart (1982) found that female students belonging to a sorority felt there was a good deal of variety in their own sorority regarding issues like fashion and study habits, but that members of a rival sorority were more similar to each other in their attitudes about these issues. In short, we tend to exaggerate differences between groups and minimize those

Figure 8.1

(a) Actual spatial locations of fourteen nonsense syllables

(b) Subjects' estimates of the locations of middle E and terminal X syllables at an intermediate stage of learning.

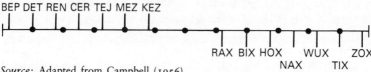

Source: Adapted from Campbell (1956)

differences that exist within groups, particularly out-groups. While such views allow us to maintain a tidy and simplified view of the world, they also often lead us to make unwarranted generalizations that can be used to justify intergroup hostility and prejudice. (They are not like us. They are hostile and dishonest. All of them are. We must protect ourselves by striking first.)

The preceding points suggest that human tendencies to simplify their social environment contribute to stereotyping and social bias. Is there any proof of this assertion? Several recent studies do, indeed, provide support for this view. These studies utilize the fact that various forms of arousal are known to limit attentional capacity, thereby increasing our tendency to process events at a simplistic level. If so, arousal should elevate group bias and stereotyping if such bias is a reflection of simplistic thinking. In one such study, Kim and Baron (1988) found that subjects were more likely to make judgments based on stereotypes if they were aroused by vigorous exercise. In related work, Wilder and his associates (e.g. Wilder and Shapiro 1988, 1989) found that emotional arousal such as fear or embarrassment led subjects to judge others primarily on the basis of what group they belonged to rather on the basis of their own behavior. For example, a smart juror embedded in a dumb jury was more likely to be labeled as dumb by emotionally aroused observers than by control subjects (Wilder and Shapiro 1988). These studies are quite congruent with the view that one ingredient that contributes to out-group bias is the tendency to simplify the world. Such bias is of course often a prerequisite for intergroup aggression.

Illusory correlation

The illusory correlation is another cognitive bias that combines with intergroup processes to promote negative views about out-groups. Perceivers overestimate the frequency with which members of a smaller, more distinct group engages in less frequent kinds of behaviors. In one illustrative study, subjects read a series of thirty-nine sentences. Each described a person by first name, his membership in group A or B, and a moderately positive or negative behavior he performed (e.g. John, a member of Group A, raked the lawn before dinner; Harry, a member of Group B, sarcastically chided his secretary). Two-thirds of the desirable behaviors, however, which were more frequent than the undesirable ones, were ascribed to Group A (see Table 8.1).

As shown, the frequencies of *both* desirable *and* undesirable behavior patterns for Group A were double those for Group B. As a result, the ratio of good to bad behavior was the same in the two groups, thereby controlling the relationship between group membership and relative desirability. Note, however, that Group B is smaller than Group A and that, in this setting, undesirable behavior is less frequent than desirable actions. Thus, Group B is more distinctive here, as is undesirable behavior. Apparently, this distinctive information 'sticks in our minds' and we tend to associate the two distinctive elements together (i.e. Group B with undesirable action). Therefore, subjects overestimate the co-occurrence of instances of a Group B person performing an undesirable behavior. That is, they perceive an illusory association between membership in Group B and the desirability of the behavior of persons in that group, even though no such relationship exists in the information that is presented to them. Consequently, Group A was rated more favorably than Group B on various evaluative traits (Hamilton and Gifford 1976).

Such a misperception provides a cognitive basis for intergroup bias. Most human behavior, day to day or month to month, is positive. Since contact with out-group members in everyday life is less frequent than with in-group members and since negative behavior is less common, there are now two distinctive events and, therefore, the ingredients for a negative stereotype based on an illusory correlation are in place. Even if whites and blacks behave negatively equally often, the illusory correlation effect will act to augment negative valuation of blacks by whites. Moreover, the

Table 8.1 Number of desirable and undesirable traits attributed to members of each group

Desirability	Group A	Group B
Desirable	18	9
Undesirable	8	4

illusory correlation effect is stronger when the distinctive (infrequent) traits are negative, as opposed to positive (Mullen and Johnson 1990). Finally, the effect generalizes to other negative trait dimensions in addition to those specifically observed, creating an overall devaluation of the out-group (Acorn *et al.* 1988).

Cognitive processes like the illusory correlation, however, cannot explain all prejudice. Therefore, we now consider additional factors that contribute to intergroup bias and aggression.

Ethnocentrism

Ethnocentrism refers to the universal strong liking of one's own group and the concomitant negative evaluation of out-groups. Presumably such feelings are based on intergroup competition and conflict. Consequently, they are thought to operate most strongly toward proximal groups, i.e. those we encounter frequently (Sumner 1906). As such, ethnocentric bias involves a mutually reinforcing relationship among attitudinal, ideological and behavioral mechanisms which promotes in-group cohesiveness and out-group antagonism. The bias has a strong moral component which serves a self-esteem bolstering function, but with respect to group rather than personal identity. In a study of thirty distinct East African ethnic groups, each with well-articulated cultural identities predating European influence in the area (Brewer and Campbell 1976), and in a cross-cultural analysis of seventeen societies based on interviews with two to five elderly respondents who reported on a total of ninety-five out-groups (Levine and Campbell 1972), the one dimension that generated universal in-group bias was trustworthiness or moral virtue. The in-group is rated more highly than out-groups on traits such as peace-loving, virtuous and obedient

– traits on which all groups (e.g. a family or a religious group) typically apply normative prescriptions to its members. As Campbell (1967) noted, ethnocentrism generates a set of universal reciprocal stereotypes in which each group, sees itself as good and the out-group as bad, even in cases where both groups emit the same behavior patterns. While the behavior may be similar, the interpretation is not: we are loyal, they are clannish; we are brave and willing to defend our rights, they are hostile and treacherous to outsiders. When there are real differences between groups, these, too, are depicted with group-serving evaluative connotation: we are responsible with our money, they are spendthrifts; or, from the other group's perspective, we are generous to all, they are stingy, selfish, hoarders.

The basic categorization processes of exaggerated homogeneity within categories and exaggerated differentiation between them are accentuated by the motivational forces implicit in ethnocentrism (Eiser and Stroebe 1972; Judd and Harackiewicz 1980; Reid 1983). Brown (Brown 1984; Brown and Abrams 1986) shows how egotistic tendencies seen among individuals (the boastful tendency to differentiate self from others in terms of one's positive attributes) extends to intergroup differentiation as well. To gain prize money for sports equipment, children in one school were cooperatively or competitively paired with those in another. These other children were alleged to be either equivalent to, above or below the subjects in ability. A key manipulation was whether students at the paired school were described as similar or different in their attitude about the importance of Mathematics and English in school. (In the dissimilar condition, the students of the other school supposedly thought science and practical subjects were most important.) In their estimates of their respective levels of performance on a Math/English test, when paired either with a lower or a higher status school, the children showed more in-group bias when the other school differed in attitude about what was important. This fits in with other research showing that dissimilarity typically is associated with decreased liking. When the ability status of the two groups was identical, however, more bias was shown when the out-group had similar than different attitudes, suggesting the need for the in-group to establish positive distinctiveness from the out-group when it is similar to the in-group.

Social identity theory

Why do we have such pervasive tendencies to both overvalue our own groups and simultaneously see them as different from other groups? Why, in the minimal groups research of Tajfel and his associates, do subjects seem more intent on maximizing differences between their in-group and the out-group than in maximizing payments to the in-group? As we have seen, at least one answer appears to be that we prefer to view the world in simple, categorical terms in which there are large differences between categories. Social identity theory suggests an additional explanation (cf. Tajfel and Turner 1986). According to this view, the quality and accomplishments of the groups we belong to are a crucial source of our self-esteem. If we wish to feel good about ourselves it is important to feel that our group is adequate and preferably superior. This view explains a good deal of the data on minimal group research and on ethnocentric bias as well as offering an interpretation of why individuals are inclined to perceive, preserve and exaggerate positive distinctions between their groups and others. Indeed, the research of Brown and Abrams 1986 (cited just above) illustrates how important the need for distinctiveness can be for group members.

A key idea for social identity theory is that positive intergroup social comparison (we are better than they are) represents a powerful means of establishing or maintaining an adequate 'social' identity for group members. Various findings and observations support this view. For example, minimal group studies by Oakes and Turner (1980), and Lemyre and Smith (1985) indicate that subjects who are prevented from making reward allocations (and thereby positively differentiating their group from the outgroup) report lower self-esteem than subjects who did make such allocations. Complementing these laboratory studies, Clark and Clark (1947) found that disadvantaged minorities (black children) showed evidence of low self-concept (actually preferring white dolls to black ones). Here then is evidence that chronic negative intergroup social comparisons produces dysfunctional effects on self-esteem.

As a final note, Brown (1988) suggests that one reason ethnic groups in larger societies (e.g. Mexican–Americans, French–Canadians, Welsh nationalists) are so concerned about their ability to cling to their language and customs has to do with the importance of these noticeable group distinctions for maintaining self-esteem and a positive sense of social identity. In short, social identity theory offers an interesting account of intergroup conflict and prejudice, and is currently generating a good deal of research and excitement among groups researchers.

The social construction of intergroup aggression

These various sources and types of intergroup bias have important implications for our understanding group aggression both in terms of how each form of bias operates in isolation and in combination with each other. Some of these implications are as follows.

Ethnocentric judgments of aggressiveness

We have already seen that each in-group judges its own behavior as good, the out-group's as bad. Aggressiveness is a bad trait. After a roughly played football game between Dartmouth and Princeton, two Ivy League colleges, members of each school were shown a film of the game. Princeton students 'saw' the Dartmouth team commit more than twice as many infractions as their own team. Dartmouth students 'saw' their own team commit only half as many infractions as the Princeton students saw them commit (Hastorf and Cantril 1954). Similarly, students with a negative attitude towards the police, judged police behavior during demonstrations to be violent, but judged student demonstrators like themselves non-aggressive (Blumenthal et al. 1972). Yet, an external observer might note that the students' sit-in behavior was the instigating action for the police behavior.

The ultimate attribution error

Pettigrew (1979) described a form of bias which he labeled *the ultimate attribution error*. When members of the out-group behave reprehensibly, it is seen as due to features of their character or personality. In contrast, the same action by an in-group member is interpreted as having been caused by situational factors. The opposite direction of bias occurs with positively evaluated behaviors.

Good acts by in-group members reflect their character, whereas the same acts by out-group members are merely due to special circumstances.

Reciprocity

The norm of reciprocity (Gouldner 1960), understood most simply as tit for tat, strongly governs a wide array of human behavior. When students watched an actor physically attack another in response to provocation, the actor was judged to be behaving defensively and fairly, presumably because the reciprocity norm dictates that it is appropriate for the victim of aggression to retaliate (Brown and Tedeschi 1976).

Combining the processes

We can now combine the preceding three ingredients. In accord with ethnocentric bias, in any (potential) conflict, the out-group is seen as behaving aggressively (whereas we are defensively and appropriately responding to their attack). Furthermore, in accord with the ultimate attribution error, their aggressiveness is ascribed to their character (whereas ours is attributed to the situation that they created). Finally, according to the norm of reciprocity, intended harm is a strong initiator of retaliation. Because the out-group's aggression is seen as internal, i.e. as part of their character, it must necessarily also be judged as behavior that was intended. Thus, whereas the out-group is viewed as intending to harm, our own aggressive response is merely justified retaliation.

Our discussions of such processes as ethnocentrism, perceived out-group homogeneity, illusory correlations, the ultimate attributional error and the need for positive social identity should provide some clarification about why dislike and lack of trust often exists between groups. In the next few sections we discuss factors that increase the likelihood that this dislike will escalate into violence and aggression.

Eliciting intergroup aggression

Equity

Notions of fairness will frequently play a key role in triggering aggression between groups. Equity is a circumstance in which the ratio of own outcomes to own inputs is equal to that of another relevant person. Deviation in either direction can be aversive. If you work harder than I at the same job, but get less income, I may feel guilty. If the situation is reversed, I may feel angry. Where there is inequity, individuals will differ in what they consider relevant inputs. Newly hired workers are less likely than long time workers to consider seniority important. Those with high status or power readily convince themselves that they deserve bigger shares than others. Their time is 'worth more'. Thus, guilt can be assuaged by devaluing the perceived value of another's contributions or augmenting one's own. Belief in a just world is a symptom of such rationalization (Lerner 1980). A person who receives a bad outcome is judged as deserving it. In contrast, an exploited person can justify her poor outcome to herself ('I'm glad I'm not an assertive, aggressive person') or attempt to restore equity either by making demands or increasing another's costs (e.g. requesting longer lunch breaks or stealing merchandise).

A feeling of inequity arises over time, as one compares oneself to another. Alone or combined with an immediate instigating event, it can be a potent source of angry or instrumental aggression. Outcomes perceived as unfair elicit stronger aggression than those that are simply unpleasant. Even when the unpleasantness of two events is equal, a negative *social* experience leads to substantially more aggression than a non-social event. On the average, across numerous studies, social provocation elicited twice as much aggressiveness as non-social negative events (Carlson and Miller 1988). The experience of unfairness almost always results from the actions of another person rather than a nonsocial cause.

When inequity exists in interpersonal relations, as in an inequitable dating relationship, the relationship is often terminated (Berscheid and Walster 1978). In intergroup settings, however, short of secession or mass migration (e.g. as when Pakistan was created and Buddhists migrated from the new country into India, while Moslems in India fled to Pakistan), such dissolution is much more difficult. As will be seen, inequity, often also described as *relative deprivation*, can contribute powerfully to intergroup hostility and conflict.

Relative deprivation

In our preceding discussion of equity, unfairness was seen as a strong contributor to anger. As previously noted, fairness also strongly figured among the moral components invoked in ethnocentric comparisons. After first being instructed to start each of an array of sentences with 'I' if it described something which they did more often than others, and if not with 'they', Dutch, as well as American subjects began more sentences describing fair behavior with 'I' than with 'they' and began more descriptions of unfair behavior with 'they' than with 'I'. In other words, unfair action is seen as more characteristic of an out-group ('they'). Behavior of the 'they'/unfair type were also rated as more salient and recalled substantially more frequently than behavior in any of the other three categories (viz. the 'they'/fair, 'I'/fair, and 'I'/unfair categories). Also, there was a strong negative correlation between rated frequency of a behavior and its salience (Liebrand *et al.* 1986a). The experience of unfair behavior from others may occur infrequently, but it stands out in memory.

Not surprisingly, when in-group members feel that they have been treated unfairly by out-group members, in-group/out-group bias becomes intensified. Students in two small face-to-face groups were given two tasks to perform: drawing a map of the school grounds and answering a football quiz. Ability status between the two groups was manipulated by indicating that one group had done considerably better than the other. A second manipulation concerned the legitimacy of this outcome. In one condition, legitimacy was reinforced by indicating that the superior group remained superior once again on yet a third task. To introduce illegitimacy, the experimenter called attention to the fact that the winning group had an easier task. The unfairness was further enhanced by creating the impression that the winning group seemed unwilling to give the other group a chance with the easier task. When asked to evaluate their own and the other group's performance on the initial map drawing task, each group exhibited in-group bias, although the winners were more biased than the losers. When the status difference was illegitimate, however, the winning groups increased their bias three-fold, whereas the losers increased it approximately ten-fold (Caddick 1982).

Intergroup bias will contribute to, but not by itself explain intergroup aggression. Also necessary are inequities at the group level – relative deprivation. In the United States, despite the recent progress of minorities in employment, income level and occupational distribution due to affirmative action (Smith and Welch 1984), the gaps that remain exceed the gains of recent years. Average black incomes have only risen from about 60 to 75 per cent of average white incomes. Furthermore, there has been no improvement in unemployment levels. Blacks comprise 10 per cent of those employed, but 22 per cent of those unemployed. They make up only 3 per cent of all lawyers, 2.3 per cent of all real estate salesmen, 7.4 per cent of all accountants, and 5.6 per cent of managers and executives. Exclusion is strongest in the higher executive levels. Less than 1 per cent of corporate vice-presidents are minorities (Farnham 1989).

To the extent that the plight of minority groups has improved, should they feel that much more content? Perhaps, but in periods where the low status of one's group is no longer seen as stable and untractable, attention focuses on the residual inequality rather than the improvements compared to the plight of one's grandparents. Moreover, when group-level discrepancies with whites are seen by blacks as illegitimate or unfair, feelings of relative deprivation become an even stronger source of anger and fuel for intergroup conflict.

Like inequity, relative deprivation is caused by the gap between expectations and achievement – own input and outcome in comparison to others'. With its emphasis on expectations, however, relative deprivation theory considers contributions to unfairness beyond those that stem directly from own inputs. In a period of relative improvement, when a subgroup of a minority group is doing relatively better than the rest of its members, that subgroup's expectations (based on their improved status) will be particularly high. During the 1950s and 1960s a black middle class emerged in the United States to form the core of the militant civil rights protest movement – a movement in which instrumental aggression disrupted ordinary life in countless US cities. The continued slow progress for most blacks in basic areas of opportunity such as education and civil rights was perhaps particularly discrepant from this subgroup's own rising expectations. Like the illegitimate losers in Caddick's experiment, they saw that, as a group, blacks were not only not getting that to which they were entitled, but that they were unfairly being deprived of it. The rash of recent national and ethnic movements within the Soviet bloc may reflect the rising expectations produced by Gorbachev's earlier relaxation of civil oppression and censorship and his promised economic improvement.

Triggering events

In contemporary United States, perhaps especially on college campuses, most people know that it is wrong to be prejudiced. Consequently, they mask prejudice or negative behavior toward blacks and other minorities. When put into the teacher–learner paradigm, white students administered less shock to a black than to a white learner. However, when the whites had been angered by the victim, they behaved quite differently, administering far more shock when angered by a black, than a white victim (Rogers and Prentice-Dunn 1981). In other words, justification for anger or aggression triggers bias toward out-group members that is masked under other circumstances (Dollard 1938).

What we are arguing here is that intergroup bias can help to set the stage for intergroup aggression, but it is not a sufficient condition for it. Also necessary are motivational forces. Perceptions of unfairness and group-level inequity (relative deprivation) can also contribute by providing motivational impetus. They too, however, though necessary, are not by themselves sufficient. Such general social inequities typically have persisted over a period of time without eliciting collectively organized conflict. The critical question is why group protest or rebellion becomes mobilized at any particular point during the period in which group-level inequity or unfairness exists? Even when social forces create an increase in relative deprivation, it is usually a gradual one, making it difficult for any single moment to be seized on as the time for action, rather than the preceding one or the next. These considerations argue for the additional necessity of specific triggering events – events that are a vivid, dramatic, and specific instance of unfairness or instigation. Such triggering events may not, if taken in isolation, justify social rebellion, but rather they mobilize action that is based on a combination of the other factors that we have discussed. Finally, they must also occur at a time when collective action and rebellion seem feasible or likely to succeed. The political, ideological or social climate must appear to be ripe for change.

The brutal Hawkins murder mentioned at the start of this chapter – unjust in any event, but even more so in its mistakenness – might have qualified as a triggering event. So too, might the seeming unfairness (to the black community) of Keith Mondello's acquittal. The additional impetus of inflammatory action by a charismatic or instrumental leader, such as the Reverend Sharpton, who can incite a crowd into a sufficiently high level of arousal, might also be required. The outbreak of any specific mass movement or insurrection, however, will not be easily predicted. It will depend on a confluence of many of the factors that we have discussed.

Adaptation level effects

Each new experience is evaluated against the background of prior experience. The upshot is that past experience defines the neutral point or the meaning of any particular point on a psychological scale. One might ordinarily think that with more personal income people would feel happier. The average after-tax income per person in the United States has approximately doubled between 1958 and 1988 (in constant dollars). Although there is a slight tendency for the very wealthy to be happier than the very poor, the percentage of people describing themselves as very happy remains stable across a two-decade time period at approximately 30 per cent (Smith 1979). By implication, with increasing income, each individual's standard for what is adequate gradually shifts upward in perfect correlation with the increase – an adaptation level effect.

TV programming, being saturated with violence and aggression, should affect adaptation levels and, consequently, the meaning of any aggressive act – its aggressiveness. Constant exposure desensitizes people to the experience of violence. Since the purpose of angry aggression is to elicit pain in another, the desensitization implicit in such a shifting adaptation level requires induction of a higher level of pain in the victim in order for it to be 'sufficient'. In areas of chronic intergroup conflict or war, such as Ireland, Nicaragua, Israel or Sri Lanka, adaptation-level desensitization may contribute to the tolerance for continued aggression.

Reduction of intergroup conflict

Cooperative strategies

It should be clear that once intergroup hostility becomes established it is no simple matter to reduce it. As we have argued, due to ethnocentrism and other cognitive biases, views of the out-group will tend to be biased and distorted, and these selective perceptions are apt to be intensified by processes of group polarization. Add to this a history of mutual hostility and desires for revenge (equity), and one faces a serious challenge if one wishes to de-escalate the conflict.

One technique that has been used with some success is to induce groups to engage in cooperative problem-solving (e.g. Brown and Abrams 1986). As we have seen, Sherif *et al.* (1961) found that this procedure produced rapid and dramatic drops in intergroup tension in their summer camp study. Aronson and his associates (1978) used related strategies to reduce racial tension in US high schools. Aronson *et al.* instituted what they called a jigsaw technique which required students of differing races to work cooperatively during class. Students would first master one part of an assignment working in one group. They then would join their 'jigsaw group' where each member would have information about different segments of the assignment and the information would be shared. Groups were, of course, racially mixed, requiring students to cooperate at all stages. The results of this and similar cooperative learning procedures (e.g. DeVries and Edwards 1974; Johnson and Johnson 1981; Slavin 1985) have been generally positive in terms of reducing racial hostility (Aronson *et al.* 1978).

The reason for these results is less clear. Such cooperation may break down group boundary lines (the 'us *v.* them' mentality) to some degree. Additionally, close cooperative contact with out-group members may do much to dispel our stereotyped characterizations and the view that 'they' are all alike. Wilder (1981) describes several studies in which bias towards out-group members is reduced if those members are somehow individuated. For example, in one study the usual in-group/out-group bias was much lower in conditions where the out-group was described as being in disagreement on certain issues. Thus, cooperative learning may reduce prejudice by simply undermining one's tendency to view out-group members simply as interchangeable members of a disliked category. Finally, cooperative contact may lead to simple positive association between out-group members, and various rewards and accomplishments. Hopefully, these various mechanisms can work in combination. This is tacitly assumed by most researchers in this field who tend to agree that cooperation is most likely to reduce intergroup hostility when group members have equal status, social norms and authority figures support the cooperative effort, cooperation produces a successful or rewarding outcome, out-group members come to be viewed as individuals and some degree of intimacy occurs (e.g. Brewer and Miller 1984).

GRIT

A somewhat different strategy based more on equity and bargaining considerations has been suggested by Osgood (1980). Described as the Gradual and Reciprocal Concession Technique (GRIT), this procedure, aimed primarily at de-escalating international conflict, seems appropriate to intergroup problems of smaller scale as well. The goals of this strategy are to increase communication and reciprocity between groups while reducing mistrust, thereby allowing for de-escalation of hostility and creation of a greater array of possible options. What is unique about this strategy is that it can be initiated unilaterally. One group (or county) can decide to try GRIT even without agreement from the other. The strategy is as follows:

1 Announce your general intentions to de-escalate tensions and your specific intention to make an initial concession.
2 Execute the initial concession unilaterally, completely and, of course, publicly. Provide as much verification as possible.
3 Invite reciprocity from the out-group. Expect the out-group to react to these steps with mistrust and skepticism. To overcome this, continued concessions should be made.
4 Match any reciprocal concessions made by the out-group and invite more.
5 Diversify the nature of your concessions.
6 Maintain your ability to retaliate if the out-group escalates tension. Any such retaliation should be carefully calibrated to match the intensity of the out-group's transgression.

Data on the utility of GRIT is scarce. Perhaps this is to be expected of a technique created to de-escalate international tension.

Meaningful laboratory studies on such procedures would be hard to design. Note, however, that Mikhail Gorbachev's decisions in the period 1986–1989 closely resemble the GRIT model. Gorbachev made a number of unilateral concessions that resulted in serious de-escalation of world tensions in this period. First, on two occasions, the Soviets stalled resumptions of atmospheric nuclear testing despite their inability to extend the prior treaty with the Reagan administration. They then agreed twice to summit meetings despite the Reagan administration's refusal to discuss the Star Wars defense system. They then agreed to the Intermediate and Strategic Range Nuclear Missile (INF) Treaty (exceeding US requests for verification) with continued refusal by the US to bargain about Star Wars. Next came agreements on the Berlin Wall and the unification of Germany. Eventually, even the staunchly anti-Communist/anti-Soviet Reagan–Bush regime had to take notice. This led to a period of mellowing tensions between these two superpowers.

Summary

To understand group aggression we first discussed those variables which contribute to individual aggression, but are also particularly important for group aggression. Here, we considered both direct and misdirected psychological arousal; the effect of cues, such as the sight of weapons; and the capacity of models to elicit or inhibit aggression.

In our discussion of group aggression, we noted that real similarity among group members results both from the selection process that produces group membership and from members' subsequent influence on one another. In addition, however, a pervasive tendency to assume similarity to others exaggerates the true degree of similarity. Together, these factors strengthen modeling effects within the group. Consequently, when, for whatever reason, a group member behaves aggressively or destructively, others are likely to join in quickly. The group polarization effect, discussed in Chapter 5, extends to group aggression as well. Finally, we discussed two alternative accounts of group aggression, the deindividuation and emergent norm models. We suggested that the latter is more likely to apply when a strong group identity becomes salient, as when group aggression becomes an intergroup process.

In considering intergroup aggression, basic cognitive processes, such as categorization effects that organize and simplify the social as well as the physical world, and other distortions in judgment, such as the illusory correlation effect contribute to intergroup bias. However, motivational forces implicit in ethnocentrism shape the valence of bias. In their social construction of aggression, in-groups see out-groups as hostile and aggressive toward them and view their own aggressive behavior merely as justified retaliation. Finally, to understand insurrections and rebellions we argued that in addition to the previously discussed factors, the existence of group level inequities that are implicit in relative deprivation provide the basic motivational impetus. Also necessary, however, are specific provocations – triggering events that can be seized on to justify the initiation of an aggressive uprising.

Finally, we discussed two approaches to reducing intergroup conflict. One is especially useful in situations where despite ethnic or racial heterogeneity participants essentially share a common goal, as in work teams in industrial, military or school settings. It uses small, cooperative, racially or ethnically heterogeneous teams in which group members share resources, have intimate face-to-face contact and produce a team product. These procedures are likely to work best when applied pro-actively to settings in which acts of flagrant hostility, strife and aggression have not become a routine aspect of intergroup relations. A second approach, the Gradual Reciprocal Concession Technique, applies to situations in which high levels of intergroup conflict and overt hostility are ongoing features of the relationship between two groups. It calls for a series of steps on the part of one group that are designed to lower intergroup aggression and tension irrespective of the actions of the other group.

Notes

1 Critics claimed this weapons effect was due to experimental demand – the tendency of subjects, being cooperative and reasonable, to figure out what the experimenter wants them to do and then do it. In this view, the weapons cue subjects that the experimenter wants them to be aggressive. They comply more, not because the weapons remind them of aggression, but because the weapons instruct them that the experimenter wants them to administer lots of shock (Page and Scheidt 1971;

Zillmann 1979). If true, this argument requires that those most clearly aware of the purpose of the research (as shown by post-experimental interviews) exhibit a larger weapons effect. In fact, the opposite occurs. Those least aware and most inaccurate in guessing that the experiment was intended to demonstrate the facilitating cue function of weapons, exhibit a stronger weapons effect, ruling out the demand explanation (Carlson *et al.* 1990).

2 Of course, to add co-action, as when people in the crowd move, act and shout collectively, introduces modeling effects too, a factor that must be kept conceptually and experimentally distinct from anonymity effects.

Suggestions for further reading

Aronson, E., Blaney, N., Stephan, C., Sikes, J. and Snapp, M. (1978). *The Jig-Saw Classroom*. London: Sage.

Diener, E. (1980). Deindividuation: The absence of self-awareness and self-regulation in group members. In P. Paulus (ed.) *The Psychology of Group Influence*. Hillsdale, NJ: Erlbaum.

Hastorf, A. H. and Cantril, H. (1954). They saw a game. A case study. *Journal of Abnormal and Social Psychology*, **49**, 129–134.

LeBon, G. (1895). *The Crowd: A Study of the Popular Mind*. New York: Viking Press, 1960.

Marks, G. and Miller, N. (1987). The 'false consensus effect': An empirical and theoretical view. *Psychological Bulletin*, **102**, 72–90.

Tajfel, H. and Turner, J. C. (1986). The social identity theory of intergroup behavior. In S. Worchel and W. G. Austin (eds) *Psychology of Intergroup Relations*, pp. 7–24. Chicago: Nelson Hall.

9 / STRESS AND SOCIAL SUPPORT

One of the most primitive human tendencies is for individuals to huddle together in times of fear, sorrow or extreme excitement. This tendency to seek out others in times of stress reflects one of the most documented psychological phenomena of recent years. Indeed, recent research indicates that those people who are strongly supported by friends and family are less devastated by a wide variety of stressors, including death or illness of a spouse (Pennebaker and O'Heeron 1984; Baron *et al.* 1990), job loss (Linn *et al.* 1985), and learning that one's child has cancer (Morrow *et al.* 1984).

Affiliation research

One of the earliest researchers to examine this group effect was Stanley Schachter. His initial interest in this topic was captured by reports that after periods of prolonged isolation, individuals often experienced unexplained anxiety. Schachter reasoned that if isolation produced anxiety, perhaps the opposite was true, i.e. that affiliation reduced it. Schachter's initial experiments were quite simple. He frightened subjects with the threat of shock and then examined the extent to which they chose to be with others. As predicted, over 60 per cent of these people chose to wait with others before the shock began. In a low fear control group, the equivalent figure was 33 per cent.

After replicating this phenomenon in several studies, Schachter argued that there were at least two reasons fear produced this desire to affiliate with others. First, he felt that fearful people were particularly interested in information about the stressful situation (how bad will this be?) and their response to it (am I over-reacting here?). Other people are an important source of this type of information and, as a result, Schachter felt one reason we prefer to be in groups in times of stress is in order to engage in social comparison. Social comparison, as you may remember from Chapter 1, involves comparing your feelings, behavior and opinions to those of others in order to get a fix on the accuracy of your opinions and the relative strength of your reactions. Secondly, Schachter argued that having other people present served to reduce fear directly even when no direct communication was possible. Presumably, this direct fear reduction was based in large part on early childhood conditioning since, for most individuals, parents are so often associated with the prevention or cessation of stressful stimuli during childhood.

Schachter's suggestions have received a good deal of support. In one very dramatic series of case study reports, Lynch *et al.* (1974) closely observed the heart activity of three severely injured patients as a female ward nurse sat down and held the patient's hand. All three patients had been paralyzed with the drug Curare for medical reasons. In some cases the nurse spoke soothingly to the patient while holding his/her hand, but in others he/she was silent. These periods of human contact both with and without verbal reassurance produced substantial reduction in heart rate for all three patients. For example, one patient reduced her heart rate from 125 BPM to approximately 110 BPM due to having her hand held (silently). Although these data are provocative, they are based on case study reports with limited subjects and few controls. Fortunately, in addition to case study data, there are a number of carefully controlled laboratory studies which indicate that direct fear reduction does occur when individuals affiliate with others, particularly if the companions are themselves acting calmly (cf. Epley 1974). Probably the most compelling and carefully documented study of this type using human subjects was conducted by Amoroso and Walters (1969). In the first stage of this study, women volunteers received a series of moderate electric shocks while they worked on a learning task. Not surprisingly, this shock elevated subjects' heart rate and self-reports of anxiety, and also interfered with their task performance. After the first series of shocks, one group of women waited alone for a 5-minute period before the second shock series began. The second group of women waited silently with three other individuals. At the end of this 5-minute waiting period, the experimenter assessed the subject's anxiety, heart rate and task skill. As expected, those who waited alone had greater heart rate and self-reported anxiety, and performed worse than those who waited with companions. Thus, in this study, the soothing effects of affiliation could be inferred from the subjects' physiological reactions and task performance as well as their self-reports.

This use of multiple measures is important. The earliest research on this issue relied primarily on fear questionnaires. These can easily be falsified. Amoroso and Walter's results seem free of such problems. An additional strength of this study is that it seems clear that the subjects experienced stress in this situation whereas in earlier studies, people were only threatened with shock; a threat they may have doubted. Moreover, their results complement several other studies that also used actual shock exposure as a stressor. Seidman et al. (1957) found that individuals tolerated more shock when in the presence of a non-shocked companion. Similarly, Ader and Tatum (1963) found that shock avoidance (i.e. fear) was more pronounced when people were tested as individuals rather than in pairs. A number of studies, however, indicate that the soothing effects of companions are most likely to occur if the companions appear calm (e.g. Latané et al. 1966). Indeed, in some cases, openly fearful companions have been found to increase the fear level of individuals. Imagine yourself in the study run by Shaver and Liebling (1976). First you learn you will receive a series of painful injections. Then you are joined by a companion who reacts by muttering such things as 'Oh my God' and 'No'. Not surprisingly, subjects in this condition made 40 per cent more errors on a maze task than those tested alone. Obviously, not all companionship is comforting. For the most part, however, calm companionship has proven to be beneficial. On balance then, there is a good deal of evidence for Schachter's argument that affiliation can reduce fear in human subjects. Indeed, similar effects have also been widely reported among a variety of animals. For example, young goats are less upset by darkness and unpredictable shock if they are accompanied by their mother; chickens are less immobilized by a 'shock signal' when in the presence of a calm companion and rats appear less stressed by exposure to a wide open space when they are with a partner (Epley 1974). This apparently is due, at least in part, to the fact that rats are distracted from the fearful situation by their companions (Moore *et al.* 1981).

However, what about Schachter's arguments regarding social comparison? Remember, he argued that fear-based affiliation was caused at least in part by needs for social comparison information, in addition to the direct effect that groups had on fear reduction. Here too, the data support his view. The social comparison view assumes that fear produces a variety of uncertainties which the individual attempts to resolve by social comparison. According to this view, greater uncertainty should produce greater desire to be with others with whom one can make comparisons. Several studies find this to be true. For example, in one study, Gerard (1963) gave people the impression that they were connected via electrodes to an 'emotion meter'. In one condition, the readings from this emotion meter were made to appear steady and, therefore, implied a consistent emotional reaction. In a second condition, the readings from the emotion meter varied a good deal. Since this made the reading hard to interpret, it elevated uncertainty. As predicted, those in this latter condition exhibited stronger desires to affiliate with others.

In another study, Mills and Mintz (1972) had subjects ingest a strong dose of caffeine. Half of these subjects were told that they had ingested a mild sedative, whereas others were correctly told that the caffeine would arouse them. Mills and Mintz reasoned that those given the 'sedative' instructions would feel a good deal of surprise, confusion and uncertainty when they experienced the strong arousal caused by the caffeine. The question was, would this uncertainty produce a stronger desire to be with others? This result is just what Mills and Mintz observed, suggesting again that social comparison needs are an important reason for grouping together in stressful situations. In summary, stress has generally been found to increase affiliative tendency and seems to do so because affiliation provides individuals with both direct stress reduction and an opportunity to gain information from others. What is noteworthy about most of the findings stemming from Schachter's affiliation work is that the research concerns the effects of affiliating with total strangers. Indeed, many studies did not even permit direct verbal exchanges between subjects (although admittedly much information can be gained just by looking at one's companions in a stressful situation). If total strangers are comforting in times of stress, the effects of good friends and family should, if anything, be extremely powerful.

Studies of *social support* (the soothing impact of friends, family and acquaintances) show just such results. Social support has been found helpful with a very wide range of stressors and subject populations (cf. Cohen and Syme 1985; House *et al.* 1988, for reviews).

The broken heart effect

Some of the most dramatic social support evidence concerns what happens when longstanding companionship is suddenly removed. Several studies indicate that individuals are far more likely to suffer illness and death in the years just following the death of their spouse. In one study this 'broken heart' effect reflected the fact that, averaging over all age categories, bereaved spouses were three times more likely to die than a similarly aged married control group (Stroebe *et al.* 1982). Indeed, for those between the ages of 20 and 29, the bereaved were almost ten times more likely to die. However, a result this astounding should not be accepted at face value without some form of corroboration. When we examine similar studies, the results are rather more modest, but the differential death rate among bereaved and non-bereaved samples is, nevertheless, most remarkable. For example, a study by Rees and Lutkins (1967) reported that in one town in South Wales, 12.2 per cent of bereaved spouses died within 1 year of the original death while only 1.2 per cent of controls passed away. Indeed, in this study, even bereaved relatives were more likely to die (4.76 per cent) than those in the control group. Apparently, the impact of physical and psychologically based illness is much stronger for those who find themselves deprived of a major source of social support.

The surprisingly high mortality of people mourning the death of their spouse has prompted a good deal of careful analysis. In a recent view of this topic, Stroebe *et al.* (1982) document some interesting facts. First, males seem more affected by the loss of their spouse than are women. Secondly, although there are some differences from study to study, grief seems to have its major effect on health and mortality within the first 6 months of the partner's death. Finally, people seem to be far more affected by their spouse's death the younger they are. Although, widowers aged 50–54 are 1.66 times more likely to die than same-aged married individuals, those only aged 25–29 are 6.27 times more likely to die.

Researchers are currently exploring the basis of 'The Broken Heart' phenomenon. One strong possibility is that the immune and neuroendocrine system are less effective in the absence of strong social support (Jemmott and Locke 1984). Another possibility is that one tends to neglect one's health more in the absence of strong social support (or during periods of grief) (Krantz *et al.* 1985). Future research will undoubtedly shed light on such explanations.

Social support research

Research on loss of a spouse has some unique properties since such a loss is in itself an extremely powerful stressor. Most social support research examines how the presence of friends and family protect the individual and minimize the effects of other stressors such as combat, illness, job loss, relocation, etc. For example, Janis (1968) argued that belonging to a close-knit combat unit provided soldiers with soothing feelings of control and power. He felt that in a very real sense, the group served to replace the family unit as a source of security.

Cobb (1976) also comments on the sense of control we may gain through group membership. The reason why this emphasis on control is important is that stress research indicates that simply thinking one has some control over stress renders that stress far more tolerable (Geer *et al.* 1970). For example, using severe noise as a stressor, Glass and Singer (1972) found that providing people with a 'cut-off switch' almost completely eliminated the negative effects of the noise. What was interesting is that individuals never used the switch. Just knowing it was available was comforting enough. In short, if social support does raise feelings of control, we would expect it to reduce stress. However, Cobb (1976) also alludes to another factor. He feels when we are accepted by a group, we are more likely to feel important, worthy and loved. As a result we are likely to be more upbeat, optimistic and confident, and this, too, may play a crucial role in adapting to stressful events. As we will see later in this chapter, there is a good deal of data supporting this view (e.g. Linn *et al.* 1985).

The support we receive from friends, family and loved ones can be complex and multi-faceted. In one case a friend might provide us with temporary housing, in another, crucial advice, and in yet another, the knowledge that we are accepted, loved or cared for. Theorists differ in their analyses of social support, but certain common components can be identified (Weiss 1974; Cobb 1976; Cohen and McKay 1984). We list them using the labels identified by Weiss (1974).

Attachment
This refers to the feelings of emotional support, intimacy and liking that exist in a group. It is fostered by the love, caring and attention group members provide for each other.

Guidance
This refers to information, advice and feedback provided by the group.

Tangible assistance
This refers simply to material aid whether it be financial or in the form of service.

Embeddedness in a social network
This refers to simply feeling part of a cohesive or well defined group. Often such feelings contribute to an individual's sense of identity.

Opportunity to Provide Nurturance
This refers to the extent to which the individual feels that others are dependent on him or her for support. [Note: this component is identified only by Weiss (1974) among the major social support writers.]

These various components have proven quite useful in developing measures of social support. With these measures researchers have been able to examine the relationship between social support and various stress related outcomes. This research clearly supports the arguments of Cobb, Janis and others that social support should improve one's ability to cope with stress. For example, Nuckolls *et al.* (1972) examined the rate of pregnancy complications occurring among 170 pregnant army wives who had reported experiencing major life changes during their pregnancy. Those who had strong social support had a relatively low rate of complication (33 per cent). The rate was almost three times higher (91 per cent) for women who had low social support. Gore (1978) found that among unemployed males low social support was associated with higher rates of cholesterol and more illness symptoms.

Indeed, in various studies over the years, low social support has been linked to such conditions as high blood pressure, tuberculosis, depression, low birth weight in children, arthritis and even death (cf. Cobb 1976). Admittedly, these are correlational findings and it is, therefore, hard to be sure whether the lack of social support causes these effects on health. For example, it is possible that once someone is ill, one simply *reports* fewer friendships due to depression or as an attempt to gain sympathy.

In order to address this type of problem, a series of studies in the mid 1960s utilized *prospective* research designs. This involves assessing social support at one point in time and then examining the extent to which it is associated with health outcomes in the years which followed. One of the earliest of these extensive projects was completed in the Oakland, California area by Berkman and Syme (1979). Over 4000 individuals were first classified in terms of their degree of social support, as measured by their marital status, membership of clubs and church groups, and the extent of their contact with friends and relatives. A 9-year follow-up indicated that males with least social support were 2.3 times more likely to die over the period than those with substantial social support. For women who lacked social support, this disadvantage was 2.8. The researchers were careful to control for a wide range of variables such as socioeconomic status, obesity, physical exercise, smoking, use of alcohol, etc.

These dramatic findings would be less plausible if they were not well corroborated by at least six similar reports from regions as diverse as Michigan and Georgia in the United States, Gothenberg in Sweden, and Eastern Finland (cf. House *et al.* 1988). In the Swedish study, for example, males who were lowest in social support had death rates four times higher than those with highest social support (Tibblin *et al.* 1986).

As we noted, Berkman and Syme (1979) controlled for variables such as smoking, obesity, etc. These controls are crucial in research of this type because people are not randomly assigned to the high and low social support conditions, but rather 'select themselves' to these conditions. Consequently, individuals in these two conditions are not strictly comparable. For example, it is conceivable that it is easier to find social support if one is healthy, attractive, a non-smoker, etc. If so, those high in social support may have been 'healthier' than others at the beginning of the study, suggesting that the health of these subjects causes social support, rather than vice versa. Therefore, careful researchers assess such confounding variables as smoking, obesity, etc., so that statistical procedures can be used to control for their influence. Unfortunately, these statistical techniques have limits. No matter how many confounding variables are assessed for use as statistical controls, it is possible to omit the key variable. Thus, for example, Berkman and Syme (1979) were unable to assess serum cholesterol as a control variable (unlike Tibblin *et al.* 1986). On the other hand, when one reviews all the studies on social support and mortality, a wide range of confounding variables have been considered overall and none has eliminated the relationship between social support and mortality. Thus, if there is a key confounding variable, it is not an obvious one. More important, as we already know from lab research, people who are randomly assigned to receive social support (in the form of simple companionship) experience less distress during stressful procedures than those tested alone (e.g. Amoroso and Walters 1969). Note that the use of random assignment in experimental studies *does* produce initial comparability among the subjects in various conditions. Therefore, combining these data with the large scale field studies on mortality make it quite likely that social support does have some causal role in health status. Indeed, after an extensive review of this literature, House *et al.* (1988) conclude that the evidence favoring a causal link between social support and health status is at least as strong as that used originally to link smoking and cancer. Currently, researchers are examining which aspects of social support are most important in this relationship and how they have the effect they do.

Pets as sources of social support

Humans are not the only source of love and friendship. Who among us has not known someone who has been devoted to a cat, a dog or a horse? Since love and friendship are key aspects of social support, researchers have begun to explore whether animal 'social support' has the type of therapeutic effect found for human social support. Research with children (Friedmann *et al.* 1983), terminal cancer patients (Muschel 1984), heart attack victims

(Friedmann *et al.* 1980) and the elderly (Mugford and McComisky 1975; Brickel 1984; Garrity *et al.* 1989) all support the conclusion that contact with pets has therapeutic effects (see Lago *et al.* 1983; Robb and Stegman 1983 for some exceptions). For example, Friedmann *et al.* (1980), examined the survival rate of over ninety individuals released from hospital following a heart attack. Ninety-four per cent of those patients who owned pets were still alive 1 year after their hospital admission. In the non-pet group, only 70 per cent were still alive. Similarly, Siegel (1990), in a carefully controlled field study, found elderly pet owners made fewer visits to the doctor over a 1-year period and responded to stress with less illness than non-pet owners. Interestingly, these effects were strongest when the pets were dogs. Other research indicates that contact with pets reduces blood pressure, heart rate and skin conductance (Baun *et al.* 1984; Allen *et al.* 1991). Allen *et al.* (1991), for example, found that blood pressure and skin conductance of dedicated pet owners was lower during a stressful mental task if their pet was present. Indeed, physiological responding in this condition was lower than in conditions where human friends were present. Consequently, it appears that pet ownership provides some of the same benefits produced by human social support and in fact, may provide superior benefits under certain conditions.

Explaining the relationship between social support and health

The dramatic impact of social support on mortality and other stress-related variables has prompted a good deal of discussion and research. Some has been directed at investigating *why* social support has this comforting effect. Research on this topic has focused on the role of advice and material aid, as well as how social support affects feelings of control and self-esteem. Not surprisingly, it indicates that those who report having more social support feel more capable and better about themselves. This has been found to be true for adult males (Linn *et al.* 1985), high school students (Cauce *et al.* 1982) and nursing students (Hilbert and Allen 1985), among others. This relationship between support and esteem is a two-way street. Being liked and accepted by others should lift self-esteem; at the same time those with high self-esteem are probably more attractive to others. It does appear, however, that self-esteem does play a key role in social support effects. Recent studies by Cutrona and Troutman (1986) indicate that when social support does serve to reduce a stressful experience (parenting a difficult child), it primarily does so not only by affecting feelings of self-control as previously argued, but also by bolstering self-esteem.

In addition, several recent studies suggest that high social support may improve health-related outcomes due to its effect on the immune system. For example, in one very recent study, Baron et al. (1990) examined the immune responses of subjects whose spouses were hospitalized for treatment of serious cancers. Observing the side-effects of cancer treatment on a loved one is in itself quite stressful (as is the threat of losing one's mate to cancer) and as a result all subjects were experiencing at least moderate to intense psychological distress.

Baron et al. took blood samples and measured two basic forms of immune functioning: the ability of blood lymphocytes to reproduce and their ability to kill target cells. The results indicated that both these forms of immune function were superior among those who had substantial social support. At least one study reports similar results among people caring for spouses or relatives with Alzheimer's disease (Kiecolt-Glaser et al. 1987), and Jemmott and Magliore (1988) report a positive relationship between social support and immune function in a sample of college students. Thus, there is converging evidence that the immune system may play a mediating role in the strong association seen between social support and health.

The buffering hypothesis

Additional research is currently examining the kinds of actions (on the part of companions) that most effectively produce feelings of social support (e.g. Costanza et al. 1988) and under which circumstances different types of social support will provide greatest benefit (Cutrona 1990). One intriguing idea, the 'buffering hypothesis', states that social support only provides benefit in times of stress. Although the buffering hypothesis has some support, other studies find that high social support contributes to health even when stress is absent. The reason for these inconsistent outcomes may be that some forms of social support are generally beneficial even in times of low stress whereas other forms only heighten well-being if stress is present (Cohen and Wills 1985). Rook (1987) argues that when social contact takes the form of shared recreation, humor and affection, it will have beneficial effects on well-being and psychological adjustment whether stress is present or not. She labels this type of social contact 'companionship'. In contrast, more problem orientated actions, such as offering guidance, material aid, reassurance and sympathy are most likely to prove beneficial in stressful periods. Rook labels this form of contact 'social support'. Thus, the inconsistent data regarding the buffering hypothesis may reflect differences in the way researchers measure or define social support.

Can social support be harmful?

Although friends and relatives can offer aid, reassurance and love, they can also be a source of criticism, thoughtlessness, pity, disagreement and selfishness. Melamed and Brenner (1990), for example, found that married couples often do not even agree which types of behaviors are supportive and which are not. In a similar vein, Dakof and Taylor (1990) document the irritation cancer patients experience when well-meaning visitors and staff attempt to cheer them up by minimizing the extent of their illness. In short, sources of support often cause substantial upset and irritation (Rook 1990). In a study conducted with elderly widows, negative social interactions affected their psychological well-being more than positive ones (Rook 1984). Spouses caring for a husband or wife with Alzheimer's disease over a 10-month period showed similar effects (Pagel *et al.* 1985). Alzheimer's patients place very strong demands on caregivers, who themselves are often elderly; as a result, these caregivers suffer substantial distress. Pagel *et al.* found that when members of a social network managed to upset the caregiver, this was associated with increases in depression in the caregiver. Indeed, some of the largest increases in caregiver depression occurred when friends or relatives were helpful to the caregiver, but also served as a source of irritation. Quite possibly, this result occurred because the caregiving spouse cannot easily avoid these upsetting personal contacts because she or he needs the help provided by the source of the irritation.

Other researchers have found that being part of a social network can increase depressive symptoms if the network is characterized by behaviors such as criticism and overinvolvement (e.g. Hooley *et al.* 1986). Problems can also occur if members of a network are all victims of stress. Hobfoll and London (1986) found that among Israeli women, those who had more friends with whom to talk felt more concerned and distressed about their boyfriends and husbands during wartime. They suggest that friends may have fed each other's fears – a result quite consistent with those of laboratory studies we discussed earlier, in which companionship reduced stress most effectively for an individual if the companions were not stressed themselves. Obviously, being part of a strong social network does not necessarily imply that individuals will receive effective social support. As noted, positive social support serves to bolster self-esteem and feelings of control, as well as providing advice, affection and tangible assistance. Clearly, some social networks do this more effectively than others.

Summary

A large number of studies indicate that the presence of others makes a variety of stressors easier to tolerate. Moreover, non-human species exhibit similar effects. These benefits occur most reliably when the stressed individual (rat or human) has companions who remain calm. In some of the earliest research on this issue, Schachter (1959) found that frightened people wished to be with others. He argued this occurred because frightened people desired to engage in social comparison and because fear levels would be reduced in groups. Research has supported both views, even in cases of simple affiliation (i.e. where group members are strangers to each other). However, the truly dramatic instances of stress reduction occur in studies of social support that examine the stress-reducing properties of friends, loved ones and family. These studies have examined the effects of losing social support, as well as having it available in times of stress. Both approaches indicate that social support is an important factor, not only in psychological adjustment, but in physical adjustment as well. Losing one's spouse increases one's likelihood of contracting a number of ailments and can substantially increase risk of death, particularly among males. In contrast, those who report high social support seem less susceptible to such problems. Recent attempts to explain this relationship between social support and health have investigated variables such as perceived control, self-esteem, and the possible effects of social support on the immune system. In addition, researchers have begun to examine ways in which social conditions can interfere with stress-related coping. Given the wide variety of stressful settings that are affected by strong social support, it seems likely that researchers will continue to study this variable in the coming years.

Suggestions for further reading

Cobb, S. (1976). Social support as a moderator of life stress. *Psychosomatic Medicine*, 38, 300–14.

Cohen, S. and Syme, S. C. (1985). *Social Support and Health*. New York: Academic Press.

House, J. S., Landis, K. R. and Umberson, D. (1988). Social relationships and health. *Science*, 241, 540–5.

Janis, I. L. (1963). Group identification under conditions of external danger. *British Journal of Medical Psychology*, 36, 227–38.

Schachter, S. (1959). *The psychology of affiliation*. Stanford, CA: Stanford University Press.

/10/ CROWDING

The population problem

We have seen in the last chapter that in many stressful settings social groups can have soothing and therapeutic effects. There is an important exception to this generalization, however. This exception occurs when group conditions cause overcrowding. Social scientists have become increasingly concerned with problems caused by uncontrolled population growth, and with ample reason. Population growth is geometric. Consider a case where an average family size in a culture is four children and two adults. Assume all four children from one of these families marry and have 'average size' families themselves. The result is that the two original adult parents contribute at least 20 new individuals to the population, i.e. their four children and their 16 grandchildren. (We will ignore any possible great grandchildren.) This geometric progression, combined with rapid medical advances that lowered the death rate, produced a population increase of some 1 billion persons in the 15 years between 1960 and 1975. Stated differently, during those 15 years the world increased its population by 25 per cent.

This rampant overpopulation has created shortages of food, water and territory in many areas of the world. Worse yet, the rate of this population increase has been growing steadily. As a result, the time needed for the world to double its population has become progressively shorter (Erlich 1968). While awareness of the population problem has lowered birth rates in most industrialized countries, current birth rates are still alarming. Every 3 years some 230 million individuals (the current population of the USA) are added to the world population, and some projections argue that by the year 2000 the world population will be some 6 billion people; this would be an increase of almost 50 per cent from its present population of 4½ billion. What does this mean? Just imagine your parking problems or the crowds you encounter on public transit being 50 per cent worse and you begin to get the picture. In light of these disturbing statistics, a good deal of psychological research has examined the effects of overcrowding in an attempt to discover which conditions increase or decrease its impact.

Animal data

For anyone who has lived in a major city, the experience of intense overcrowding on highways, parks and city streets is all too familiar. However, the results of the earliest research with animals startled even those intimately familiar with the population problem. In an early study, Calhoun (1962) found that when a rat colony became overcrowded it developed what he referred to as a *behavioral sink*. This can best be described as a general deterioration in the social behavior of the overcrowded animals. Some animals displayed inappropriate, unprovoked, random aggression, while others became passive and withdrawn. Female rats were inattentive to their young, many of whom were trampled or eaten by other rats. Indeed, the infant mortality rate exceeded 80 per cent. Sexual behavior became disordered and abnormal with some males attempting romantic advances to females who were not on heat while other males completely refrained from sexual behavior. Females who came into heat were pursued by packs of aggressive males who ignored normal mating rituals in attempting intercourse. Finally, crowded animals developed a number of biological maladies often associated with extreme stress. Other researchers have found related outcomes (e.g. Marsden 1972; Dahlof *et al.* 1977; Lobb and McCain 1978). These startling results prompted researchers to examine human reactions to overcrowding.

Human research on task performance

The earliest studies of Freedman and his colleagues were some-what reassuring. In one study, Freedman *et al.* (1971) exposed people to a variety of mental tasks (e.g. listing unique uses for a given object; forming words from a list of letters) and found that crowding had little effect on how well people completed these tasks. Freedman's group used a careful crowding manipulation, placing individuals in groups of either five or nine in laboratory rooms varying in size for a period of 4 hours.

In crowded conditions, people were seated so as to be almost touching, but factors such as temperature, the availability of ma-terials and the need to move around others were kept constant in crowded and uncrowded conditions. In this way, Freedman *et al.* (1971) hoped to study how crowding in its 'pure form' affected performance. In a second study, Freedman's team used a similar manipulation to study the effect of crowding on competition and aggression using a Prisoner's Dilemma game (see Chapter 7). Freedman's team found that crowding decreased cooperative re-sponding among men, but had the opposite effect among women. Related findings occurred on a further task in which subjects made judgments about punishments to be used in a series of criminal cases (e.g. hit and run death, rape). Crowded women were less punitive than non-crowded women. Men's ratings were unaffected by crowding on this variable. Added to these results, males liked their group mates less when crowded, while women liked their group mates more under crowded conditions. From these results, Freedman *et al.* (1972) concluded that crowding, at least in its pure form, could not truly be considered a stressor. It had little effect on performance and inconsistent effects on liking, competi-tion and punitiveness (considering both men and women together). Freedman did suggest that crowding might intensify behavior, but noted that this could often result in positive behavior (as indicated by female responses to crowding) as well as negative.

Freedman's arguments were provocative ones which encouraged continued work on crowding. The thrust of this research indicates that, contrary to Freedman's arguments, crowding does provoke stress-related responding. First, laboratory studies closely exam-ined the connection between crowding and task performance. These studies found that when investigators took care to use tasks and testing procedures that are well known to produce poor

performance under stress, crowding does, in fact, lower performance. For example, Paulus et al. (1976) found that subjects had
less ability to solve a pencil-maze type problem under crowded
conditions. In a similar vein, Evans (1975) found that ten subjects
working in crowded conditions showed poor performance at a
secondary task (monitoring a tape-recorded story). Worchel and
Teddlie (1976) found that subject's ability to create new words
out of groups of letters was poorer under crowded conditions.
Finally, several studies (e.g. Heller et al. 1977) found that task
performance tends to drop on tasks that come just after an experience of crowding. This is a well established stress pattern (Cohen
1978; Paulus 1980).

In fairness, although many studies report that crowding inter-
feres with task performance, several laboratory studies besides
Freedman's failed to find poor performance under crowded conditions. What could cause such inconsistency? There are several
possible explanations. Some studies that fail to find crowding
effects have not used tasks known to be sensitive to stress. As a
result, part of the problem in these studies may just be the use of
tasks that are unaffected by any kind of stress. Secondly, research
by Paulus and his associates (Paulus 1980) indicates that crowding
hurts performance most when the situation encourages competition between individuals. Studies that fail to find crowding effects
may have subtly deemphasized a competitive atmosphere.

In addition to these problems, task complexity and difficulty
may be an important consideration. If crowding is a stressful
experience it should increase arousal and bodily tension. As we have
noted in our discussion of social facilitation, arousal primarily
impairs complex or difficult tasks. Those studies that fail to find
that crowding hurts task performance may be using tasks that
do not have these features. Indeed, most crowding studies that do
report task impairment employ complex tasks (Fisher et al. 1984)

Finally, and most crucially, crowding seems to have its most
pronounced effects in settings in which individuals must attend to
and deal with their fellow humans. In a clever study, Heller et al.
(1977) arranged a collating and adding task so that in one condition subjects could work easily without negotiating their way
around the other subjects. In the other condition, things were
arranged so that a substantial amount of social contact and
maneuvering was necessary. Heller et al. found that crowding in
the social contact condition produced far more errors than crowding

in the no social contact condition. Moreover, these errors in the social contact condition occurred even after people were past the stage of social contact and were seated comfortably at their desks. Since the early laboratory studies on crowding explicitly prevented the type of complex social contact manipulated by Heller *et al.*, it is not wholly surprising that the effects of crowding were not particularly pronounced in these early experiments.

For the most part, however, laboratory research indicates that crowding has negative effects on task performance. This laboratory research is complemented by field studies conducted in naturalistic settings. Brown and Poulton (1961), for example, found that drivers made more errors on a mental task while they were in areas of heavy traffic. Saegert (1973) brought individuals to the shoe department of a large department store and found that under crowded conditions, they were less able to remember accurately the prominent features of this setting. These studies indicate that crowding limits our ability to pay attention to a wide range of stimuli (events, signals, details, etc.). This is an important finding because such limits in attentional capacity are commonly associated with emotional arousal (Easterbrook 1959).

Sex differences in crowding and social behavior

One puzzle in the research on crowding and social behavior is that sex differences have frequently been reported. As noted, Freedman *et al.* (1972) found men reacting more negatively on such things as competitiveness and friendliness when crowded and women reacting more positively in crowded settings. Similar results have been reported in at least four other studies, all using same sexed groups (cf. Paulus 1980; Fisher *et al.* 1984). Freedman *et al.* (1972) argued that their results reflect the fact that crowding simply intensifies dominant emotional tendencies. This 'intensification' explanation assumes that women are generally friendly (at least toward groups of other women) while men generally harbor feelings of distrust and competitiveness when in the presence of other males. Crowding simply amplifies these tendencies. A serious problem with this analysis is that in several of these studies males in uncrowded settings were more *positive* emotionally than females (cf. Paulus 1980). Intensifying this reaction should lead the men to become even more positive.

An alternative view that seems more plausible is that men and women adopt different coping strategies when stressed (Epstein and Karlin 1975). Women may react to stress, especially interpersonal stress, by utilizing social skills to mend fences and by finding common ground. This would easily account for the heightened cooperation and greater friendship found among women under crowded conditions. Males, in turn, may react to interpersonal stress with competitive tendencies for mastery and dominance. In fact, there is a good deal of evidence congruent with this perspective. Several studies indicate that crowded women engage in more mutual eye contact and self-disclosure than do uncrowded women (e.g. Ross *et al.* 1973). In addition, a series of studies by Hokanson and his colleagues (e.g. Hokanson *et al.* 1968) indicate that males prefer aggressive forms of coping when insulted (a form of interpersonal stress) while women prefer cooperative forms of coping in such situations.

In Hokanson's research, people found themselves insulted, betrayed or attacked by an instigator. This stress caused rapid increases in blood pressure. In one study, subjects were required to shock the instigator in a second part of the study. This opportunity to retaliate against the instigator lowered the blood pressure of male subjects, but not that of females. In a second study, people were given a choice between retaliation or cooperation following social stress. Women preferred a cooperative strategy and this served to lower their blood pressure. By contrast, males preferred to retaliate and, as before, this reduced the elevation in their blood pressure.

It seems, then, that males and females have been trained to manage social stress using very different strategies. Indeed Hokanson *et al.* (1968) demonstrated that these sex-based patterns could be reversed on the basis of careful conditioning, suggesting that training plays a key role in these sex differences. The observed sex differences in crowded settings seem linked to these different coping styles. From this perspective, the cooperative, non-punitive and friendly behavior of crowded women hardly indicates that they are experiencing crowding as a non-stressful experience as argued by Freedman *et al.* (1972). Rather, it is just the type of responding one would expect to see if crowding *is* stressful. This accounts for the fact that when one examines measures of task performance and physiology, both males and females show evidence that crowding is a disruptive experience (Paulus 1980).

Crowding and altruism

Crowding also has effects on our social behavior. Griffith and Veitch (1971) found that individuals rated another person more negatively in crowded conditions. Several other studies show that crowding leads to less cooperative and friendly actions in a variety of settings (college dorms, playgrounds, laboratories, etc.; cf. Paulus 1980). Crowding also appears to reduce feelings of social responsibility. Steblay (1987) reviewed some 35 studies, using a meta-analytic strategy, and found that prosocial behavior (e.g. cooperation/helpfulness) was more likely in smaller rather than in larger cities. In individual studies, Bickman *et al.* (1973) found that those living in a crowded dorm were less likely to go to the effort to mail a lost letter. Similarly, Cohen and Spacapan (1978) found that people emerging from a crowded shopping mall were less likely than uncrowded people to offer aid to an individual searching for a contact lens. As a final example, Jorgenson and Dukes (1976) found that in crowded periods, cafeteria users were less responsible when it came to returning their trays to the requested area. One reason crowding may suppress these forms of social behavior is that crowded situations threaten individuals with *attentional overload*. If one attended to everyone and all their demands, one would be overwhelmed (Milgram 1970). In this sense, the unfriendliness, callousness and noninvolvement seen in crowded settings (e.g. cities) may simply represent attempts to reduce or avoid overload (Milgram 1970).

Crowding and aggression

There is also some evidence that under certain conditions crowding heightens aggression and feelings of anger. Such affects have been observed in children (e.g. Rohe and Patterson 1974), prison inmates (e.g. Megargee 1977) and college students (e.g. Schettino and Bordon 1976). Not all studies find such results, however. Why this is true is not yet clear but several writers speculate that under certain conditions crowding produces withdrawal rather than aggression (cf. Paulus 1980) and this may account for some of the uneven results. Another key variable appears to be the availability of resources. Crowding, at least among children, is more likely to produce aggression if there are not enough toys to go around

(Rohe and Patterson 1974; Smith and Connolly 1977). Finally, gender is an important determinant of whether aggression will be increased by crowding. As we note above, a number of studies show that crowding heightens aggression, anger and feelings of hostility primarily among males. Thus, while aggression will not inevitably occur in crowded conditions, it does seem to increase in likelihood under certain conditions.

Crowding and physiology

Perhaps the most convincing research on the negative effects of crowding are studies that focus on how crowding affects health and physiology. Not surprisingly, the results indicate that crowding is not very good for you. In an interesting and humorous study, Middlemist et al. (1976) studied how crowding effects the onset of urination in public restrooms. The researchers, using a sort of periscope apparatus, determined that when men were crowded in a public restroom, urination onset was delayed. You may well wonder why the researchers would conduct such a bizarre investigation. In point of fact, urination onset is known to be delayed by the physiological arousal accompanying stress. As a result, this procedure provided a simple, if unusual means of establishing that crowding increased arousal. Moreover, the procedure used a natural setting and did not involve the elaborate and noticeable measurement procedures usually associated with physiological measurement (e.g. placing electrodes, drawing blood, taking blood pressure, etc.). There is a criticism we could direct at this study, however. Being crowded in a public bathroom is a very unique form of crowding that may trigger feelings of embarrassment rather than simple feelings of being crowded. Fortunately, there are several studies which provide corroboration for Middlemist et al.'s argument using less controversial crowding techniques. These studies examine crowding in laboratories (e.g. Aiello et al. 1979), in college dorms (Ray 1978) and prisons (e.g. D'Atri and Ostfeld 1975) and find that crowding elevates more traditional physiological indices such as skin conductance (Aiello et al. 1979) blood pressure (D'Atri and Ostfeld 1975; Ray 1978) pulse rate (Evans 1979) and palmar sweat (Saegert 1974). Finally, Lundberg (1976) collected urine samples from passengers as they exited from Swedish commuter trains and found that crowding elevated the level of epinephrine, a symptom of stress-related arousal. In short, crowding had been found to produce a variety of stress-related bodily reactions.

Crowding and health

As these data suggest, long-term crowding has also been associated with negative health-related outcomes. Crowding has been found to be related to increased complaints of illness in college dormitories (Ray 1978) and prisons (McCain *et al.* 1976; Ruback and Carr 1984), and increased illness on board navy ships (Dean *et al.* 1975). One study conducted in The Netherlands found that elderly men who lived in relatively crowded neighborhoods were more likely to be admitted to hospitals and were also more likely to die from heart disease (Levy and Herzog 1974). One particularly interesting project (Paulus *et al.* 1978; Cox *et al.* 1984) examined prison records for an entire prison system for an 8-year period. This project found that the death rate from various forms of cardiovascular disease was substantially higher in those years where the prison population was high. A skeptic might still argue that this result occurred more because of inadequate staffing in those years or some other coincidental form of stress. To address that issue, Paulus *et al.* (1978) examined prisoners at one point in time and found those living in the more crowded areas to have elevated levels of systolic blood pressure – an index of arousal. Despite these data, there are still those who remain skeptical of the assertion that crowding has negative effects on health and mortality (Ruback and Innes 1988). However, this skeptical stance is seriously challenged by the converging findings from field research, laboratory studies and archival investigations, indicating that long-term crowding is capable of producing negative effects on a variety of health-related measures.

Naturalistic research with children

In addition to these effects with adult populations, a few studies examine the impact of long-term crowding on children. Rodin (1976) examined the persistence and desire for control among grade school and high school children living in public low-income housing. Her hypothesis was that those living in crowded conditions would be unaccustomed to having meaningful control over their environment. Imagine being a child in an overcrowded apartment trying to sleep or study or read while someone, perhaps in the same room, is arguing, playing music or just having an animated conversation on the phone. Rodin hypothesized that such children would eventually resign themselves to a world where they feel little sense of control or power; a state that psychologists refer to as learned helplessness. Learned helplessness is thought to lead to feelings of apathy, depression, low creativity and poor task persistence. The child feels, 'Why try? What I do never has any impact'. Rodin found several of these effects. Those children who lived in the most crowded apartments persisted less at a task following an initial failure. Moreover, when they were successful, they were more likely to let the experimenter select the rewarding treat rather than select it themselves. Thus, they were more likely to relinquish control to the experimenter.

In short, children from chronically crowded homes showed several signs of learned helplessness in this study. Other studies on children by Cohen and his associates have focused on the effects of noise, an important byproduct of overcrowding. One project (Cohen et al. 1980) examined the effects of sudden uncontrollable noise by studying children who attended schools located in the glide path of Los Angeles International, one of the world's largest airports. These children showed greater elevations in blood pressure and lower task persistence on a maze puzzle than children in comparison schools. This last finding resembles the results reported by Rodin (1976). In a second project, Cohen et al. (1973) examined children who lived in a high-rise public housing building that spanned a major urban interstate highway. As you can imagine, the noise levels in this building were far above normal. Cohen et al. tested children in the relative quiet of their school. They found those children living on the lower floors of the apartment building, where the noise was higher, had poorer ability at auditory discrimination and lower reading ability than those on the higher floors. These effects were not due to loss of hearing on the part of the children but rather to their failure, even in a quiet environment, to discriminate accurately between spoken words that sounded quite similar (e.g. ice and nice).

Mediating variables

This array of findings should make it clear that despite the early optimism of Freedman et al.'s (1972) arguments, a good deal of evidence illustrates that crowding can have a variety of negative and serious effects, particularly on health and social behavior. In fairness, however, the crowding data are consistant with Freedman's view that high social density does not invariably produce negative effects on behavior. Indeed, researchers have emphasized that some forms of crowding seem more distressing than others, and are more likely to trigger negative effects and psychological feelings of crowding (Fleming et al. 1987). Not surprisingly, one goal of social researchers has been to determine which conditions seem likely to minimize such negative effects. As we have already seen, two factors that seem to elevate crowding stress are competitive situations and the extent to which physical contact seems hard to avoid. Another key factor appears to be how much control individuals have over such things as who they must interact with and how long they must remain in the crowded or stressful setting (Rodin et al. 1978).

In the last chapter we saw that the negative after-effects of stressful noise could be almost completely eliminated if people felt that they could stop the noise if they wanted to (Glass and Singer 1972). Several crowding studies show quite similar effects. Sherrod (1974) found that control over crowding reduced negative after-effects such as those found in Glass and Singer's (1972) noise research. Rodin et al. (1978) ran a crowding study on an elevator using a team of confederates. In one key condition, the subject was maneuvered so that she or he stood next to the control panel of the lift. This gave the subject the option of pushing a button and exiting at any floor. These subjects reported feeling much less crowded than subjects who did not have such control. In a second experiment people worked on a prolonged task under very crowded conditions. One person was given control over when the group session ended. This individual felt less crowded than people who had no control. Finally, by analyzing urine samples, Singer et al. (1978) found that on crowded Swedish commuter trains, passengers who boarded the train first showed the lowest levels of epinephrine. Presumably, this occurred since these passengers had time to 'stake out' and arrange their territory during a relatively uncrowded period, thereby elevating their feelings of control.

While these studies examine the effects of actually controlling the duration and nature of the crowding experience, other forms of control exist. We can simply have knowledge about what the crowding experience will feel like, where and when it will be worst, why it exists and how long it will last. This form of coping is referred to as informational control. A number of studies indicate that such control is beneficial (e.g. Baum *et al.* 1981). For example, Langer and Saegert (1977) informed shoppers how they were likely to feel just before they entered a crowded shopping area. These people performed 'shopping tasks' better and reported feeling more positive about their time in the store than shoppers not provided with such forewarning.

Crowding and architecture

The fact that control appears to soften the impact of crowding has led researchers to examine architectural features that might increase or decrease the possibility of control. Baum and Valins (1977) hypothesized that living on long corridor dormitories is a situation that minimizes control over whom one comes into contact with. This is because these settings limit residents to one or two major exits, a single large cooperative bathroom, and one shared lounge per floor. Suites of rooms, in contrast, provide substantially more control (i.e. privacy). Suites are usually three or four sleeping rooms sharing a common living room, bath and exit. These researchers took advantage of the fact that college students at a certain campus lived either in traditional dorm rooms or in a suite. As they predicted, dorm residents reported greater feelings of crowding and helplessness than suite residents, and were generally more withdrawn and less friendly with their floormates than suite residents. Even when these people were tested in the laboratory, dorm residents sat further away from others and generated less eye contact than suite residents when waiting for an experiment to begin. Additionally, dorm residents were less disturbed than suite residents when they were consistently ignored during laboratory group discussions. Clearly, suite residents seemed less withdrawn and generally were less disturbed by their campus housing than were dorm residents. These results were recently replicated in a study of urban poor males in India. In this research Evans *et al.* (1989) found that those who lived in particularly crowded conditions reported greater desires to be left alone and lower levels of social support. These data suggest that crowding may disrupt social support and this in turn could well have effects on psychological and physical health.

In a related study, Fleming *et al.* (1987) reasoned that residents of an urban neighborhood would feel that they had less control over public and semi-public areas in their neighborhood (sidewalks, front yards, streets and porches) in cases where there were markets and pharmacies at the end of the block. This prediction was based on the fact that there would be more pedestrian traffic on sidewalks and a higher proportion of 'strangers to the neighborhood' on 'store streets'. As a result, residents would have less control over whom they met on a given day. These notions were strongly supported. Residents on store streets felt more crowded, and reported more depression, anxiety and physical symptoms than those on non-store streets. In addition, on a urinary measure, those living on store streets showed elevated counts of epinephrine and norepinephrine, suggesting chronic physiological signs of stress. In short, two studies indicate that architectural and structural features which reduce uncontrollable contact with others are effective factors in reducing the potential stress of crowded settings. Thus, it would appear that manipulating architectural features may prove useful as one means of modifying the effects of crowding.

One architectural strategy seems particularly promising. A good deal of research indicates that a very common response to crowding is to reduce our eye contact with others (e.g. Argyle and Dean 1965; Baum and Koman 1976). Notice the number of people carefully studying the floor number display in any crowded elevator if you wish to see evidence of this phenomenon. This suggests that crowding will be less stressful if there is an easy and socially graceful way to avoid eye contact. There are a variety of strategies that can be employed for such a purpose. Windows, interesting pictures, graphics and video displays could be quite useful here. In public transportation and office settings, we may be able to reduce feelings of crowding by the careful use of partitions and by placing chairs at different levels or at varying directions to minimize eye contact. L-shaped rooms also hold promise since people in one 'leg' of the L are not capable of seeing those in the other leg. For the same reason, thin rectangular rooms seem preferable to square rooms because fewer people can be seen in the former (Desor 1972). Preliminary research on some of these features already exists

(Desor 1972; Worchel and Teddlie 1976; Baum and Davis 1980), but a good deal more will be necessary before we fully understand the possibilities of architectural interventions.

Summary

It seems likely that the world will face serious problems of over-crowding by the year 2000. Research on animals indicates that crowding can have very serious effects on mating, social behavior, care of the young and health status. Research with humans also indicates that crowding can have a number of negative effects. Crowding has been shown to impair task performance on certain (stress-sensitive) tasks, depress helping behavior, increase social withdrawal and increase feelings of hostility. In addition, crowding has been found to be associated with poorer health outcomes and a variety of biological changes including increased blood pressure, skin conductance and palmar sweat. Indeed, several studies of prolonged crowding have reported greater death rates in crowded settings.

One major consequence of chronic overcrowding appears to be feelings of learned helplessness and low personal control. This suggests that increasing feelings of control may be a particularly effective strategy for minimizing the stress of crowding. Several studies support this view. These studies suggest why high social density has not always been found to produce negative effects (e.g. Freedman et al. 1971). High social density may provoke feelings of crowding and consequent stress reactions only when it decreases feelings of control by raising the likelihood of unpredictable and unwanted social intrusions (e.g. Heller et al. 1977; Fleming et al. 1987). Thus, there is some basis for Freedman's early arguments that high social density, by itself, has few serious effects on health and behavior. This argument, however, offers small solace. If crowding is severe enough, feelings of low control will often be inevitable. Imagine you have driven for two hours on a sweltering day in heavy traffic to get to the beach only to find there is nowhere to park. Nowhere! A good reason perhaps to go *out of control* and park on the sidewalk. In short, the crowding data when viewed as a whole have ominous implications for a population that seems ordained to experience serious overcrowding in most sections of the world. Even in the 'wide open spaces' of the

American Midwest, signs of this crowding crunch can be seen. One of the co-authors lives some 10 miles from his Midwestern university. Ten years ago these miles were filled with gently rolling farm fields, pasture and open woodland. Currently, they are filled with housing tracts. He now has a bumper sticker which reads 'There's nothing in Iowa – Stay away!!'

Suggestions for further reading

Calhoun, J. B. (1962). Population density and social psychology. *Scientific American*, 206, 139–48.

Erlich, P. (1968). *The Population Bomb*. New York: Ballantine.

Heller, J. F., Groff, B. D. and Solomon, S. H. (1977). Toward an understanding of crowding: The role of physical interaction. *Journal of Personality and Social Psychology*, 35, 183–90.

Paulus, P. B., McCain, G. and Cox V. C. (1978). Death rates, psychiatric commitments, blood pressure, and perceived crowding as a function of institutional crowding. *Environmental Psychology and Nonverbal Behavior*, 3, 107–16.

Rodin, J., Solomon, S. and Metcalf, J. (1978). Role of control in mediating perceptions of density. *Journal of Personality and Social Psychology*, 36, 988–99.

/11/ CONCLUDING THOUGHTS

At one level, research on groups is loaded with apparent para-
doxes. The social support literature indicates that groups can have
a soothing influence while research on social facilitation and
crowding suggests that others can elevate arousal and tension;
sometimes group settings can elevate performance while at other
times social loafing and free riding are induced by groups; groups
can dramatically elevate aggressive behavior, but cooperative group
experiences represent one of the most powerful means of reducing
prejudice and hostility. These superficial contradictions, however,
seem less 'paradoxical' once one considers why each phenomenon
occurs. Thus, for example, a careful consideration of task and
situational variables makes it clear that social loafing occurs in
some settings and social facilitation occurs in others because on
some tasks, co-workers enhance comparability and evaluative concerns while on other tasks, co-workers minimize these factors.

In short, if you ask how groups effect motivation, perception,
performance, behavior, aggression and problem solving you will
not receive a simple answer. There are, however, a few conclusions that do seem valid. First, group settings can have dramatic
effects on all these phenomena. Predicting precisely what type of
effect this will be requires a careful analysis of situational and task
features as well as some understanding of the structure and composition of the group in question. Secondly, it seems clear that
groups can have a profound impact on what we think is true and
good; what we think we should do; indeed, even on what we think
we are seeing and hearing. Groups can not only contribute to
our initial impressions but group discussion can also produce

polarization of those impressions under appropriate conditions. Major contributing factors to these social influence phenomena are our tendencies to trust a consensus of our peers and our reluctance to incur their wrath. These tendencies can lead us to suppress our private reservations (e.g. Janis 1972), to refrain from offering information that we feel is not commonly shared (e.g. Stasser and Titus 1985) and to perform extreme behaviors that violate our own private values (e.g. Milgram 1974). Thirdly, groups are a major source of comfort, orientation and sense of identity for us. This would seem to explain why even rejection and ridicule from total strangers are so avidly avoided. Our inclination to please those around us is apparently so deeply overlearned that we reflexively avoid offending others with deviant opinions and actions even when the consequences for doing so would be fairly minimal.

Fourthly, it seems clear that group process phenomena have a good deal of significance for many contemporary world problems. Research on conformity, groupthink, social decision schemes and group polarization have direct relevance for problems ranging from jury work to international policy decision-making. Research on social support, social dilemmas, social loafing, free riding and crowding has obvious relevance for a variety of health, economic and environmental issues. For example, given the powerful therapeutic effect of social support, should hospitals provide a more structured means of incorporating family members into health treatment? Alternatively, can we successfully apply principles developed in social dilemma research so that we as a species can act as more careful stewards of our dwindling planetary resources?

Research on group aggression and cooperative problem solving offer insights which we hope aid us in alleviating racial, ethnic, religious and nationalistic hostility. These, of course, are all large and complex applied problems that will not be solved by any one academic discipline. Nevertheless, research on group processes can make a distinct contribution to better understanding and controlling a number of these contemporary challenges.

REFERENCES

Acorn, D. A., Hamilton, D. L. and Sherman, S. J. (1988). Generalization of biased perceptions of groups based on illusory correlations. *Social Cognition*, 6, 345–72.

Adams, J. S. (1963). Toward an understanding of inequity. *Journal of Abnormal and Social Psychology*, 67, 422–36.

Adams, J. S. (1965). Inequity in social exchange. In L. Berkowitz (ed.) *Advances in Experimental Social Psychology*, Vol. 2. New York: Academic Press.

Adams, J. S. and Rosenbaum, W. B. (1962). The relationship of worker productivity to cognitive dissonance about wage inequities. *Journal of Applied Psychology*, 46, 161–4.

Ader, R. and Tatum, R. (1963). Free-operant avoidance conditioning in individual and paired human subjects. *Journal of the Experimental Analysis of Behavior*, 6, 357–9.

Aiello, J. R., Nicosia, G. and Thompson, D. E. (1979). Physiological, social, and behavioral consequences of crowding on children and adolescents. *Child Development*, 50, 195–202.

Allen, K. M., Blascovich, J., Tomaka, J. and Kelsey, R. M. (1991). The presence of human friends and pet dogs as moderators of autonomic responses to stress in women. *Journal of Personality and Social Psychology: Interpersonal Relations and Group Processes*, 61, 582–9.

Allison, S. T. and Messick, D. M. (1985). Effects of experience on performance in a replenishable resource trap. *Journal of Personality and Social Psychology*, 49, 943–8.

Allport, F. H. (1924). *Social psychology*. Boston: Houghton-Mifflin.

Amoroso, D. and Walters, R. (1969). Effects of anxiety and socially mediated anxiety reduction on paired-associate learning. *Journal of Personality and Social Psychology*, 11, 388–96.

Argyle, M. and Dean, J. (1965). Eye-contact, distance and affiliation. *Sociometry*, 28, 289–304.

Aronson, E. (1968). Dissonance theory: Progress and problems. In R. P. Abelson, E. Aronson, W. J. McGuire, T. M. Newcomb, M. J. Rosenberg and P. H. Tanenbaum (eds) *Theories of Cognitive Consistency: A Sourcebook*, pp. 5–28. Chicago: Rand McNally & Company.

Aronson, E., Blaney, N., Stephan, C., Sikes, J. and Snapp, M. (1978). *The Jig-Saw Classroom*. London: Sage.

Asch, S. E. (1955). Opinions and social pressure. *Scientific American*, 193, 31–55.

Asch, S. E. (1956). Studies of independence and submission to group pressure: I. On minority of one against a unanimous majority. *Psychological Monographs*, 70 (9, Whole N. 417).

Axelrod, R. (1984). *The evolution of cooperation*. New York: Basic Books.

Back, K. W. (1951). Influence through social communication. *Journal of Abnormal and Social Psychology*, 46, 9–23.

Bales, R. F. (1958). Task roles and social roles in problem-solving groups. In E. E. Maccoby, T. M. Newcomb and E. L. Hartley (eds) *Readings in Social Psychology*. New York: Holt.

Bales, R. F. and Strodtbeck, F. L. (1951). Phases in group problem solving. *Journal of Abnormal and Social Psychology*, 46, 485–95.

Bales, R. F., Strodtbeck, F. L., Mills, T. M. and Roseborough, M. E. (1951). Channels of communication in small groups. *American Sociological Review*, 16, 461–8.

Ballew v. Georgia (1978). *United States Reports*, 435, 222–45.

Bandura, A., Ross, D. and Ross, S. A. (1961). Transmission of aggression through imitation of aggressive models. *Journal of Abnormal and Social Psychology*, 63, 575–82.

Baron, R. A. and Kepner, C. R. (1970). Model's behavior and attraction toward the model as determinants of adult aggressive behavior. *Journal of Personality and Social Psychology*, 14, 335–44.

Baron, R. S. (1970). *Anonymity, deindividuation and aggression*. Unpublished doctoral dissertation, University of Minnesota.

Baron, R. S. (1986). Distraction-conflict theory: Progress and problems. In L. Berkowitz (ed.) *Advances in experimental social psychology*, Vol. 19, pp. 1–40. New York: Academic Press.

Baron, R. S. and Roper, G. (1976). Reaffirmation of social comparison views of choice shifts: Averaging and extremity effects in an autokinetic situation. *Journal of Personality and Social Psychology*, 33, 521–30.

Baron, R. S., Baron, P. H. and Miller, N. (1973). The relation between distraction and persuasion. *Psychological Bulletin*, 80, 310–23.

Baron, R. S., Roper, G. and Baron, P. H. (1974). Group discussion and the stingy shift. *Journal of Personality and Social Psychology*, 30, 538–45.

Baron, R. S., Moore, D. L. and Sanders, G. S. (1978). Distraction as a source of drive in social facilitation research. *Journal of Personality and Social Psychology*, 36, 816–24.

Baron, R. S., Cutrona, C. E., Hicklin, D., Russell, D. W. and Lubaroff, D. M. (1990). Social support and immune function among spouses of cancer patients. *Journal of Personality and Social Psychology*, 59, 344–52.

Baum, A. and Davis, G. E. (1980). Reducing the stress of high-density living: An architectural intervention. *Journal of Personality and Social Psychology*, 38, 471–81.

Baum, A. and Koman, S. (1976). Differential response to anticipated crowding: Psychological effects of social and spatial density. *Journal of Personality and Social Psychology*, 34, 526–36.

Baum, A. and Valins, S. (1977). *Architecture and Social Behavior: Psychological Studies in Social Density*. Hillsdale, NJ: Erlbaum.

Baum, A., Fisher, J. D. and Solomon, S. (1981). Type of information, familiarity, and the reduction of crowding stress. *Journal of Personality and Social Psychology*, 40, 11–23.

Baun, M., Bergstrom, N., Langston, N. and Thoma, L. (1984). Physiological effects of human/companion animal bonding. *Nursing Research*, 33 (3).

Beaman, A. L. and Klentz, B. (1983). The supposed physical attractiveness bias against supporters of the women's movement: A meta-analysis. *Personality and Social Psychology Bulletin*, 9, 544–50.

Beaman, A. L., Klentz, B., Diener, E. and Svanum, S. (1979). Objective self-awareness and transgression in children: A field study. *Journal of Personality and Social Psychology*, 37, 1835–46.

Berk, R. (1974). *Collective behavior*. Dubuque, IA: Wm. C. Brown.

Berkman, L. F. and Syme, L. S. (1979). Social networks and mortality. *American Journal of Epidemiology*, 109, 186–204.

Berkowitz, L. (1989). Frustration-aggression hypothesis: Examination and reformulation. *Psychological Bulletin*, 106, 59–73.

Berkowitz, L. and LePage, A. (1967). Weapons as aggression-eliciting stimuli. *Journal of Personality and Social Psychology*, 7, 202–7.

Bermant, G. and Coppock, R. (1973). Outcomes of six- and twelve-member jury trials: An analysis of 128 civil cases in the State of Washington. *Washington Law Review*, 48, 593–6.

Berscheid, E. and Walster (Hatfield), E. (1978). *Interpersonal Attraction*. Reading, Mass: Addison-Wesley.

Bickman, L., Teger, A., Gabriele, T., McLaughlin, C., Berger, M. and Sunaday, E. (1973). Dormitory density and helping behavior. *Environment and Behavior*, 5, 465–90.

Blascovich, J., Ginsburg, G. P. and Veach, T. L. (1975). A pluralistic explanation of choice shifts on the risk dimension. *Journal of Personality and Social Psychology*, 31, 422–9.

Blumenthal, K., Kahn, L., Andrews, F. M. and Head, K. B. (1972). *Justifying Violence: The Attitude of American Men*. Ann Arbor Institute for Social Research.

Bond, C. F. (1982). Social facilitation: A self-presentational view. *Journal of Personality and Social Psychology*, 42, 1042–50.

Bond, C. F. and Titus, L. J. (1983). Social facilitation: A meta-analysis of 241 studies. *Psychological Bulletin*, 94, 265–92.

Boster, F. and Hale, J. (1990). Responsive scale ambiguity as a moderator of the choice shift. *Communication Research*, in press.

Bowlby, J. (1958). The nature of a child's tie to his mother. *International Journal of Psycho-Analysis*, 39, 350–73.

Brann, P. and Foddy, M. (1987). Trust and the consumption of a deteriorating common resource. *Journal of Conflict Resolution*, 31, 615–30.

Braver, S. L. and Wilson, L. (1984). A laboratory study of social contracts as a solution to public goods problems: Surviving on the lifeboat. Paper presented at the Western Social Science Association, San Diego, April, 1984.

Bray, R. M. (1974). *Decision rules, attitude similarity, and jury decision making*. Unpublished doctoral dissertation, University of Illinois, Urbana.

Bray, R. M. and Kerr, N. L. (1982). Methodological considerations in the study of the psychology of the courtroom. In N. Kerr and R. Bray (eds) *The Psychology of the Courtroom*. New York: Academic Press.

Bray, R. M., Kerr, N. L. and Atkin, R. S. (1978). Group size, problem difficulty, and group performance on unitary disjunctive tasks. *Journal of Personality and Social Psychology*, 36, 1224–40.

Brewer, M. B. (1981). Ethnocentrism and its role in interpersonal trust. In M. Brewer and B. Collins (eds) *Scientific Inquiry and the Social Sciences*. San Francisco: Jossey-Bass.

Brewer, M. B. and Campbell, D. T. (1976) *Ethnocentrism and intergroup attitudes: East African Evidence*. New York: Halsted.

Brewer, M. B. and Kramer, R. M. (1986). Choice behavior in social dilemmas: Effects of social identity, group size, and decision framing. *Journal of Personality and Social Psychology*, 50, 543–9.

Brewer, M. B. and Miller, N. (1984). Beyond the contact hypotheses: Theoretical perspectives on desegregation. In N. Miller and M. B. Brewer (eds) *Groups in Contact: The Psychology of Desegregation* (pp. 281–302). New York: Academic Press.

Brickel, C. (1984). The clinical use of pets with the aged. *Clinical Gerontologist*, 2 (4).

Brickner, M. A. (1987). *Locked into performance: Goal setting as a moderator of the social loafing effect.* Paper presented at the annual meeting of the Midwestern Psychological Association, Chicago.

Brickner, M. A., Harkins, S. and Ostrom, T. (1986). Personal involvement: Thought provoking implications for social loafing. *Journal of Personality and Social Psychology*, 51, 763–9.

Brown, I. D. and Poulton, E. C. (1961). Measuring the spare 'mental capacity' of car drivers by a subsidiary task. *Ergonomics*, 4, 35–40.

Brown, R. (1987). *Social Psychology: The second edition*. New York: Free Press.

Brown, R. C. and Tedeschi, J. T. (1976). Determinants of perceived aggression. *Journal of Social Psychology*, 100, 77–87.

Brown, R. J. (1984). The effects of intergroup similarity and cooperative vs. competitive orientation on intergroup discrimination. *British Journal of Social Psychology*, 23, 21–33.

Brown, R. J. (1988). *Group Processes: Dynamics within and between groups*. New York: Basil Blackwell.

Brown, R. J. and Abrams, D. (1986). The effects of intergroup similarity and goal interdependence on intergroup attitudes and task performance. *Journal of Experimental Social Psychology*, 22, 78–92.

Brown, R. W. (1954). Mass phenomena. In G. Lindzey (ed.) *Handbook of Social Psychology*, Vol. 2, pp. 833–76. Cambridge, MA: Addison-Wesley.

Bruning, J. L., Capage, J. E., Kozuh, J. F., Young, P. F. and Young, W. E. (1968). Socially induced drive and range of cue utilization. *Journal of Personality and Social Psychology*, 9, 242–4.

Burch v. Louisiana (1979). *United States Reports*, 441, 130–9.

Burnstein, E. and Vinokur, A. (1973). Testing two classes of theories about group induced shifts in individual choice. *Journal of Experimental Social Psychology*, 9, 123–37.

Burnstein, E. and Vinokur, A. (1977). Persuasive argumentation and social comparison as determinants of attitude polarization. *Journal of Experimental Social Psychology*, 13, 315–32.

Bushman, B. J. and Cooper, H. M. (1990). Effects of alcohol on human aggression: an integrative research review. *Psychological Bulletin*, 107, 341–54.

Business Week (1985). The double standard that's setting worker against worker. *Business Week*, April 8, p. 70.

Business Week (1983). The revolutionary wage deal at G. M.'s Packard Electric. *Business Week*, August 29, p. 54.

Cacioppo, J. T., Rourke, P., Tassinary, L., Marshall-Goodall, B. and Baron, R. S. (1990). Rudimentary physiological effects of mere observation. *Psychophysiology*, 27, 177–86.

Caddick, B. (1982). Perceived illegitimacy and intergroup relations. In H. Tajfel (ed.) *Social Identity and Intergroup Relations*. Cambridge: Cambridge University Press.

Calhoun, J. B. (1962). Population density and social psychology. *Scientific American*, 206, 139–48.

Callaway, M. R., Marriott, R. G. and Esser, J. K. (1985). Effects of dominance on group decision making: Toward a stress-reduction explanation of groupthink. *Journal of Personality and Social Psychology*, 49, 949–52.

Campbell, D. T. (1956). Enhancement of contrast as a compositive habit. *Journal of Abnormal and Social Psychology*, 53, 350–5.

Campbell, D. T. (1961). Conformity in psychology's theories of acquired behavioral dispositions. In I. A. Berg and B. M. Bass (eds) *Conformity and Deviation*. New York: Harper.

Campbell, D. T. (1967). Stereotypes and the perception of group differences. *American Psychologist*, 22, 812–29.

Campbell, J. D. and Fairey, P. J. (1989). Informational and normative routes to conformity: The effect of faction size as a function of norm extremity and attention to the stimulus. *Journal of Personality and Social Psychology*, 57, 457–68.

Cantor, J. R., Zillman, D. and Einsiedel, E. F. (1978). Female responses to provocation after exposure to aggressive and erotic films. *Communication Research*, 9, 177–86.

Cappelli, P. and Sherer, P. D. (1990). Assessing worker attitudes under a two-tier wage plan. *Industrial and Labor Relations Review*, 43, 225–44.

Carlson, M. and Miller, N. (1988). The differential effects of social and nonsocial negative events on aggressiveness. *Sociology and Social Research*, 72, 155–8.

Carlson, M., Marcus-Newhall, A. and Miller, N. (1990). The effects of situational aggression cues: A quantitative review. *Journal of Personality and Social Psychology*, 58, 622–33.

Carver, C. S. and Scheier, M. F. (1981). The self-attention-induced feedback loop and social facilitation. *Journal of Experimental Social Psychology*, 17, 545–68.

Cass, R. C. and Edney, J. J. (1978). The commons dilemma: A simulation testing resource visibility and territorial division. *Human Ecology*, 6, 371–86.

Cauce, A. M., Felner, R. D. and Primavera, J. (1982). Social support in high-risk adolescents: Structural components and adaptive impact. *American Journal of Community Psychology*, 10, 417–28.

Clark, J. V. (1958). *A preliminary investigation of some unconscious assumptions affecting labor efficiency in eight supermarkets*. Unpublished Ph.D. dissertation, Harvard University.

Clark, K. B. and Clark, M. P. (1947). Racial identification and preference in Negro children. In. T. M. Newcomb and E. D. Hartley (eds) *Readings in Social Psychology*. NUC: Holt, Rinehart & Winston.

Cobb, S. (1976). Social support as a moderator of life stress. *Psychosomatic Medicine*, 38, 300–14.

Cohen, S. (1978). Environmental load and the allocation of attention. In A. Baum, J. E. Singer and S. Valins (eds) *Advances in environmental psychology*, Vol. 1. Hillsdale, NJ: Erlbaum.

Cohen, S. (1980). After effects of stress on human performance and social behavior: A review of research and theory. *Psychological Bulletin*, 88, 82–108.

Cohen, S. and McKay, G. (1984). Social support, stress and the buffering hypothesis: A theoretical analysis. In A. Baum, J. E. Singer and S. E. Taylor (eds) *Handbook of Psychology and Health*, Vol. 4. Hillsdale, NJ: Erlbaum.

Cohen, S. and Spacapan, S. (1978). The after effects of stress: An attentional interpretation. *Environmental Psychology and Nonverbal Behavior*, 3 (1), 43–57.

Cohen, S. and Syme, S. C. (1985). *Social Support and Health*. New York: Academic Press.

Cohen, S. and Wills, T. (1985). Stress, social support, and the buffering hypothesis. *Psychological Bulletin*, 98, 310–57.

Cohen, S., Glass, D. C. and Singer, J. E. (1973). Apartment noise, auditory discrimination, and reading ability in children. *Journal of Experimental Social Psychology*, 9, 407–22.

Cohen, S., Evans, G. W., Krantz, D. S. and Stokols, D. (1980). Physiological, motivational and cognitive effects of aircraft noise on children. *American Psychologist*, 35, 231–43.

Costanza, R. S., Derlega, V. J. and Winstead, B. A. (1988). Positive and negative forms of social support: Effects of conversational topics on coping with stress among same-sex friends. *Journal of Experimental Social Psychology*, 24, 182–93.

Cotton, J. L. and Baron, R. S. (1980). Anonymity, persuasive arguments and choice shifts. *Social Psychology Quarterly*, 43 (4), 391–404.

Cottrell, N. B. (1972). Social facilitation. In C. G. McClintock (ed.) *Experimental Social Psychology*, pp. 185–236. New York: Holt.

Cottrell, N. B., Wack, D. L., Sekerak, G. J. and Rittle, R. H. (1968). Social facilitation of dominant responses by the presence of an audience and the mere presence of others. *Journal of Personality and Social Psychology*, 9, 245–50.

Courtright, J. A. (1978). A laboratory investigation of groupthink. *Communication Monographs*, 43, 229–46.

Cox, V. C., Paulus, P. B. and McCain, G. (1984). Prison crowding research: The relevance for prison housing standards and a general approach regarding crowding and phenomena. *American Psychologist*, 39, 1148–60.

Crook, J. H. (1981). The evolutionary ethology of social processes in man. In H. Kellerman (ed.) *Group Cohesion*. New York: Grune & Stratton.

Cunha, D. (1985). *Interpersonal trust as a function of social orientation.* Unpublished doctoral dissertation, University of Delaware.

Cutrona, C. E. (1990). Stress and social support: In search of optimal matching. *Journal of Social and Clinical Psychology*, 9, 3–14.

Cutrona, C. E. and Troutman, E. (1986). Social support, infant temperament, and parenting self-efficacy. *Child Development*, 57, 1507–18.

Dahlof, L., Hard, E. and Larsson, K. (1977). Influence of maternal stress on offspring sexual behavior. *Animal Behavior*, 25, 958–63.

Dakof, G. A. and Taylor, S. E. (1990). Victims' perceptions of social support: What is helpful from whom? *Journal of Personality and Social Psychology*, 58, 80–9.

Darley, J. M. (1966). Fear and social comparison as determinants of conformity behavior. *Journal of Personality and Social Psychology*, 4, 73–8.

Darley, J. M. and Latané, B. (1968). Bystander intervention in emergencies: Diffusion of responsibility. *Journal of Personality and Social Psychology*, 8, 377–83.

D'Atri, D. A. and Ostfeld, A. M. (1975). Crowding: Its effects on the elevation of blood pressure in a prison setting. *Preventative Medicine*, 4, 550–66.

Davis, J. H. (1969). *Group performance.* Reading, MA: Addison-Wesley.

Davis, J. H. (1973). Group decision and social interaction: A theory of social decision schemes. *Psychological Review*, 80, 97–125.

Davis, J. H. (1982). Social interaction as a combinational process in group decision. In H. Brandstatter, J. Davis and G. Stocker-Kreichgauer (eds) *Group Decision Making.* London: Academic Press.

Davis, J. H. and Restle, F. (1963). The analysis of problems and prediction of group problem solving. *Journal of Abnormal and Social Psychology*, 66, 103–16.

Davis, J. H. and Kerr, N. L. (1986). Thought experiments and the problem of sparse data in small-group performance research. In P. Goodman (ed.) *Designing effective work groups.* New York: Jossey-Bass.

Davis, J. H., Kerr, N. L., Atkin, R., Holt, R. and Meek, D. (1975). The decision processes of 6- and 12-person mock juries assigned unanimous and 2/3 majority rules. *Journal of Personality and Social Psychology*, 32, 1–14.

Dawes, R. M. (1989). Statistical criteria for establishing a truly false consensus effect. *Journal of Experimental Social Psychology*, 25, 1–17.

Dawes, R. M., McTavish, J. and Shaklee, H. (1977). Behavior, communication, and assumptions about other people's behavior in a commons dilemma situation. *Journal of Personality and Social Psychology*, 35, 1–11.

Dean, L. M., Pugh, W. M. and Gunderson, E. K. (1975). Spatial and perceptual components of crowding: Effects on health and satisfaction. *Environment and Behavior*, 7, 225–36.

Desmond, E. W. (1987). Out in the open. *Time*, Nov. 30, pp. 80–90.

Desor, J. A. (1972). Toward a psychological theory of crowding. *Journal of Personality and Social Psychology*, 21, 79–83.

Deutsch, M. (1973). *The Resolution of Conflict: Constructive and Destructive Processes*. New Haven: Yale University Press.

Deutsch, M. and Gerard, H. B. (1955). A study of normative and informational social influence upon individual judgement. *Journal of Abnormal and Social Psychology*, 51, 629–36.

DeVries, D. L. and Edwards, K. J. (1974). Student teams and learning games: Their effects on cross-race and cross-sex interaction. *Journal of Educational Psychology*, 66, 741–9.

Diehl, M. and Stoebe, W. (1987). Productivity loss in brainstorming groups: Toward solution of a riddle. *Journal of Personality and Social Psychology*, 53, 497–509.

Diener, E. (1976). Effects of prior destructive behavior, anonymity, and group presence on deindividuation and aggression. *Journal of Personality and Social Psychology*, 33, 497–507.

Diener, E. (1980). Deindividuation: The absence of self-awareness and self-regulation in group members. In P. Paulus (ed.) *The Psychology of Group Influence*. Hillsdale, NJ: Erlbaum.

Diener, E. and Wallboom, M. (1976). Effects of self-awareness on antinormative behavior. *Journal of Research in Personality*, 10, 107–11.

Diener, E., Fraser, S. C., Beaman, A. L. and Kelem, R. T. (1976). Effects of deindividuating variables on stealing by Halloween trick-or-treaters. *Journal of Personality and Social Psychology*, 33, 178–83.

Dion, K. L., Baron, R. S. and Miller, N. (1970). Why do groups make riskier decisions than individuals? In L. Berkowitz (ed.) *Advances in Experimental Social Psychology*, Vol. 5, pp. 306–77. New York: Academic Press.

Dollard, J. (1938). Hostility and fear in social life. *Social Forces*, 17, 15–25.

Doms, M. and van Avermaet, E. (1980). Majority influence, minority influence, and conversion behavior: A replication. *Journal of Experimental Social Psychology*, 16, 283–92.

Donnerstein, E. and Hallum, J. (1978). Facilitating effects of erotica on aggression against women. *Journal of Personality and Social Psychology*, 36, 1270–7.

Donnerstein, E., Donnerstein, M., Simons, S. and Dittrichs, R. (1972). Variables in interracial aggression. *Journal of Personality and Social Psychology*, 22, 236–45.

Duval, S. and Wicklund, R. A. (1972). *A Theory of Objective Self-awareness*. New York: Academic Press.

Eagly, A. H. (1978). Sex differences in influenceability. *Psychological Bulletin*, 85, 86–116.

Eagly, A. H. and Steffen, V. J. (1986). Gender and aggressive behavior: A meta-analytic review of the social psychological literature. *Psychological Bulletin*, 100, 309–30.

Eagly, A. H., Wood, W. and Fishbaugh, L. (1981). Sex differences in conformity: Surveillance by the group as a determinant of male non-conformity. *Journal of Personality and Social Psychology*, 40, 384–94.

Easterbrook, J. A. (1959). The effects of emotion on cue-utilization and the organization of behavior. *Psychological Review*, 66, 183–201.

Ebbesen, E. B. and Bowers, R. J. (1974). Proportion of risky to conservative arguments in a group discussion and choice shifts. *Journal of Personality and Social Psychology*, 29, 316–27.

Eiser, J. R. and Stroebe, W. (1972). *Categorization and Social Judgment*. London: Academic Press.

Epley, S. W. (1974). Reduction of the behavioral effects of aversive stimulation by the presence of companions. *Psychological Bulletin*, 81, 271–83.

Epstein, Y. M. and Karlin, R. A. (1975). Effects of acute experimental crowding. *Journal of Applied Social Psychology*, 5, 34–53.

Erlich, P. (1968). *The Population Bomb*. New York: Ballantine.

Evan, W. M. and Simmons, R. G. (1969). Organizational effects of inequitable rewards: Two experiments in status inconsistency. *Administrative Science Quarterly*, 14, 224–37.

Evans, G. W. (1975). *Behavioral and Physiological Consequences of Crowding in Humans*. Unpublished doctoral dissertation, University of Massachusetts.

Evans, G. W. (1979). Behavioral and physiological consequences of crowding in humans. *Journal of Applied Social Psychology*, 9, 27–46.

Evans, G. W., Palsane, M. N., Lepore, S. J. and Martin, J. (1989). Residential density and psychological health: The mediating effects of social support. *Journal of Personality and Social Psychology*, 57, 994–9.

Farnham, A. (1989). Holding firm on affirmative action: *Fortune*, 119, 87–8.

Festinger, L. (1954). A theory of social comparison processes. *Human Relations*, 7, 117–40.

Fiedler, F. E. (1967). *A Theory of Leadership Effectiveness*. New York: McGraw-Hill.

Fisher, J. D., Bell, P. A. and Baum, A. (1984). *Experimental Psychology*, 2nd edn. New York: Holt, Rinehart & Winston.

Fiske, S. T. and Taylor, S. E. (1984). *Social Cognition*. Reading, Mass.: Addison-Wesley.

Fleming, R. and Baum, A. (1986). Social support and stress: The buffering effects of friendship. In V. J. Deriega and B. A. Winstead (eds) *Friendship and Social Interaction*, pp. 207–26. New York: Springer-Verlag.

Fleming, I., Baum, A. and Weiss, L. (1987). Social density and perceived control as mediators of crowding stress in high-density residential neighborhoods. *Journal of Personality and Social Psychology*, 52, 899–906.

Flowers, M. L. (1977). A laboratory test of some implications of Janis' groupthink hypothesis. *Journal of Personality and Social Psychology*, 35, 888–96.

Fodor, E. M. (1978). Stimulated work climate as an influence on choice of leadership style. *Personality and Social Psychology Bulletin*, 4, 111–14.

Forgas, J. P., Brennan, G., Howe, S., Kane, J. F. and Sweet, S. (1980). Audience effects on squash players' performance. *Journal of Social Psychology*, 111, 41–7.

Forsyth, D. R. (1983). *An Introduction to Group Dynamics*. Monterey, CA: Brooks/Cole Publishing Company.

Fox, D. R. (1985). Psychology, ideology, utopia, and the commons. *American Psychologist*, 40, 48–58.

Freedman, J. L. and Doob, A. N. (1968). *Deviancy: The psychology of being different*. New York: Academic Press.

Freedman, J. L., Klevansky, S. and Ehrlich, P. R. (1971). The effect of crowding on human task performance. *Journal of Applied Social Psychology*, 1, 7–25.

Freedman, J. L., Levy, A. S., Buchanan, R. W. and Price, J. (1972). Crowding and human aggressiveness. *Journal of Experimental Social Psychology*, 8, 528–48.

Friedmann, E., Katcher, A. H., Lynch, J. J. and Thomas, S. A. (1980). Animal comparisons and one year survival of patients after discharge from a coronary care unit. *Public Health Reports*, 95, 307–12.

Friedmann, E., Katcher, A., Thomas, S., Lynch, J. and Messent, P. (1983). Social interaction and blood pressure: Influence of animal companions. *Journal of Nervous and Mental Disease*, 171(8).

Gabrenya, W. K., Jr, Wang, Y. E. and Latané, B. (1981). *Social loafing among Chinese overseas and U.S. students*. Paper presented at the Asian Conference of the International Association for Cross-Cultural Psychology, Taipei, Taiwan, R.O.C.

Garrity, T. F., Stallones, L., Marx, M. B. and Johnson, T. P. (1989). Pet ownership and attachment as supportive factors in the health of the elderly. *Anthrozoos*, 3, 35–44.

Gastorf, J. W., Suls, J. and Sanders, G. S. (1980). Type A coronary-prone behavior pattern and social facilitation. *Journal of Personality and Social Psychology*, 38, 773–80.

Geen, R. G. (1976). Text anxiety, observation, and range of cue utilization. *British Journal of Social and Clinical Psychology*, 15, 253–9.

Geen, R. G. (1980a). Test anxiety and cue utilization. In I. G. Sarason (ed.) *Test anxiety: Theory, Research, and Applications*, pp. 43–61. Hillsdale, NJ: Erlbaum.

Geen, R. G. (1980b). The effects of being observed on performance. In P. Paulus (ed.) *Psychology of Group Influence*, pp. 61–97. Hillsdale, NJ: Erlbaum.

Geen, R. G. (1985). Evaluation apprehension and response withholding in solution of anagrams. *Personality and Individual Differences*, 6, 293–8.

Geen, R. G. (1989). Alternative conceptions of social facilitation. In P. Paulus (ed.) *Psychology of Group Influence*, 2nd ed. Hillsdale, NJ: Erlbaum.

Geen, R. G. and Gange, J. J. (1977). Drive theory of social facilitation: Twelve years of theory and research. *Psychological Bulletin*, 84, 1242–88.

Geer, J. H., Davison, G. C. and Gatchel, R. I. (1970). Reduction of stress in humans through nonveridical perceived control of aversive stimulation. *Journal of Personality and Social Psychology*, 16, 731–8.

Gerard, H. B. (1963). Emotional uncertainty and social comparison. *Journal of Abnormal and Social Psychology*, 66, 568–73.

Gergen, K. J., Morse, S. J. and Bode, K. (1974). Overpaid or overworked? Cognitive and behavioral reactions to inequitable rewards. *Journal of Applied Social Psychology*, 4, 259–74.

Gergen, K. J., Ellsworth, P., Maslach, C. and Seipel, M. (1975). Obligation, donor resources, and reactions to aid in three cultures. *Journal of Personality and Social Psychology*, 31, 390–400.

Gibb, J. R. (1951). The effects of group size and of threat reduction upon creativity in a problem solving situation. *American Psychologist*, 6, 324. (Abstract)

Gil, D. G. (1970). *Violence Against Children: Physical Child Abuse in the United States*. Cambridge, MA: Harvard University Press.

Glaser, A. N. (1982). Drive theory of social facilitation: A critical reappraisal. *British Journal of Social Psychology*, 21, 265–82.

Glass, D. C. and Singer, J. E. (1972). *Urban Stress*. New York: Academic Press.

Goethals, G. R., Messick, M. M. and Allison, S. T. (1990). The uniqueness bias: Studies of constructive social comparison. In J. Suls and T. Wills (eds) *Social Comparison: Contemporary Theory and Research*. Hillsdale, NJ: Erlbaum.

Goodman, P. S. and Friedman, A. (1971). An examination of Adams' theory of equity. *Administrative Science Quarterly*, 16, 271–88.

Gore, S. (1978). The effect of social support in moderating the health consequences of unemployment. *Journal of Health and Social Behavior*, 19, 157–65.

Gouldner, A. W. (1960). The norm of reciprocity: A preliminary statement. *American Sociological Review*, 25, 161–78.

Griffith, W. E. and Veitch, R. (1971). Influences of population density and interpersonal affective behavior. *Journal of Personality and Social Psychology*, 17, 92–8.

Groff, B. D., Baron, R. S. and Moore, D. L. (1983). Distraction, attentional conflict, and drivelike behavior. *Journal of Experimental Social Psychology*, 19, 359–80.

Guerin, B. (1983). Social facilitation and social monitoring: A test of three models. *British Journal of Social Psychology*, 22, 203–14.

Guerin, B. and Innes, J. M. (1982). Social facilitation and social monitoring: A new look at Zajonc's mere presence hypothesis. *British Journal of Social Psychology*, 21, 7–18.

Haas, J. and Roberts, G. C. (1975). Effects of evaluative others upon learning and performance of a complex motor task. *Journal of Motor Behavior*, 7, 81–90.

Hackman, J. R. and Morris, C. G. (1975). Group tasks, group interaction process and group performance effectiveness: A review and proposed integration. In L. Berkowitz (ed.) *Advances in Experimental Social Psychology*, Vol. 8. New York: Academic Press.

Hamilton, D. L. and Gifford, R. K. (1976). Illusory correlation and the maintenance of stereotypic beliefs. *Journal of Experimental Social Psychology*, 12, 392–407.

Hardin, G. (1968). The tragedy of the commons. *Science*, 162, 1243–8.

Harkins, S. (1987). Social loafing and social facilitation. *Journal of Experimental Social Psychology*, 23, 1–18.

Harkins, S. and Jackson, J. (1985). The role of evaluation in eliminating social loafing. *Personality and Social Psychology Bulletin*, 11, 457–65.

Harkins, S. and Petty, R. E. (1982). Effects of task difficulty and task uniqueness on social loafing. *Journal of Personality and Social Psychology*, 43, 1214–30.

Harkins, S. and Szymanski, K. (1987a). Social loafing and social facilitation: New wine in old bottles. In C. Hendrick (ed.) *Group Processes and Intergroup Relations*. Newbury Park, CA: Sage.

Harkins, S. and Szymanski, K. (1987b). Social loafing and self-evaluation with an objective standard. *Journal of Experimental Social Psychology*, 24, 354–65.

Harkins, S. and Szymanski, K. (1989). Social loafing and group evaluation. *Journal of Personality and Social Psychology*, 56, 934–41.

Harvey, O. J. and Consalvi, C. (1960). Status and conformity to pressures; in informal groups. *Journal of Abnormal and Social Psychology*, 60, 182–7.

Hastie, R., Penrod, S. D. and Pennington, N. (1983). *Inside the Jury*. Cambridge, MA: Harvard University Press.

Hastorf, A. H. and Cantril, H. (1954). They saw a game. A case study. *Journal of Abnormal and Social Psychology*, 49, 129–34.

Hawkins, C. (1962). Interaction rates of jurors aligned in factions. *American Sociological Review*, 27, 689–91.

Hearst, P. C. (1982). *Every Secret Thing*. Garden City, NY: Doubleday.

Heller, J. F., Groff, B. D. and Solomon, S. H. (1977). Toward an understanding of crowding: The role of physical interaction. *Journal of Personality and Social Psychology*, 35, 183–90.

Herek, G., Janis, I. L. and Huth, P. (1987). Decisionmaking during international crises: Is quality of process related to outcome? *Journal of Conflict Resolution*, 31, 203–26.

Hilbert, G. A. and Allen, L. R. (1985). The effect of social support on educational outcomes. *Journal of Nursing Education*, 24, 48–52.

Hinkle, L. E. and Wolff, H. G. (1956). Communist interrogation and indoctrination. *Archives of Neurology and Psychiatry*, 76, 115–74.

Hinsz, V. (1990). Cognitive and consensus processes in group recognition memory performance. *Journal of Personality and Social Psychology*, October, 1990.

Hobbes, T. (1974). *Leviathan*. London: Kent (1651).

Hobfoll, S. E. and London, P. (1986). The relationship of self-concept and social support to emotional distress among women during war. *Journal of Social and Clinical Psychology*, 4, 189–203.

Hobfoll, S. and Walfisch, S. (1984). Coping with a threat to life: A longitudinal study of self-concept, social support, and psychological distress. *American Journal of Community Psychology*, 12, 87–100.

Hogg, M. A. and Turner, J. C. (1987). Social identity and conformity: A theory of referent informational influence. In W. Doise and S. Moscovici (eds) *Current Issues in European Social Psychology*, Vol. 2. Cambridge: Cambridge University Press.

Hokanson, J. E., Willers, K. R. and Koropsak, E. (1968). The modification of autonomic responses during aggressive interchange. *Journal of Personality*, 36, 386–404.

Hooley, J. M., Orley, J. and Teasdale, J. D. (1986). Levels of expressed emotion and relapse in depressed patients. *British Journal of Psychiatry*, 148, 642–7.

House, J. S., Landis, K. R. and Umberson, D. (1988). Social relationships and health. *Science*, 241, 540–5.

Ingham, A. G., Levinger, G., Graves, J. and Peckham, V. (1974). The Ringelmann effect: Studies of group size and group performance. *Journal of Experimental Social Psychology*, 10, 371–84.

Isenberg, D. J. (1986). Group polarization: A critical review and meta-analysis. *Journal of Personality and Social Psychology*, 50, 1141–51.

Jackson, J. M. and Williams, K. D. (1985). Social loafing on difficult tasks. *Journal of Personality and Social Psychology*, 49, 937–42.

Jackson, J. M. and Williams, K. D. (1986). *A review and theoretical analysis of social loafing*. Unpublished manuscript, Fordham University.

Jacobs, R. and Campbell, D. T. (1961). The perpetuation of an arbitrary tradition through several generations of a laboratory microculture. *Journal of Abnormal and Social Psychology*, 62, 649–58.

Jaffe, Y. and Yinon, Y. (1983). Collective aggression: The group-individual paradigm in the study of collective anti-social behavior. In H. H. Blumberg, A. P. Hare, V. Kent and M. Davies (eds) *Small Groups and Social Interaction*, Vol. 1. Cambridge: Wiley.

Janis, I. L. (1968). Group identification under conditions of external danger. In D. Cartwright and A. Zander (eds) *Group Dynamics*, pp. 80–90. New York: Harper & Row.

Janis, I. L. (1972). *Victims of Groupthink*. Boston: Houghton Mifflin.

Jemmott, J. and Locke, S. (1984). Psychosocial factors, immunologic mediation, and human susceptibility to infectious diseases: How much do we know? *Psychological Bulletin*, 95, 78–108.

Jemmott, J. and Magliore, K. (1988). Academic stress, social support and secretory immunoglobin A. *Journal of Personality and Social Psychology*, 55, 803–10.

Johnson v. Louisiana (1972). *United States Reports*, 406, 356–403.

Johnson, B. T. and Eagly, A. H. (1989). Effects of involvement on persuasion: A meta-analysis. *Psychological Bulletin*, 106, 290–314.

Johnson, D. W. and Johnson, R. T. (1981). Effects of cooperative and individualistic learning experiences on interethnic interaction. *Journal of Educational Psychology*, 73, 444–9.

Johnson, D. W., Maruyama, G., Johnson, R., Nelson, D. and Skon, L. (1981). Effects of cooperative, competitive, and individualistic goal structures on achievement: A meta-analysis. *Psychological Bulletin*, 89, 47–62.

Johnson, H. H. and Torcivia, J. M. (1967). Group and individual performance on a single-stage task as a function of distribution of individual performance. *Journal of Experimental Social Psychology*, 3, 266–73.

Johnson, R. D. and Downing, L. J. (1979). Deindividuation and valence of cues: Effects of pro-social and anti-social behavior. *Journal of Personality and Social Psychology*, 37, 1532–8.

Jorgenson, D. O. and Dukes, F. O. (1976). Deindividuation as a function of density and group membership. *Journal of Personality and Social Psychology*, 34, 24–39.

Judd, C. M. and Harackiewicz, J. M. (1980). Contrast effects in attitude judgment: An examination of the accentuation hypothesis. *Journal of Personality and Social Psychology*, 34, 24–9.

Judd, C. M. and Park, B. (1988). Out-group homogeneity: Judgments of variability at the individual and group levels. *Journal of Personality and Social Psychology*, **54**, 778.

Kahan, J. P. and Rapoport, A. (1984). *Theories of coalition formation*. Hillsdale, NJ: Erlbaum.

Kahn, A. S. and Ryen, A. H. (1972). Factors influencing the bias towards one's own group. *International Journal of Group Tensions*, **2**, 33–50.

Kahneman, D. and Tversky, A. (1984). Choices, values and frames. *American Psychologist*, **39**, 341–50.

Kalven, H. and Zeisel, H. (1966). *The American Jury*. Boston: Little-Brown.

Kaplan, M. F. and Miller, C. E. (1987). Group decision making and normative versus information influence: Effects of type of issue and assigned decision rule. *Journal of Personality and Social Psychology*, **53**, 306–13.

Kelley, H. H., Condry, J. C., Jr, Dahlke, A. E. and Hill, A. H. (1965). Collective behavior in a simulated panic situation. *Journal of Experimental Social Psychology*, **1**, 20–54.

Kerr, N. L. (1981). Social transition schemes: Charting the group's road to agreement. *Journal of Personality and Social Psychology*, **41**, 684–702.

Kerr, N. L. (1983). Motivation losses in task-performing groups: A social dilemma analysis. *Journal of Personality and Social Psychology*, **45**, 819–28.

Kerr, N. L. (1992). Issue importance and group decision-making. In S. Worchel, W. Wood and J. Simpson (eds) *Productivity and Process in Groups*. Newberry Park, CA: Sage.

Kerr, N. L. (1986). Motivational choices in task groups: A paradigm for social dilemma research. In H. Wilke, D. Messick and C. Rutte (eds) *Experimental Social Dilemmas*. Frankfurt am Main: Lang GmbH.

Kerr, N. L. (1989). Illusions of efficacy: The effects of group size on perceived efficacy in social dilemmas. *Journal of Experimental Social Psychology*, **25**, 287–313.

Kerr, N. L. and Bruun, S. (1981). Ringelmann revisited: Alternative explanations for the social loafing effect. *Journal of Personality and Social Psychology*, **7**, 224–31.

Kerr, N. L. and Bruun, S. (1983). The dispensability of member effort and group motivation losses: Free rider effects. *Personality and Social Psychology Bulletin*, **44**, 78–94.

Kerr, N. L. and MacCoun, R. (1984). Sex composition of groups and member motivation II: Effects of relative member ability. *Basic and Applied Social Psychology*, **5**, 255–71.

Kerr, N. L. and MacCoun, R. J. (1985). The effects of jury size and polling method on the process and product of jury deliberation. *Journal of Personality and Social Psychology*, **48**, 349–63.

Kerr, N. L., Atkin, R., Stasser, G., Meek, D., Holt, R. and Davis, J. H.

(1976). Guilt beyond a reasonable doubt: Effects of concept definition and assigned decision rule on the judgments of mock jurors.
Journal of Personality and Social Psychology, 34, 282–94.

Kerr, N. L., Stasser, G. and Davis, J. H. (1979). Model-testing, model-
fitting, and social decision schemes. *Organizational Behavior and
Human Performance*, 23, 339–410.

Kerr, N. L., MacCoun, R., Hansen, C. H. and Hymes, J. A. (1987).
Gaining and losing social support: Momentum in decision-making
groups. *Journal of Experimental Social Psychology*, 23, 119–45.

Kessler, J. J. and Wiener, Y. (1972). Self-consistency and inequity dissonance as factors in undercompensation. *Organizational Behavior and
Human Performance*, 8, 456–66.

Kiecolt-Glaser, J. K., Glaser, R., Dyer, C., Shuttleworth, E., Ogrocki, P.
and Speicher, C. E. (1987). Chronic stress and immunity in family
caregivers of Alzheimer's disease victims. *Psychosomatic Medicine*, 49,
523–35.

Kim, H. S. and Baron, R. S. (1987). Exercise and the illusory correlation:
Does arousal heighten stereotypic processing? *Journal of Experimental Social Psychology*, 24, 366–80.

Knox, R. E. and Safford, R. K. (1976). Group caution at the race track.
Journal of Experimental Social Psychology, 12, 317–24.

Kohlfeld, D. L. and Weitzel, W. (1969). Some relations between personality factors and social facilitation. *Journal of Experimental Research
in Personality*, 3, 287–92.

Komorita, S. S., Sweeney, J. and Kravitz, D. A. (1980). Cooperative choice
in the N-person dilemma situation. *Journal of Personality and Social
Psychology*, 38, 504–16.

Korsch, B. M., Christian, J. B., Gozzi, E. K. and Carlson, P. U. (1965).
Infant care and punishment: A pilot study. *American Journal of Public
Health*, 55, 1880–8.

Kramer, R. M. and Brewer, M. B. (1984). Effects of group identity on
resource use in a simulated commons dilemma. *Journal of Personality and Social Psychology*, 46, 1044–57.

Kramer, R. M. and Brewer, M. B. (1986). Social group identity and the
emergence of cooperation in resource conservation dilemmas. In H.
Wilke, D. M. Messick and C. G. Rutte (eds) *Experimental Social
Dilemmas*. Frankfurt am Main: Verlag Peter Lang.

Kramer, R. M., Messick, D. M. and McClintock, C. G. (1986). Social
values and cooperative response to a simulated resource conservation
crisis. *Journal of Personality*, 54, 576–92.

Krantz, D., Grundberg, N. and Baum, A. (1985). Health psychology.
Annual Review of Psychology, 36, 349–83.

Kravitz, D. A. and Martin, B. (1986). Ringelmann rediscovered: The
original article. *Journal of Personality and Social Psychology*, 50,
936–41.

Kruglanski, A. W. and Mackie, D. M. (1990). Majority and minority influence: A judgmental process analysis. In W. Strobe and M. Hewstone (eds) *European Review of Social Psychology*, Vol. 1, pp. 229–61. Chichester: Wiley.

Kuhlman, D. M. and Marshello, A. (1975). Individual differences in game motivation as moderators of preprogrammed strategic effects in prisoner's dilemma. *Journal of Personality and Social Psychology*, 32, 922–31.

Lago, D., Connell, C. M. and Knight, B. (1983). A companion animal program. In M. A. Smyer and M. Gatz (eds) *Mental Health and Aging*, pp. 165–84. Beverly Hills, CA: Sage.

Lamm, H. and Trommsdorff, G. (1973). Group versus individual performance on tasks requiring ideational proficiency (brainstorming). *European Journal of Social Psychology*, 3, 361–87.

Langer, E. J. and Saegert, S. (1977). Crowding and cognitive control. *Journal of Personality and Social Psychology*, 35, 175–82.

Lanzetta, J. T., Haefner, D., Langham, P. and Axebrod, H. (1954). Some effects of situational threat on group behavior. *Journal of Abnormal and Social Psychology*, 49, 445–53.

Larsson, K. (1956). *Conditioning and Sexual Behavior in the Male Albino Rat*. Stockholm: Almqvist & Wiksell.

Latané, B. (1969). Gregariousness and fear in laboratory rats. *Journal of Experimental Social Psychology*, 5, 61–9.

Latané, B. (1981). The psychology of social impact. *American Psychologist*, 36, 343–56.

Latané, B. and Nida, S. (1981). Ten years of research on group size and helping. *Psychological Bulletin*, 89, 308–24.

Latané, B., Eckman, J. and Joy, V. (1966). Shared stress and interpersonal attraction. *Journal of Experimental Social Psychology, Supplement 1*, 92–102.

Latané, B., Williams, K. and Harkins, S. (1979a). Many hands make light the work: The causes and consequences of social loafing. *Journal of Personality and Social Psychology*, 37, 822–32.

Latané, B., Williams, K. and Harkins, S. (1979b). Social loafing. *Psychology Today*, 13, 104–10.

Laughlin, P. R. (1980). Social combination process of cooperative, problem-solving groups at verbal intellective tasks. In M. Fishbein (ed.) *Progress in Social Psychology*, Vol. 1. Hillsdale, NJ: Erlbaum.

Laughlin, P. R. and Early, P. C. (1982). Social combination models, persuasive arguments theory, social comparison theory and choice shift. *Journal of Personality and Social Psychology*, 42, 273–80.

Laughlin, P. R. and Ellis, A. L. (1986). Demonstrability and social combination processes on mathematical intellective tasks. *Journal of Experimental Social Psychology*, 22, 177–89.

Laughlin, P. R., Kerr, N. L., Davis, J. H., Halff, H. M. and Marciniak, K. A. (1975). Group size, member ability, and social decision schemes on an intellective task. *Journal of Personality and Social Psychology*, 31, 522–35.

Laughlin, P. R., Kerr, N. L., Munch, M. and Haggerty, C. A. (1976). Social decision schemes of the same four-person groups on two different intellective tasks. *Journal of Personality and Social Psychology*, 33, 80–8.

Leana, C. R. (1985). A partial test of Janis' groupthink model: Effects of group cohesiveness and leader behavior on defective decision making. *Journal of Management*, 11, 5–17.

Leavitt, H. J. (1951). Some effects of certain communication patterns on group performance. *Journal of Abnormal and Social Psychology*, 46, 38–50.

LeBon, G. (1895). *The crowd: A study of the popular mind.* New York: Viking Press, 1960.

Lefkowitz, M. M., Eron, L. D., Walder, L. O. and Huesmann, L. R. (1977). *Growing up to be violent: A longitudinal study of the development of aggression.* New York: Pergamon.

Lemyre, L. and Smith, P. M. (1985). Intergroup discrimination and self esteem in the Minimal Groups Paradigm. *Journal of Personality of Social Psychology*, 49, 660–70.

Lerner, M. J. (1980). *The belief in a just world: A fundamental delusion.* New York: Plenum.

Levine, J. M. and Russo, E. M. (1987). Majority and minority influence. In C. Hendrick (ed.) *Review of personality and social psychology: Group process.* Vol. 8, pp. 13–54. Newbury Park, CA: Sage.

LeVine, R. A. and Campbell, D. T. (1972). *Ethnocentrism: Theories of conflict, ethnic attitudes and group behavior.* New York: Wiley.

Levy, I. and Herzog, A. N. (1974). Effects of population density and crowding on health and social adaptation in The Netherlands. *Journal of Health and Social Behavior*, 15, 228–40.

Liebrand, W. B. G. (1983). A classification of social dilemma games. *Simulation and Games*, 14, 123–38.

Liebrand, W. B. G. and van Run, G. J. (1985). The effect of social motives across two cultures on behavior in social dilemmas. *Journal of Experimental Social Psychology*, 21, 86–102.

Liebrand, W. B. G., Messick, D. M. and Wolters, F. J. M. (1986a). Why we are fairer than others: A cross-cultural replication and extension. *Journal of Experimental Social Psychology*, 22, 590–604.

Liebrand, W. B. G., Jansen, R. W. T. L., Rijken, V. M. and Suhre, C. J. M. (1986b). Might over morality: Social values and the perception of other players in experimental games. *Journal of Experimental Social Psychology*, 22, 203–15.

Lifton, R. J. (1961). *Thought Reform and the Psychology of Totalism.* NY: W. W. Norton.

Linn, M. W., Sandifer, R. and Stein, S. (1985). Effects of unemployment on mental and physical health. *American Journal of Public Health*, 75, 502–6.

Lobb, M. and McCain, G. (1978). Population density and nonaggressive competition. *Animal Learning and Behavior*, 6, 98–105.

Longley, J. and Pruitt, D. (1980). Groupthink: A critique of Janis' theory. In L. Wheeler (ed.) *Review of Personality and Social Psychology*, 1. Beverly Hills, CA: Sage.

Lorge, I. and Solomon, H. (1955). Two models of group behavior in the solution of eureka-type problems. *Psychometrika*, 20, 139–48.

Lorge, I., Fox, D., Davitz, J. and Brenner, M. (1958). A survey of studies contrasting the quality of group performance and individual performance, 1920-1957. *Psychological Bulletin*, 55, 337–72.

Luce, R. D. and Raiffa, H. (1957). *Games and decisions*. New York: Wiley.

Lundberg, U. (1976). Urban commuting: Crowdedness and catecholamine excretion. *Journal of Human Stress*, 2, 26–32.

Lynch, J. J., Flaherty, L., Emrich, C., Mills, M. E. and Katcher, A. H. (1974). Effects of human contact on the heart activity of curarized patients in a shock-trauma unit. *American Heart Journal*, 88(2), 160–9.

Maass, A. and Clark, R. D. (1983). Internalization versus compliance: Differential processes underlying minority influence and conformity. *European Journal of Social Psychology*, 13, 197–215.

Maass, A. and Clark, R. D. (1984). Hidden impact of minorities: Fifteen years of minority influence research. *Psychological Bulletin*, 95, 428–50.

Maass, A., Clark, R. D. and Haberkorn, G. (1982). The effects of differential ascribed category membership and norms on minority influence. *European Journal of Social Psychology*, 12, 89–104.

Maass, A., West, S. G. and Cialdini, R. B. (1987). Minority influence and conversion. In C. Hendrick (ed.) *Review of Personality and Social Psychology: Group Process*, Vol. 8, pp. 55–79. Newbury Park, CA: Sage.

MacCoun, R. J. and Kerr, N. L. (1988). Asymmetric influence in mock jury deliberations. Jurors' bias for leniency. *Journal of Personality and Social Psychology*, 54, 21–33.

Mackie, D. M. (1987). Systematic and nonsystematic processing of majority and minority persuasive communications. *Journal of Personality and Social Psychology*, 53, 41–52.

MacNeil, M. K. and Sherif, M. (1976). Norm change over subject generations as a function of arbitrariness of prescribed norms. *Journal of Personality and Social Psychology*, 34, 762–73.

Maier, N. R. F. and Solem, A. R. (1952). The contribution of a discussion leader to the quality of group thinking: The effective use of minority opinions. *Human Relations*, 5, 277–88.

Manstead, A. S. R. and Semin, G. R. (1980). Social facilitation effects: Mere enhancement of dominant responses? *British Journal of Social and Clinical Psychology*, 19, 119–36.

Marks, G. and Miller, N. (1987). The 'false consensus effect': An empirical and theoretical view. *Psychological Bulletin*, 102, 72–90.

Marsden, H. M. (1972). Crowding and animal behavior. In J. F. Wohlwill and D. H. Carson (eds) *Environment and the Social Sciences: Perspectives and Applications*. Washington, D.C.: American Psychological Association.

Martin, J. E. and Peterson, M. M. (1987). Two-tier wage structures: Implications for equity theory. *Academy of Management Journal*, 30, 297–315.

Martin, R. (1987). Influence minorite et relations entre group. In Moscovici, S. and Mugny, G. (eds) *Psychologie de la Conversion*. Paris: Cossett de Val.

Martin, R. and Young, B. P. (1979). *Escape*. Denver, Co: Accent Books.

McCain, G., Cox, V. C. and Paulus, P. B. (1976). The relationship between illness complaints and degree of crowding in a prison environment. *Environment and Behavior*, 8, 283–90.

McCauley, C. (1989). The nature of social influence in groupthink: Compliance and internalization. *Journal of Personality and Social Psychology*, 57, 250–60.

McCauley, C., Stitt, C. L., Woods, K. and Lipton, D. (1973). Group shift to caution at the race track. *Journal of Experimental Social Psychology*, 9(1), 80–6.

McClintock, C. G. (1972). Social motivation: A set of propositions. *Behavioral Science*, 17, 438–54.

McGrath, J. E. (1984). *Groups: Interaction and performance*. Englewood Cliffs, NJ: Prentice Hall.

McKelvey, W. and Kerr, N. H. (1988). Difference in conformity among friends and strangers. *Psychological Reports*, 62, 759–62.

McPhail, C. (1991). *The Myth of the Maddening Crowd*. New York: Aldine DeGruyter.

Mednick, S. A. and Mednick, M. T. (1967). *Examiner's Manual, Remote Associates Test*. Boston: Houghton-Mifflin.

Megargee, E. I. (1977). The association of population density, reduced space, and uncomfortable temperatures with misconduct in a prison community. *American Journal of Community Psychology*, 5, 289–98.

Melamed, B. G. and Brenner, G. F. (1990). Social support and chronic medical stress: An interaction-based approach. *Journal of Social and Clinical Psychology*, 9, 104–17.

Messick, D. M. (1973). To join or not to join: An approach to the unionization decision. *Organizational Behavior and Human Performance*, 10, 145–56.

Messick, D. M. (1984). Solving social dilemmas: Individual and collective approaches. *Representative Research in Social Psychology*, 14, 72–87.

Messick, D. M. and Brewer, M. B. (1983). Solving social dilemmas: A review. In L. Wheeler and P. Shaver (eds) *Annual Review of Personality and Social Psychology*, Vol. 3. Beverly Hills, CA: Sage.

Messick, D. M. and McClelland, C. L. (1983). Social traps and temporal traps. *Personality and Social Psychology Bulletin*, 9, 105–10.

Messick, D. M. and McClintock, C. G. (1968). Motivational basis of choice in experimental games. *Journal of Experimental Social Psychology*, 4, 1–25.

Messick, D. M., Wilke, H., Brewer, M. B., Kramer, R. M., Zemke, P. E. and Lui, L. (1983). Individual adaptations and structural change as solutions to social dilemmas. *Journal of Personality and Social Psychology*, 44, 294–309.

Meuman, L. (1904). Haus-und Schularbeit: Experimente on Kindern der Volkschule. *Die Deutsche Schule*, 8, 278–303, 337–59, 416–31.

Michaels, S. W., Blommel, J. M., Brocato, R. M., Linkous, R. A. and Rowe, J. S. (1982). Social facilitation in a natural setting. *Replications in Social Psychology*, 2, 21–4.

Middlemist, R. D., Knowles, E. S. and Matter, C. F. (1976). Personal space invasions in the lavatory: Suggestive evidence for arousal. *Journal of Personality and Social Psychology*, 33, 541–6.

Milgram, S. (1970). The experience of living in cities. *Science*, 167, 1461–8.

Milgram, S. (1974). *Obedience to authority*. New York: Harper & Row.

Miller, C. E. (1989). The social psychological effects of group decision rules. In P. Paulus (ed.) *Psychology of Group Influence*, 2nd edn Hillsdale, NJ: Erlbaum.

Miller, C. E., Jackson, P., Mueller, J. and Schersching, C. (1987). Some social psychological effects of group decision rules. *Journal of Personality and Social Psychology*, 52, 325–32.

Miller, N., Brewer, M. B. and Edwards, K. (1985). Cooperative interaction in desegregated settings: A laboratory analogue. *Journal of Social Issues*, 41, 63–79.

Miller, N., Gross, S. and Holtz, R. (1991). Social projection and attitudinal certainty. In J. Suls and T. A. Wills (eds) *Social Comparison: Contemporary Theory and Research*. Hillsdale, NJ: Erlbaum.

Mills, J. and Mintz, P. M. (1972). Effect of unexplained arousal on affiliation. *Journal of Personality and Social Psychology*, 24, 11–13.

Mills, L. (1973). Six-member and twelve-member juries: An empirical study of trial results. *University of Michigan Journal of Law Reform*, 6, 671–711.

Moore, D. L. and Baron, R. S. (1983). Social facilitation: A psychophysiological analysis. In J. Cacioppo and R. Petty (eds) *Social psychophysiology: A sourcebook*, pp. 434–66. New York: Guilford Press.

Moore, D. L., Byers, D. and Baron, R. S. (1981). Socially mediated fear reduction in rodents: Distraction, communication, or mere presence? *Journal of Experimental Social Psychology*, 17, 485–505.

Moore, D. L., Baron, R. S., Logel, M. L., Sanders, G. S. and Weerts, T. C. (1988). Methodological Note: Assessment of attentional processing using a parallel phenomenon strategy. *Personality and Social Psychological Bulletin*, 14, 565–72.

Morrow, G. R., Carpenter, P. J. and Hoagland, A. C. (1984). The role of social support in parental adjustment to pediatric cancer. *Journal of Pediatric Psychology*, 9, 317–29.

Moscovici, S. (1980). Toward a theory of conversion behavior. In L. Berkowitz (ed.), *Advances in Experimental Social Psychology*, Vol. 13, pp. 209–39. New York: Academic Press.

Moscovici, S. (1985). Social influence and conformity. In G. Lindzey and E. Aronson (eds) *The Handbook of Social Psychology*, 3rd edn, Vol. 2, pp. 347–412. New York: Random House.

Moscovici, S. and Lage, E. (1976). Studies in social influence: III. Majority vs. minority influence in a group. *European Journal of Social Psychology*, 6, 149–74.

Moscovici, S. and Mugny, G. (1983). Minority influences. In P. Paulus (ed.) *Basic Group Processes*. Springer Verlag: NY.

Moscovici, S. and Personnaz, B. (1980). Studies on social influence: V. Minority influence and conversion behavior in a perceptual task. *Journal of Experimental Social Psychology*, 16, 270–82.

Moscovici, S. and Zavalloni, M. (1969). The group as a polarizer of attitudes. *Journal of Personality and Social Psychology*, 12, 125–35.

Moscovici, S., Lage, E. and Naffrechoux, M. (1969). Influence of a consistent minority on the responses of a majority in a colour perception task. *Sociometry*, 32, 365–79.

Muehleman, J. T., Bruker, C. and Ingram, C. M. (1976). The generosity shift. *Journal of Personality and Social Psychology*, 34, 344–51.

Mugford, R. A. and McComisky, J. G. (1975). Therapeutic value of cage birds with old people. In R. S. Anderson (ed.) *Pet Animals and Society*. London: Bailliere and Tindall.

Mugny, G. (1975). Negotiations, image of the other and the process of minority influence. *European Journal of Social Psychology*, 5, 209–28.

Mugny, G. (1982). *The Power of Minorities*. London: Academic Press.

Mugny, G. and Papastamou, S. (1975–6). A propos du 'credit idiosynchrasique' chez Hollander: conformisme initial ou negociation? *Bulletin de Psychologie*, 29, 970–6.

Mullen, B. (1986). Atrocity as a function of lynch mob composition: A self-attention perspective. *Personality and Social Psychology Bulletin*, 12, 187–97.

Mullen, B. and Baumeister, R. F. (1987). Group effects on self-attention and performance. In C. Hendrick (ed.) *Group Processes and Intergroup Relations*, pp. 189–206. Newbury Park, CA: Sage.

Mullen, B. and Johnson, C. (1990). Distinctiveness based illusory correlations and stereotyping: A meta-analytic integration. *British Journal of Social Psychology*, 29, 11–27.

Mullen, B., Salas, E. and Driskell, J. E. (1989). Salience, motivation and artifact as contributions to the relation between participation rate and leadership. *Journal of Experimental Social Psychology*, 25, 545–59.

Muschel, I. J. (1984). Pet therapy with terminal cancer patients. *Social Casework*, 65, 451–8.

Myers, D. G. (1982). Polarizing effects of social interaction. In H. Brandstatter, J. H. Davis and G. Stocker-Kreichgauer (eds) *Group Decision Making*. New York: Academic Press.

Myers, D. G. (1987). *Social Psychology*, 2nd edn. New York: McGraw-Hill.

Myers, D. G. and Bishop, G. D. (1970). Discussion effects on racial attitudes. *Science*, 169, 778–9.

Myers, D. G. and Lamm, H. (1976). The group polarization phenomenon. *Psychological Bulletin*, 83, 602–27.

Nemeth, C. (1977). Interactions between jurors as a function of majority vs. unanimity decision rules. *Journal of Applied Social Psychology*, 7, 38–56.

Newcomb, T. M. (1943). *Personality and Social Change*. New York: Dryden.

Nuckolls, K. B., Cassel, J. and Kaplan, B. H. (1972). Psychosocial assets, life crisis and the prognosis of pregnancy. *American Journal of Epidemiology*, 5, 431–41.

Oakes, P. J. and Turner, J. C. (1980). Social categorization and intergroup behaviour: does minimal intergroup discrimination make social identity more positive? *European Journal of Social Psychology*, 10, 295–302.

Olson, M. (1965). *The logic of collective action: Public goods and the theory of groups*. Cambridge, MA: Harvard University Press.

Orbell, J. and Dawes, R. (1981). Social dilemmas. In G. Stephenson and J. H. Davis (eds) *Progress in Applied Social Psychology*, Vol. 1. Chichester: Wiley.

Orbell, J., Dawes, R. and van de Kragt, A. (1988). Explaining discussion induced cooperation. *Journal of Personality and Social Psychology*, 54, 811–19.

Orive, R. (1988). Group consensus, action immediacy, and opinion confidence. *Personality and Social Psychology Bulletin*, 14, 573–7.

Osborn, A. F. (1957). *Applied imagination*. New York: Scribners.

Osgood, C. E. (1980). *GRIT: A strategy for survival in mankind's nuclear age?* Paper presented at the Pugwash Conference on New Directions in Disarmament, Racine, Wis.

Page, M. M. and Scheidt, R. J. (1971). The elusive weapons effect: Demand awareness, evaluation, apprehension, and slightly sophisticated subjects. *Journal of Personality and Social Psychology*, 20, 304–18.

Pagel, M. D., Becker, J. and Coppel, D. (1985). Loss of control, self-blame, and depression: An investigation of spouse caregivers of Alzheimer's disease patients. *Journal of Abnormal Psychology*, 94, 169–82.

Park, B. and Rothbart, M. (1982). Perception of out-group homogeneity and levels of social categorization: Memory of the subordinate attributes of in-group and out-group members. *Journal of Personality and Social Psychology*, 42, 1051–68.

Paulus, P. B. (1980). *Psychology of Group Influence*. Hillsdale, NJ: Erlbaum.

Paulus, P. B. and Cornelius, W. L. (1974) An analysis of gymnastic performance under conditions of practice and spectator observation. *Research Quarterly*, 45, 56–63.

Paulus, P. B., Annis, A. B., Seta, J. J., Schkade, J. K. and Matthews, R. W. (1976). Density does affect task performance. *Journal of Personality and Social Psychology*, 34, 248–53.

Paulus, P. B., McCain, G. and Cox, V. C. (1978). Death rates, psychiatric commitments, blood pressure, and perceived crowding as a function of institutional crowding. *Environmental Psychology and Nonverbal Behavior*, 3, 107–16.

Pennebaker, J. and O'Heeron, R. (1984). Confiding in others and illness rate among spouses of suicide and accidental death victims. *Journal of Abnormal Psychology*, 93, 473–6.

Pessin, J. (1933). The comparative effects of social and mechanical stimulation on memorizing. *American Journal of Psychology*, 45, 263–70.

Pettigrew, T. F. (1979). The ultimate attribution error: Extending Allport's cognitive analysis of prejudice. *Personality and Social Psychology Bulletin*, 5, 461–76.

Petty, R. E., Cacioppo, J. T. and Kasmer, J. A. (1985). *Individual differences in social loafing on cognitive tasks*. Paper presented at the annual meeting of the Midwestern Psychological Association, Chicago.

Petty, R., Harkins, S. and Williams, K. (1980). The effects of diffusion of cognitive effort on attitudes: An information processing view. *Journal of Personality and Social Psychology*, 38, 81–92.

Platt, J. (1973). Social traps. *American Psychologist*, 28, 640–51.

Premeaux, S. S., Monday, R. W. and Bethke, A. L. (1986). The two-tier wage system. *Personnel Administrator*, November, 92–100.

Prentice-Dunn, S. and Rogers, R. W. (1989). Deindividuation and the self-regulation of behavior. In P. B. Paulus (ed.) *Psychology of Group Influence*, 2nd edn., Hillsdale, NJ: Erlbaum.

Pritchard, R. D., Dunnette, M. D. and Jorgenson, D. O. (1972). Effects of perceptions of equity and inequity on worker performance and satisfaction. *Journal of Applied Psychology Monograph*, 56, 75–94.

Pruitt, D. G. (1981). *Negotiation behavior*. New York: Academic Press.

Pruitt, D. G. and Kimmel, M. J. (1977). Twenty years of experimental gaming: Critique, synthesis, and suggestions for the future. *Annual Review of Psychology*, 28, 363–92.

Quattrone, G. A. and Jones, E. E. (1980). The perception of variability within in-groups and out-groups. Implications for the law of small numbers. *Journal of Personality and Social Psychology*, 38, 141–52.

Rabbie, J. M. and Horwitz, M. (1982). Conflict and aggression between individuals and groups. In H. Hiebsch, H. Brandstatter and H. H. Kelley (eds), *Social Psychology*, revised and edited version of selected papers presented at the XXII International Congress of Psychology, Leipzig, No. 8.

Rabbie, J. M. and Lodewijkx, H. (1983). *Aggression towards groups and individuals*. Paper presented to the East–West meeting of the European Journal Association of Experimental Social Psychology, Varna, Bulgaria, 17–20 May.

Rabbie, J. M., Lodewijkx, H. and Broeze, M. (1985). *Individual and group aggression under the cover of darkness*. Paper presented to the symposium on psychology of peace at the third European Congress of the International Society for Research on Aggression (ISRA), devoted to multidisciplinary approaches to conflict and appeasements in animals and men, Parma, Italy, 3–7 September.

Radloff, R. and Helmrich, R. (1968). *Groups under Stress. Psychological Stress in SEALABII*. New York: Appleton-Century-Crofts, 1968.

Rajecki, D. W., Ickes, W., Corcoran, C. and Lenerz, K. (1977). Social facilitation of human performance: Mere presence effects. *Journal of Social Psychology*, 102, 297–310.

Rapoport, An. (1973). *Experimental games and their uses in psychology*. Morristown, NJ: General Learning Press.

Rapoport, An. (1974). Prisoner's dilemma: Recollections and observations. In An. Rapaport (ed.) *Game theory as a theory of conflict resolution*. Dordrect, Holland: Reidel.

Rapoport, An. and Chammah, A. M. (1965). *Prisoner's Dilemma: A Study in Conflict and Cooperation*. Ann Arbor: University of Michigan Press.

Ray, D. W. (1978). *The effects of high density in a juvenile correctional institution*. Unpublished doctoral dissertation, George Peabody College for Teachers.

Rees, W. and Lutkins, S. (1967). Mortality of bereavement. *British Medical Journal*, 4, 13–16.

Reid, F. J. M. (1983). Polarizing effects of intergroup comparison. *European Journal of Social Psychology*, 13, 105–6.

Restle, F. and Davis, J. H. (1962). Success and speed of problem solving by individuals and groups. *Psychological Review*, 69, 520–36.

Ringelmann, M. (1913). Research on animate sources of power: The work of man. *Annales de l'Institut National Agronomique, 2e serietome XII*, 1–40.

Robb, S. and Stegman, C. (1983). Companion animals and elderly people: A challenge for evaluators of social support. *The Gerontologist*, 23(3).

Robinson-Staveley, K. and Cooper, J. (1990). Mere presence, gender, and reactions to computers: Studying human-computer interaction in the social context. *Journal of Experimental Social Psychology*, 26(2), 168–83.

Rodin, J. (1976). Crowding, perceived choice, and response to controllable and uncontrollable outcomes. *Journal of Experimental Social Psychology*, 12, 564–78.

Rodin, J., Solomon, S. and Metcalf, J. (1978). Role of control in mediating perceptions of density. *Journal of Personality and Social Psychology*, 36, 988–99.

Rogers, R. W. and Prentice-Dunn, S. (1981). Deindividuation and anger-mediated interracial aggression: Unmasking regressive racism. *Journal of Personality and Social Psychology*, 41, 63–73.

Rohe, W. and Patterson, A. H. (1974). *The effects of varied levels of resources and density on behavior in a day care center*. Paper presented at the meeting of the Environmental Design Research Association, Milwaukee, 1974.

Rohrer, J. H., Baron, S. H., Hoffman, E. L. and Swander, D. V. (1954). The stability of autokinetic judgments. *Journal of Abnormal and Social Psychology*, 49, 595–7.

Rook, K. (1984). The negative side of social interaction: Impact on psychological well being. *Journal of Personality and Social Psychology*, 46, 1097–108.

Rook, K. (1987). Social support vs. companionship: Effects on life stress, loneliness and evaluations by others. *Journal of Personality and Social Psychology*, 52, 1132–47.

Rook, K. (1990). Parallels in the study of social support and social strain. *Journal of Social and Clinical Psychology*, 9, 118–32.

Rosenbaum, L. L. and Rosenbaum, W. B. (1971). Morale and productivity consequences of group leadership style, stress, and type of task. *Journal of Applied Psychology*, 55, 343–8.

Ross, L., Greene, D. and House, P. (1977). The 'false consensus effect': An egocentric bias in social perception and attributional processes. *Journal of Experimental Social Psychology*, 13, 279–301.

Ross, M., Layton, B., Erickson, B. and Schopler, J. (1973). Affect, facial regard, and reactions to crowding. *Journal of Personality and Social Psychology*, 28, 69–76.

Roth, S. and Kubal, L. (1975). The effects of noncontingent reinforcement on tasks of differing importance. Facilitation and learned helplessness effects. *Journal of Personality and Social Psychology*, 32, 680–91.

Ruback, R. B. and Carr, T. S. (1984). Crowding in a women's prison: Attitudinal and behavioral effects. *Journal of Applied Social Psychology*, 14, 57–68.

Ruback, R. B. and Innes, C. A. (1988). The relevance and irrelevance of psychological research: The example of prison crowding. *American Psychologist*, 43, 683–93.

Rubin, J. Z. and Brown, B. R. (1975). *The Social Psychology of Bargaining and Negotiation*. New York: Academic Press.

Rule, B. G., Nesdale, A. R. and Dyck, R. (1975). Objective self-awareness and differing standards of aggression. *Representative Research in Social Psychology*, 6, 82–8.

Runkle, P. J. and McGrath, J. E. (1972). *Research on Human Behavior: A Systematic Guide to Method*. New York: Holt.

Saegert, S. (1973). Crowding: Cognitive overload and behavioral constraint. In W. F. E. Preiser (ed.) *Environmental Design Research: Proceedings of EDRA IV Conference*. Stroudsberg, PA: Dowden, Hutchinson & Ross, Inc.

Saegert, S. (1974). *Effects of spatial and social density on arousal, mood, and social orientation*. Unpublished doctoral dissertation, University of Michigan.

Saegert, S. (1978). High density environments: Their personal and social consequences. In A. Baum and Y. Epstein (eds) *Human Responses to Crowding*. Hillsdale, NJ: Erlbaum.

Saks, M. J. (1977). *Jury Verdicts: The Role of Group Size and Social Decision Rule*. Lexington, MA: Heath.

Saks, M. J. and Baron, C. (eds) (1980). *The Use/Nonuse/Misuse of Applied Social Research in the Courts*. Cambridge, MA: Abt.

Sanders, G. S. (1981). Driven by distraction: An integrative review of social facilitation theory and research. *Journal of Experimental Social Psychology*, 17, 227–51.

Sanders, G. S. and Baron, R. S. (1975). The motivating effects of distraction on task performance. *Journal of Personality and Social Psychology*, 32, 956–63.

Sanders, G. S. and Baron, R. S. (1977). Is social comparison irrelevant for producing choice shifts? *Journal of Experimental Social Psychology*, 13, 303–14.

Sanders, G. S., Baron, R. S. and Moore, D. L. (1978). Distraction and social comparison as mediators of social facilitation effects. *Journal of Experimental Social Psychology*, 14, 291–303.

Schachter, S. (1951). Deviation, rejection and communication. *Journal of Abnormal and Social Psychology*, 46, 190–207.

Schachter, S. (1959). *The Psychology of Affiliation*. Stanford, CA: Stanford University Press.

Schachter, S., Nuttin, J., de Monchaux, C., Maucorps, D. H., Osmer, D., Duijker, J., Rommetveit, R. and Israel, J. (1954). Cross-cultural experiments on threat and rejection. *Human Relations*, 7, 403–39.

Schettino, A. P. and Borden, R. J. (1976). Sex differences in response to naturalistic crowding: Affective reactions to group size and group density. *Personality and Social Psychology Bulletin*, 2, 67–70.

Schmitt, B. H., Gilovich, T., Goore, N. and Joseph, L. (1986). Mere presence and social facilitation: One more time. *Journal of Experimental Social Psychology*, 22, 242–8.

Schroeder, D. A., Jensen, T. D., Reed, A. J., Sullivan, D. K. and Schwab, M. (1983). The actions of others as determinants of behavior in social trap situations. *Journal of Experimental Social Psychology*, 19, 522–39.

Schroeder, H. E. (1973). The risky shift as a general choice shift. *Journal of Personality and Social Psychology*, 27, 297–300.

Seidman, O., Bensen, S. B., Miller, I. and Meeland, T. (1957). Influence of a partner on tolerance for a self-administered electric shock. *Journal of Abnormal and Social Psychology*, 54, 210–12.

Shaver, P. and Liebling, B. A. (1976). Explorations in the drive theory of social facilitation. *Journal of Social Psychology*, 99, 259–71.

Shaw, M. E. (1932). Comparison of individuals and small groups in the rational solution of complex problems. *American Journal of Psychology*, 44, 491–504.

Shaw, M. E. (1981). *Group Dynamics,* 3rd edn. New York: McGraw Hill.

Sherif, M. (1935). A study of some social factors in perception. *Archives of Psychology*, 27, No. 187.

Sherif, M. (1936). *The Psychology of Social Norms*. New York: Harper & Row.

Sherif, M. and Sherif, C. W. (1956). *An Outline of Social Psychology,* rev. edn. New York: Harper & Row.

Sherif, M., Harvey, O. J., White, B. J., Hood, W. R. and Sherif, C. W. (1961). *Intergroup Conflict and Cooperation. The Robber's Cave Experiment*. Norman: University of Oklahoma.

Sherrod, D. R. (1974). Crowding, perceived control and behavioral after-effects. *Journal of Applied Social Psychology*, 4, 171–86.

Siegel, J. M. (1990). Stressful life events and use of physician services among the elderly: The moderating role of pet ownership. *Journal of Personality and Social Psychology*, 58, 1081–6.

Simon, B. and Brown, R. J. (1987). Perceived intragroup homogeneity in minority-majority contexts. *Journal of Personality and Social Psychology*, 53, 703–11.

Singer, J. E., Lundberg, U. and Frankenhaeuser, M. (1978). Stress on the train: A study of urban commuting. In A. Baum, J. E. Singer and S. Valins (eds) *Advances in Environmental Psychology*, Vol. 1. Hillsdale, NJ: Erlbaum.

Slavin, R. E. (1985). Cooperative learning: Applying contact theory in desegregated schools. *Journal of Social Issues*, 16, 169–80.

Smith, A. (1976). The Wealth of Nations. Chicago: University of Chicago Press.

Smith, J. P. and Welch, F. (1984). Affirmative action and labor markets. *Journal of Labor Economics*, 2, 269–301.

Smith, P. and Connolly, K. (1977). Social and aggressive behavior in preschool children as a function of crowding. *Social Science Bulletin*, 4, 429–33.

Smith, T. W. (1979). Happiness: Time trends, seasonal variations, intersurvey differences, and other mysteries. *Social Psychology Quarterly*, 42, 18–30.

Smoke, W. H. and Zajonc, R. B. (1962). On the reliability of group judgments and decisions. In J. H. Criswell, H. Solomon and P. Suppes (eds) *Mathematical Methods in Small Group Processes*. Stanford, CA: Stanford University Press.

Sokill, G. R. and Mynatt, C. R. (1984). *Arousal and free throw shooting*. Paper presented at Midwestern Psychology Association, Chicago.

Sorrentino, R. and Boutillier, R. (1975). The effect of quantity and quality of verbal interaction on ratings of leadership ability. *Journal of Experimental Social Psychology*, 11, 403–11.

Sorrentino, R. M., King, G. and Leo, G. (1980). The influence of the minority on perception: A note on a possible alternative explanation. *Journal of Experimental Social Psychology*, 16, 293–301.

Spears, R., Lea, M. and Lee, S. (1990). Deindividuation and group polarization in computer-mediated communication. *British Journal of Social Psychology*, 29(2), 121–34.

Spence, K. W. (1956). *Behavior, Theory and Conditioning*. New Haven, CT: Yale University Press.

Stasser, G. (1988). Computer simulation as a research tool. The DICUSS model of group decision making. *Journal of Experimental and Social Psychology*, 24, 393–422.

Stasser, G. and Titus, W. (1985). Pooling of unshared information in group decision making: Biased information sampling during group discussion. *Journal of Personality and Social Psychology*, 48, 1467–8.

Stasser, G. and Titus, W. (1987). Effects of information load and percentage shared information on the dissemination of unshared information during discussion. *Journal of Personality and Social Psychology*, 53, 81–93.

Stasser, G., Kerr, N. L. and Bray, R. (1982). The social psychology of jury deliberations: Structure, process, and product. In N. Kerr and R. Bray (eds) *The Psychology of the Courtroom*. New York: Academic Press.

Stasser, G., Kerr, N. L. and Davis, J. H. (1989a). Influence processes and consensus models in decision-making groups. In P. Paulus (ed.) *Psychology of group influence*, 2nd edn. Hillsdale, NJ: Erlbaum.

Stasser, G., Taylor, L. A. and Hanna, C. (1989b). Information sampling in structured and unstructured discussions of three- and six-person groups. *Journal of Personality and Social Psychology*, 57, 67–78.

Steblay, N. M. (1987). Helping behavior in rural and urban environments: A meta analysis. *Psychological Bulletin*, 102, 346–56.

Steiner, I. D. (1966). Models for inferring relationships between group size and potential group productivity. *Behavioral Science*, 11, 273–83.

Steiner, I. D. (1972). *Group Process and Productivity*. New York: Academic Press.

Stephan, F. F. and Mishler, E. G. (1952). The distribution of participation in small groups: An exponential approximation. *American Sociological Review*, 17, 598–608.

Stephan, W. G. (1977). Cognitive differentiation in intergroup perception. *Sociometry*, 40, 50–8.

Stoner, J. A. F. (1961). *A comparison of individual and group decisions including risk*. Unpublished thesis, Massachusetts Institute of Technology, School of Management.

Straus, M. A., Gelles, R. J. and Steinmetz, S. K. (1979). *Behind Closed Doors: Violence in the American Family*. Garden City, NY: Doubleday/Anchor.

Strodtbeck, F. L. and Mann, R. (1956). Sex role differentiation in jury deliberation. *Sociometry*, 19, 3–11.

Stroebe, W. and Frey, B. S. (1982). Self-interest and collective action: The economics and psychology of public goods. *British Journal of Social Psychology*, 21, 121–37.

Stroebe, W. (1990). *The Kohler effect: Motivation gains in group performance*. Paper presented at the Annual Convention of the Society of Experimental Social Psychology, October 13, 1990, Buffalo, NY.

Stroebe, W., Stroebe, M. S., Gergen, K. J. and Gergen, M. (1982). The effects of bereavement on mortality: A social psychological analysis. In J. R. Eiser (ed.) *Social Psychology and Behavioral Medicine*. Wiley.

Stroop, J. B. (1932). Is the judgment of the group better than that of the average member of the group? *Journal of Experimental Psychology*, 15, 550–60.

Strube, M. J., Miles, M. E. and Finch, W. H. (1981). The social facilitation of a simple task: Field tests of alternative explanations. *Personality and Social Psychology Bulletin*, 7, 701–7.

Stryker, S. (1972). Coalition behavior. In C. G. McClintock (ed.) *Experimental Social Psychology*. New York: Holt.

Suedfeld, P. and Rank, A. D. (1976). Revolutionary leaders: Long-term success as a function of changes in conceptual complexity. *Journal of Personality and Social Psychology*, 34, 169–78.

Sumner, W. G. (1906). *Folkways*. New York: Ginn.

Szymanski, K. and Harkins, S. (1987). Social loafing and self-evaluation with a social standard. *Journal of Personality and Social Psychology*, 53, 891–7.

Tajfel, H. (1970). Experiments in intergroup discrimination. *Scientific American*, 223, 96–102.

Tajfel, H. (1982). Social psychology of intergroup relations. *Annual Review of Psychology*, 33, 1–39.

Tajfel, H. and Turner, J. C. (1979). An integrative theory of intergroup conflict. In W. G. Austin and S. Worchel (eds) *The Social Psychology of Intragroup Relations*, pp. 33–47. Monterey, CA: Brooks/Cole.

Tajfel, H. and Turner, J. C. (1986). The social identity theory of intergroup behavior. In S. Worchel and W. G. Austin (eds), *Psychology of Intergroup Relations*, pp. 7–24. Chicago: Nelson Hall.

Tajfel, H. and Wilkes, A. L. (1963). Classification and quantitative judgment. *British Journal of Psychology*, 54, 101–13.

Tanford, S. and Penrod, S. (1984). Social influence model: A formal integration of research on majority and minority influence processes. *Psychological Bulletin*, 95, 189–225.

Tarde, G. (1895). *Essais et me langes sociologigues*. Lyon: Storck.

Taylor, D. W. (1954). Problem solving by groups. *Proceedings of the XIV International Congress of Psychology*. Amsterdam: North Holland Publ.

Taylor, D. W. and Faust, W. L. (1952). Twenty questions: Efficiency in problem solving as a function of size of group. *Journal of Experimental Psychology*, 44, 360–8.

Taylor, S. E. and Fiske, S. T. (1978). Salience, attention, and attribution: Top of the head phenomena. In L. Berkowitz (ed.) *Advances in Experimental Social Psychology*, Vol. 11. New York: Academic Press.

Tesser, A., Campbell, J. and Mickler, S. (1983). The role of social pressure, attention to the stimulus, and self-doubt in conformity. *European Journal of Social Psychology*, 13, 217–34.

Tetlock, P. E. (1979). Identifying victims of groupthink from public statements of decision-makers. *Journal of Personality and Social Psychology*, 37, 1314–24.

Thaler, R. (1985). Mental accounting and consumer choice. *Marketing Science*, 4, 199–214.

Thibaut, J. W. and Kelley, H. H. (1959). *The Social Psychology of Groups*. New York: Wiley.

Thomas, E. J. and Fink, C. F. (1961). Models of group problem solving. *Journal of Abnormal and Social Psychology*, 63, 53–63.

Thomas, E. J. and Fink, C. F. (1963). Effects of group size. *Psychological Bulletin*, 60, 371–84.

Thompson, W. C. (1989). Death qualification after *Wainwright vs. Witt* and *Lockhart vs. McCree*. *Law and Human Behavior*, 13, 185–216.

Tibblin, G. et al. (1986). In S. O. Isacsson and Janzoc (eds) *Social Support, Health and Disease*, pp. 11–19. Stockholm: Almqvist & Wiksell.

Torrance, E. P. (1954a). The behavior of small groups under the stress of conditions of survival. *American Sociological Review*, 19, 751–5.

Torrance, E. P. (1954b). Some consequences of power differences on decision making in permanent and temporary three-man groups. *Research Studies, State College of Washington*, 22, 130–40.

Triplett, N. (1898). The dynamogenic factors in pacemaking and competition. *Journal of Psychology*, 9, 507–33.

Tuckman, B. W. (1965). Developmental sequences in small groups. *Psychological Bulletin*, 63, 384–99.

Tuckman, B. W. and Jensen, M. A. C. (1977). Stages of small group development revisited. *Group and Organizational Studies*, 2, 419–27.

Turner, R. H. and Killian, L. M. (1972). *Collective Behavior*, 2nd edn. Englewood Cliffs, NJ: Prentice-Hall.

Valenzi, E. R. and Andrews, I. R. (1971). Effect of hourly overpay and underpay inequity when tested with a new induction procedure. *Journal of Applied Psychology*, 55, 22–7.

van de Kragt, A., Dawes, R. M., Orbell, J., Braver, S. and Wilson, L. (1986). Doing well and doing good as ways of resolving social dilemmas. In H. Wilke, D. Messick and C. Rutte (eds) *Experimental Social Dilemmas*. Frankfurt am Main: P. Lang.

van de Kragt, A., Orbell, J. and Dawes, R. M. (1983). The minimal contributing set as a solution to public goods problems. *American Political Science Review*, 77, 112–22.

van Lange, P. A. M., Liebrand, W. B. G. and Kuhlman, D. M. (1990). Causal attribution of choice behavior in three N-person prisoner's dilemmas. *Journal of Experimental Social Psychology*, 26, 34–48.

Walster, E., Walster, G. W. and Berscheid, E. (1978). *Equity: Theory and Research*. Boston: Allyn & Bacon.

Weiner, N., Pandy, J. and Latané, B. (1981). *Individual and group productivity in the United States and India*. Paper presented at the American Psychological Association, Los Angeles.

Weiss, R. (1974). The provisions of social relationships. In Z. Rubin (ed.), *Doing unto Others*, pp. 17–26. Englewood Cliffs, NJ: Prentice Hall.

Wilder, D. A. (1977). Perception of groups, size of opposition, and social influence. *Journal of Experimental Social Psychology*, 13, 253–68.

Wilder, D. A. (1981). Perceiving persons as a group. In Hamilton, D. (ed.) *Cognitive Processes in Stereotyping and Intergroup Behavior*, pp. 213–57. Hillsdale, NJ: Erlbaum.

Wilder, D. A. (1986). Social categorization: Implications for creation and reduction of intergroup bias. In L. Berkowitz (ed.) *Advances in Experimental Social Psychology*, Vol. 19. New York: Academic Press.

Wilder, D. A. and Allen, V. L. (1977). Social support, extreme social support and conformity. *Representative Research in Social Psychology*, 8, 33–41.

Wilder, D. A. and Shapiro, P. (1988). Effects of anxiety on impression formation in a group of context: An anxiety-assimilation hypothesis. *Journal of Experimental and Social Psychology*, 25, 481–99.

Wilder, D. A. and Shapiro, P. (1989). Role of competition-induced anxiety in limiting the beneficial impact of positive behavior by an out-group member. *Journal of Personality and Social Psychology*, 56, 60–9.

Williams, K. D. (1981). *The effects of group cohesiveness on social loafing*. Paper presented at the annual meeting of the Midwestern Psychological Association, Detroit.

Williams, K. D. and Karan, S. J. (1991). Social loafing and social compensation: The effects of expectations of co-worker performance. *Journal of Personality and Social Psychology*, 61, 570–81.

Williams, K. D. and Williams, K. B. (1984). *Social loafing in Japan: A cross-cultural development study*. Paper presented at the Midwestern Psychological Association, Chicago.

Williams, K. D., Harkins, S. and Latané, B. (1981). Identifiability as a deterrent to social loafing: Two cheering experiments. *Journal of Personality and Social Psychology*, 40, 303–11.

Williams v. Florida. (1970). *United States Reports*, 399, 78–145.

Wills, T. A. (1990). Multiple networks and substance use. *Journal of Social and Clinical Psychology*, 9, 78–90.

Wilson, W. (1971). Reciprocation and other techniques for inducing cooperation in the prisoner's dilemma game. *Journal of Conflict Resolution*, 15, 167–95.

Wilson, W. and Wong, J. (1968). Intergroup attitudes towards cooperative vs. competitive opponents in a modified prisoner's dilemma game. *Perceptual and Motor Skills*, 27, 1059–66.

Wolf, S. (1979). Behavioral style and group cohesiveness as sources of minority influence. *European Journal of Social Psychology*, 9, 381–95.

Worchel, S. (1979). Intergroup cooperation. In W. Austin and S. Worchel (eds) *The Social Psychology of Intergroup Relations*. Monterey: Brooks/Cole.

Worchel, S. and Teddlie, C. (1976). The experience of crowding: A two-factor theory. *Journal of Personality and Social Psychology*, 34, 30–40.

Worringham, C. J. and Messick, D. M. (1983). Social facilitation of running: An unobtrusive study. *Journal of Social Psychology*, 121, 23–9.

Yaffe, Y. and Yinon, Y. (1979). Retaliatory aggression in individuals and groups. *European Journal of Social Psychology*, 9, 177–86.

Yamagishi, T. (1986). The provision of a sanctioning system as a public good. *Journal of Personality and Social Psychology*, 51, 110–16.

Zaccaro, S. J. (1984). Social loafing: The role of task attractiveness. *Personality and Social Psychology Bulletin*, 10, 99–106.

Zajonc, R. B. (1965). Social Facilitation. *Science*, 149, 269–74.

Zajonc, R. B. (1980). Compresence. In P. Paulus (ed.) *Psychology of Group Influence*, pp. 35–60. Hillsdale, NJ: Erlbaum.

Zajonc, R. B., Heingartner, A. and Herman, E. M. (1969). Social enhancement and impairment of performance in the cockroach. *Journal of Personality and Social Psychology*, 13, 83–92.

Zeisel, H. and Diamond. S. (1978). The effect of peremptory challenges on jury and verdict: An experiment in a federal district court. *Stanford Law Review*, 30, 491–531.

Ziller, R. C. (1957). Group size: A determinant of the quality and stability of group decisions. *Sociometry*, 20, 165–73.

Zillmann, D. (1979). *Hostility and Aggression*. Hillsdale, NJ: Erlbaum.

Zillmann, D., Johnson, R. C. and Day, K. D. (1974). Attribution of apparent arousal and proficiency of recovery from sympathetic activation affecting excitation transfer to aggressive behavior. *Journal of Experimental Social Psychology*, 10, 503–15.

Zimbardo, P. (1969). The human choice: Individuation, reason, and order versus deindividuation, impulse, and chaos. In W. J. Arnold and D. Levine (eds) *Nebraska Symposium on Motivation*, Vol. 17. Lincoln, NE: University of Nebraska Press.

INDEX